Gender in early childhood

Edited by Nicola Yelland

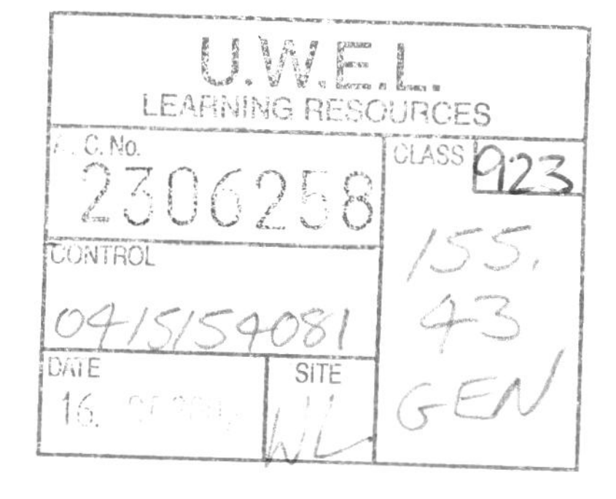

London and New York

FOR CAJA AND TAMSYN. CREATE YOUR OWN PATHS AND FOLLOW YOUR DREAMS . . .

First published 1998
by Routledge
11 New Fetter Lane, London EC4P 4EE

Simultaneously published in the USA and Canada
by Routledge
29 West 35th Street, New York, NY 10001

Typeset in Palatino by RefineCatch Limited, Bungay, Suffolk
Printed and bound in Great Britain by
Clays Ltd, St Ives PLC

British Library Cataloguing in Publication Data
A catalogue record for this book is available from the British Library

Library of Congress Cataloguing in Publication Data
Gender in early childhood / edited by Nicola Yelland.
p. cm.
1. Child development. 2. Identity (Psychology) in children.
3. Sex differences (Psychology) in children. 4. Gender identity.
5. Body image in children. 6. Self-perception in children.
I. Yelland, Nicola.
HQ772.G36 1998
305.231–dc21 97–49215
CIP

ISBN 0–415–15408–1 (hbk)
ISBN 0–415–15409–X (pbk)

Contents

Illustrations

FIGURES

TABLES

Contributors

Anna Bower is a Lecturer in Early Special Education in the School of Early Childhood at the Queensland University of Technology. Her research concerns family life and specifically mothering, both with families who may have a child with a disability and those who do not.

Virginia Casper is a developmental psychologist and educator at Bank Street College of Education in New York City, where she is co-director of the Infant and Parent Development and Early Intervention Program.

Harriet K. Cuffaro is a member of the Graduate Faculty at Bank Street College of Education in New York City. Her professional interests include the history of early education, John Dewey's philosophy and issues of equity.

Susan Danby lectures in early childhood education at the Queensland University of Technology. Her educational experience is both as a practitioner and as an academic, having taught in Australia and the United States of America.

Bronwyn Davies is Head of the School of Education at James Cook University. Her research involves analysing the ways in which individual and collective gendered identities are constructed through text and talk. Her latest research aims to theorise the particular relations between new texts, embodied subjectivity and social action within the Asia-Pacific context.

Ann Farrell is Lecturer in the School of Early Childhood at Queensland University of Technology. She has researched children and families in the criminal justice system in Australia and the United Kingdom and has an ongoing advisory role with government and community bodies on social and family policy.

Keith Gilbert is Senior Lecturer in the School of Human Movement Studies at the Queensland University of Technology. He has worked for a number of years in schools and his research interests concern cultural aspects of sport.

Susan Grieshaber lectures in the School of Early Childhood, Queensland University of Technology. Her research interests include families and gender, early childhood curriculum, and early childhood policy.

Kathy Lowe is a teacher at St Bernadette's Primary School in Ivanhoe, Victoria. She has worked as a teacher researcher with the Construction of Gender in Early Childhood Project funded by DEET and Queensland Government's Women and the World of Work programme. She is currently a doctoral student at the Queensland University of Technology.

Glenda Mac Naughton is a senior lecturer in the Department of Early Childhood, Melbourne University, with a strong interest in social justice and equity issues in early childhood. She has published widely on these issues and has recently completed a book on approaches to teaching in early childhood.

Lyn Martinez is currently the Principal Education Officer in the Equity Programs Unit. She has worked in universities and government agencies to develop gender equity policies and related issues for a number of years. She has been involved with all major Queensland and Australian gender equity policies since the early 1990s.

Steven Schultz was a Faculty member of the Bank Street College of Education in New York City. His research interests included lesbian and gay issues as they relate to early childhood education. Steven Schultz died on December 7, 1996.

Jonathan G. Silin is a Faculty member of the Bank Street College of Education in New York City. His research interests include curriculum theory, lesbian/gay studies and HIV/AIDS prevention.

Margaret White is a Lecturer and Chair of Arts Unit at the Institute of Early Childhood, Macquarie University. Margaret has experience in visual arts, music and movement and is currently researching developments in teaching in the arts in early childhood during the twentieth century. She is co-curator of Drawing on the Art of Children: An Historical Perspective of Children's Art in the Twentieth Century.

Elaine Wickens is the Faculty Director of the Bank Street College of Education/Parson School of Design Masters in Supervision and Administration in the Visual Arts program. Her professional interests include art education, equity issues and still photography.

Nicola Yelland is a Senior Lecturer at the Queensland University of Technology in the School of Early Childhood and teaches in undergraduate and graduate courses related to technology and mathematics education. Her research interests focus on the use of technology by young children in a variety of contexts.

Chapter 1

Blurring the edges

Nicola Yelland and Susan Grieshaber

Gendering occurs as an integral part of the routines of everyday life. The construction of gender is a systematic process that begins at birth and is continually shaped, moulded and reshaped throughout life, according to the sex of the newborn. Lorber and Farrell (1991) consider gender as *the* major status indicator. While this may be so for some groups in society, for others *the* major status indicator may be race or ethnicity. However, gender retains its significance, and Lorber and Farrell (1991) argue that the reason for having gender categories that are constantly constructed and reconstructed in terms of their difference occurs because, in any social group, gender is a fundamental component of the 'structure of domination and subordination and division of labour in the family and the economy' (pp. 1–2). This conceptualisation is similar to Sawicki's libidinal economy, in which women and men:

> are not automatically compared; rather gender categories (female–male, feminine–masculine, girls–boys, women–men) are analysed to see how different social groups define them, and how they construct and maintain them in everyday life.
>
> (Lorber and Farrell, 1991, p. 1)

The construction and maintenance of gender categories therefore permeates all aspects of everyday life.

According to West and Zimmerman (1991), the process of 'doing gender' is the basis on which judgements about persons are made. For example, the competence of men and women as gendered beings is determined in accordance with how well they demonstrate those qualities that have become associated with femaleness and maleness. It is at a very young age that we learn what girls and boys *should* be and what they *should* do. Institutional forces play a major role in constituting bipolar maleness and femaleness, because children learn that they must be readily identifiable through the gender characteristics they present. Individuals are immersed in modes of operation and values inherent in institutions such as the school and family and their associated social practices. These institutions seek to maintain their modes of operation and values as 'true', 'natural' or 'good'. However, Weedon (1987) cautions that appealing to the 'natural' is 'one of the most powerful aspects of commonsense thinking, but it is a way of understanding social relations which denies history and the possibility of change for the future' (pp. 3–4). Appealing to commonsense understandings of gendered social practices as normal and natural tends to blur any distinction between gender as a social construction and understanding gender as an effect of biology or nature.

Alloway (1995) has highlighted the fact that adopting an explanation of nature or biology as being responsible for differences between males and females relies on an understanding of gender that ranges from:

> genetic differences between the sexes, to gendered organisation or left–right brain hemispheres, to 'brain sex' . . . suggest[ing] that male domination of the public sphere and women's relegation to the domestic is somehow genetically justified.
>
> (p. 14)

Indeed, many people use the term gender synonymously with sex. However, gender is a *social* construct that is constantly under modification via human interactions that occur in the myriad social contexts in which we engage.

In Western societies, we tend to have two categories of gender, male and female, which are based on biological features pertaining to genitalia/sex organs. However, other societies (Lorber, 1994) have more categories that include variations of 'male women' and 'female men'. These are people who are biologically categorised into one sex, but enact their lives according to the social/behavioural characteristics of the other, as predetermined by the 'norms' of the group. An important feature here is that members of all categories created are accepted by their society. Western societies do not seem to have achieved the same conditions with regard to the transvestites who do not 'fit' into either of our existing categories.

For the benefit of both the individual and the culture, it is vital that children get their gender right, because getting it right means being seen as normal, and also allows others to interpret 'themselves in relation to it [gender]' (Davies, 1989, p. 20). In many western societies, those who adopt identities outside the dominant versions of gender, that is those who do not perform within the socially accepted boundaries of masculinity and femininity, risk marginalisation. In the case of young children, socially constructed gender boundaries are closely monitored and maintained by children themselves (Boldt, 1997; Lloyd and Duveen, 1992), as well as by teachers (Davies, 1989, 1993; Kamler, Maclean, Reid and Simpson, 1994), family members (Casper *et al.*, Chapter 5, this volume; Davies, 1989, 1993; Grieshaber, Chapter 2, this volume), and the media (Grace and Tobin, 1997).

Reliance on discourses of psychology to understand child development has privileged certain ways of thinking about young children and gendering. For example, understanding the construction of gender as sex-role stereotyping tends to reinforce biological understandings of being female and being male. Any deviation from the established standard of ways in which girls and boys *should* behave (the authoritative versions of it mean to be female and male) is therefore treated as questionable. So within the paradigm of child development, children who are able to move between the binary categories of what girls and boys are supposed to do, or who haven't got their gender quite right according to these categories, are often treated with suspicion by peers, teachers, family and society. Davies (1989) and Boldt (1997) have documented cases of gender bending by young children in institutional settings such as pre-schools and schools, and the subsequent responses by their peers and teachers.

Despite the importance of 'getting gender right', children learn to move between and adopt different gender positions for purposes of strategic advantage. This suggests that the concept of gender identity encompasses multiple relational and reflexive texts and discourses, a kind of 'heteroglossia' (Volosinov, 1986). For example, Davies (1989) talks about how children use different gender positions when they are in the presence and absence of adults; and how positions may change when in the presence of peers. Selection from the multiplicity of available discourses and positions is relational because there are different things at stake in each situation. Each identity therefore needs to be constructed appropriately in order to 'get it right' for that particular context.

Another way of understanding the adoption of different gender identities at distinct points in time is through Butler's (1990; 1993) notion of gender as performance. Butler (1990) understands the creation of truths or commonsense understandings attached to gender to be illusions that are the product of specific circumstances in space and time. The illusions create immutable truths about gender that are then performed on a regular basis. This is reason enough for Butler (1990) to argue that 'gender is always a doing' (p. 25). If gendered identities are always being created and recreated, then opportunities must invariably exist for alternative ways of doing gender to flourish. However, commonsense assumptions about how gendering should be done can obstruct the adoption of positions that differ from what is considered normal.

The employment of males to work with young children and their families in early childhood educational settings is not always considered normal. Male teachers are often treated with scepticism and sometimes distrust because they are seen as not having got their gender right. Doing gender outside the boundaries of how it *should* be done creates doubts about the suitability of such people for employment with young children. Domination of the early childhood field by women, and societal positioning of children as innocents to be nurtured and protected, help to reinforce such doubts. Silin (1997) has argued that it is women who are 'charged with protecting the child's (and their own) innocence from those who seduce them away from their "natural" heterosexuality' (p. 219). Thus, those considered as likely to seduce children away from their natural heterosexuality are those who haven't got their own gender right: the perverts. Silin (1997) identifies this homophobic stereotype as the pervert–child dyad. Linking perversion with the innocence of children perpetuates stereotypes of, for example, 'gay men as sex-obsessed child molesters' and 'preserves the belief in family innocence. It enables us to locate potentially unregulated and unruly desires outside the home [and therefore with the pervert]' (p. 219). Those involved with young children and their families need to be aware of such stereotypes and the potency with which they permeate early childhood services and settings.

What are regarded as socially acceptable, idealised gender identities are dynamic and do change, albeit slowly. Over the last twenty years, for example, we have seen evidence of this, whereby fathers have taken a more active role in the parenting process, women now work in professions that have been traditionally considered as male occupations, and we dress our children in 'unisex' outfits such as jeans and sweatshirts. The gendering process is validated by institutions such as the government and the Church and is embedded in complex value systems. Bem (1981) has noted the salience of gender as a powerful cognitive organiser, and her work highlights the need for us to ensure that we do not passively accept stereotypical gender roles in terms of what is acceptable behaviour but actively challenge them. In school contexts, for example, we can challenge the notion that girls cannot do science as well as boys and that boys are less adept in the humanities, and promote the idea that gender typing of curriculum areas is a nonsense.

While acknowledging that gender is a major characteristic of western society and the focus of this book, we also endorse the notion that gender is but one of the aspects contributing to the multiple identities of persons. Many of the chapters in this book lend weight to the idea that contextual factors such as immediate environmental circumstances are significant. Similarly, we acknowledge the importance of other major characteristics such as race, class, ethnicity and age, and the ways in which these factors are actively involved in constructing the gendered identities of young children and those with whom they interact. We endorse the notion that the construction of gender occurs in concert with other aspects of personal identity and that the process of gendering is an integral part of the politics of everyday life (Connell, 1995). However, in this volume we seek further understanding of those parts of children's lives that relate specifically to the process of gendering.

As previously stated, societies tend to prescribe behaviours according to the gender of the individual, and those who do not get it right are often marginalised. The seemingly tacit acceptance of such behaviours by the majority of members of the society as being the norm for males and females has resulted in the creation of separate and distinguishable groups who have been assigned corresponding roles and responsibilities. What is apparent, however, is that the status of the groups is not equal. In our society, what men do tends to be valued more highly than the occupations of women, not only in terms of power and prestige but also in relation to economic rewards. (For a more detailed explanation of the notion of hegemonic masculinity, see Connell, 1995.) Many tend to adhere to societal mandates for gender roles, as they want to fulfil the norms and expectations of their group to feel a sense of worth. More recently, however, we have come to challenge traditional notions of gender with the aim of creating a society based on equality of opportunity, irrespective of gender.

It has been nearly two decades since the first gender equity programmes were conceptualised and implemented (Cohen and Martin, 1976; Davis, 1979). The effect of such programmes coupled with social change during the period would seem to indicate that we have made significant advances in terms of providing girls with opportunities to participate in activities that had hitherto been considered as inappropriate for girls. Indeed, more recently there has been a call for equivalent programmes for boys, because we seem to have been so successful in improving the academic performance of girls at the secondary school level. It is interesting to note that what started as the provision of equality of *opportunity* for boys and girls has since shifted focus to equality of *outcomes* in debates where girls are achieving more success in terms of higher scores at the end of schooling. This was highlighted in New South Wales, Australia, at the end of 1996, when girls continued to outperform boys by achieving the highest scores in the High School Certificate, as they had done for a number of years since the results of humanities subjects were included in the overall calculation of scores and the impact of gender equity programmes, such as all-girl science classes, began to take effect. Reports in newspapers at the time contended that there should be equivalent programmes for boys to achieve equality of outcomes for both genders. In fact, in Australia, as a result of such public outpourings in the media, a parliamentary inquiry was set up in 1994 with a mandate to investigate the situation. The report, entitled *Challenges and Opportunities: A Discussion Paper*, recommended that it was not necessary to create a specific policy related to educational opportunities for boys, but rather encouraged that concern for boys should be incorporated into gender equity policies.

The education of boys in Australian schools is currently the subject of ongoing controversial debate, set within the recent spate of literature about men, boys and masculinity (for example, Connell, 1995, 1996; Lloyd and Wood, 1996; May, Strikwerda and Hopkins, 1996). According to Kenway (1997, p. 57), the current debate often produces 'more heat than light'. Much of the argument is about educational opportunities for boys in the context of wider gender reform agendas (see, for example, Connell, 1996; Fitzclarence, Hickey and Matthews, 1997; Kenway, 1997; Kenway, Watkins and Tregenza, 1997; Kenway, Willis, Blackmore and Rennie, 1997; Mclean, 1997; Pallotta-Chiarolli, 1997). As the debate is framed within the years of secondary schooling, the issue of gender in the early childhood years is not confronted. A similar situation has existed in relation to national policy and the early years. Alloway (1995) has shown that national policies provide implementation strategies that relate mostly to the secondary and upper primary years of schooling. Despite the exclusion of the early years from policy implementation, the significance of young children and their families, and institutional services such as childcare centres, pre-schools, kindergartens and schools, in the social construction of gendered identities cannot be underestimated.

At the same time, the situation of females both in schools and universities remains a concern. A national survey of students aged 9 to 15 years, sponsored by the American Association of University Women (AAUW), found that, as girls reach adolescence, they experience a dramatic drop in self-esteem, and are systematically discouraged from particular academic subjects, most notably mathematics and science. The report, entitled *How schools shortchange girls* (1992), concluded that girls received an inferior education to boys in America's schools. This was based on evidence that girls receive less attention in the classroom than boys and were still not pursuing careers in areas related to mathematics and science. Furthermore, African American girls were more likely than Caucasian girls to be rebuffed by teachers, ignored in curricula and stereotyped. Another major finding pertains to the issue of sexual harassment, reports of which are increasing and therefore helping to contribute to the undermining of girls' self-esteem and their confidence to pursue non-traditional roles and job opportunities.

The debate has continued to focus on the impact of gender equity programmes in secondary education, when patterns and practices pertaining to gender have been firmly entrenched in the minds of all the players in students' lives. However, it is also apparent that girls' success at the end of secondary school has not been reflected in corresponding opportunities to excel in life after school. For example, a recent study of the lifetime earnings of men and women graduates from the Northern Illinios University maintains that women will earn over $300, 000 less than their male counterparts in their lifetime (Campus Review, 1997). There still seems to be an expectation that men and women will take on certain types of employment, based on their gender, and that women will take off time to 'stay at home' as the primary caregiver of children. Such expectations mean that women frequently experience interruptions to their careers that correspond to a decrease in financial recompense during the time period as well as the lack of opportunity to build equivalent experience to a male counterpart who has been working continuously. However, the study also shows that women are still not seeking the same kinds of jobs that men are interested in (that is, those valued by society as being important and thus tend to be accompanied by high [corporate] salaries). The researchers concluded that they thought that many young women tended to think that 'judgements are based on merit and qualifications, but in reality, gender plays a huge role in employment opportunity, financial stability and future savings' (Campus Review, May 1997, p. 13). It would thus seem that we still have not achieved the status of equality of opportunity for both genders in our society, and that media complaints about equality of outcomes are relevant only to secondary schools contexts, where girls are performing better than boys in terms of academic scores. Additionally, it would seem that although gender equity programmes have had an effect in improving attitudes and academic performance at the secondary school level, we still have problems with conceptualisations of positions and personal/power relations that are disadvantageous to girls in subtle and unequal ways. What would seem to be necessary is a change of mind set about the construction of gender so that, from the beginning of their lives, children are exposed to social contexts that enable them to develop as human beings irrespective of their sex. Where better to start to look critically at how we interact with children than in the early childhood years?

This volume presents research that invites the reader to examine practices that occur with young children in the early childhood years with respect to the construction of gender and the expectations of society, schools and families on their lives. The different chapters have, as their focus, the ways in which people, practices and policy impact on the lives of young children to effect their view of themselves, how they interact with others and artefacts of their culture.

The book is organised into two main areas. The first part considers the *family, community and society* as contexts for developing notions about gender and how it is enacted in our daily lives. Susan Grieshaber talked with first-time parents about the expectations, hopes and aspirations for their new child. She illustrates how the gendering process begins from birth and how parental dispositions and values influence the environment into which their baby is born. Anna Bower's study of the expectations of parents of children with a disability provides a fascinating insight into parenting practices of an often neglected group. Her work focuses on issues of independence and how these are linked to employment, self-care and personal autonomy for both male and female children. Keith Gilbert examines the ways in which various media, the sport and fashion industries influence children's perceptions of their bodies. His chapter reveals that children as young as 6 and 7 years of age are already concerned about the way that they appear to others and that their perceptions are informed to a large extent by the popular media. Gilbert maintains that an understanding of the impact of the issues of popular culture and the effect it has on young children's perceptions of the body should be impressed upon the educators of the young in order to assist children to feel confident about such issues.

The group from Bank Street College (Virginia Casper and colleagues) have written a sensitive insight into an often overlooked issue, that is sexual orientation in early childhood education. They describe work that they have conducted with early childhood teachers and children to explore thoughts and attitudes about sexual orientation in relation to the children's sexuality and parents' sexual orientation. The authors share with us the transformation process in their own institution with regard to their struggles to include gay and lesbian lives into their curriculum. They present a persuasive argument for inclusion of the issues raised for the creation of a more just and equitable society.

In the final chapter of this section, Ann Farrell examines the human rights agenda with respect to the gendering of young children and their families. Farrell highlights that fact that the legislation is enacted in gendered settings, and provides two examples – the treatment of women and children in the criminal justice system and the positioning of children as gendered consumers in a materialistic/capitalistic culture – in order to challenge us to reflect on the content of the legislation and how it is manifested in real life settings with young children.

The second part of the book examines the role of schools in relation to the construction of gender and the expectations that are placed on students, based on the gender group that they have been assigned to. It contains research that has focused on policy and practice in a variety of curriculum contexts. Lyn Martinez has developed gender equity policy statements for schools, community and higher education institutions. Her summary of the role of early childhood professionals in the arena of educational policy making for gender equity highlights the ways in which early childhood education has been marginalised to outsider status within the apparatus of the State. She recommends that the only way forward is for policy makers and early childhood educators to form strategic alliances so that the voices of the sector are recognised and heard. She also maintains that it is essential for gender issues to remain at the forefront of discussion within the early childhood community, as pressure mounts to undercut gender equity policies in all areas of education.

Bronwyn Davies and the teachers that she collaborated with interrogate the ways in which we ascribe people to categories and perpetuate binary conceptualisations of membership and power. Workshop discussions are examined to reveal the struggles they had concerning category membership and the power relations between individuals as they interacted in various school contexts. The chapter highlights the need to enable students, teachers and principals to find ways both to question the ideas and assumptions that we take for granted and to develop new patterns of making meaning that go beyond binary interpretations.

The chapters by Glenda Mac Naughton, Susan Danby and Kathy Lowe pertain to teachers and children in pre-school settings. Mac Naughton describes the work of one early childhood educator/worker who adopted a liberal feminist approach to gender equity in an early childhood setting. For those readers who work with young children, the chapter provides valuable tools for analysing the actions they take, and suggests alternative ways of viewing what they do in the creation of learning environments for young children in the name of gender equity.

Susan Danby focuses on the social interactions of pre-school children during play in a day care centre. In this chapter she presents a scene from a pre-school that illustrates the way in which a play situation constitutes an important site where the identification and maintenance of gendered behaviours are challenged. Susan considers play to be the real life work of young children as they construct and maintain the gendered social orders in their everyday worlds.

Kathy Lowe examines some of the features that contribute to how young children construct gendermaps of themselves and describes the ways in which she, as their teacher, helped children to make sense of gender in their daily interactions in the pre-school setting.

The chapters by Margaret White and Nicola Yelland examine different curriculum contexts where gendered practices are evident. In 'The pink's run out!', Margaret White describes the context of children's artmaking and illustrates how it plays an important role in children's negotiation of their position in society. She also considers ways in which we should carefully observe and interact with young children during the artmaking process in order to develop an understanding of how children come to perceive themselves as gendered entities in this context.

Nicola Yelland questions the notion that the performance of girls is inferior to that of boys in mathematics and the use of computers by reviewing the literature to show that such assumptions are not warranted. Yelland presents research that shows how young children collaborate in different ways in computer based tasks. She suggests that the 'male way' of doing work with technology often dominates descriptions of performance and thus gives advantage to boys in educational settings. Yelland contends that all children should work with a variety of technological applications that may enhance learning in the early childhood years in contexts that offer opportunties for collaborations with partners and in groups, as well as on an individual basis.

What we have attempted to create in this book is a volume dedicated to challenging traditional ways of viewing gender in the early childhood years. We describe practices, highlight issues and suggest ways in which practice may be changed so that those who interact with young children can treat them with empathy, equity and understanding. We want to keep blurring the edges so that the categories will ultimately fade.

REFERENCES

Alloway, N. (1995) *Foundation stones: The construction of gender in early childhood.* Carlton, Victoria: Curriculum Corporation.

American Association of University Women (1995) *How schools shortchange girls.* New York: Marlow & Co.

Bem, S.L. (1981) Gender schema theory: A cognitive account of sex typing. *Psychological Review*, 88, 354–364.

Boldt, G. (1997) Sexist and heterosexist responses to gender bending. In J. Tobin (ed.) *Making a place for pleasure in early childhood education.* (pp. 188–213). New Haven: Yale.

Butler, J. (1990) *Gender trouble: Feminism and the subversion of identity.* New York: Routledge.

Butler, J. (1993) *Bodies that matter: On the discursive limits of 'sex'.* London: Routledge.

Campus Review (1997) Female grads typically prepare for lesser paying jobs, study finds.

Cohen, M. and Martin, L. (1976) *Growing free: Ways to help children overcome sex-role stereotypes.* Washington, DC: Association Childhood Education International.

Connell, R.W. (1995) *Masculinities.* St Leonards, NSW: Allen & Unwin.

Connell, R.W. (1996) Teaching the boys: New research on masculinity, and gender strategies for schools. *Teachers College Record* 98 (2), 206–235.

Davies, B. (1989) *Frogs and snails and feminist tales: Preschool children and gender.* Sydney: Allen & Unwin.

Davies, B. (1993) *Shards of glass: Children reading and writing beyond gendered identities.* St Leonards, NSW: Allen & Unwin.

Davis, W. (1979) *Towards a non-sexist classroom.* Adelaide, SA: Department of Education, Women's Advisory Unit.

Fitzclarence, L., Hickey, C. and Matthews, R. (1997) Getting changed for football: Challenging communities of practice. *Curriculum Perspectives* 17 (1), 69–73.

Grace, D.J. and Tobin, J. (1997) Carnival in the classroom. In J. Tobin (ed.) *Making a place for pleasure in early childhood education.* (pp. 159–187). New Haven: Yale.

Kamler, B., Maclean, R., Reid, J. and Simpson, A. (1994) *Shaping up nicely: The formation of schoolgirls and schoolboys in the first month of school.* A report to the gender equity and curriculum reform project. DEET. Canberra.

Kenway, J. (1997) Boys' education, masculinity and gender reform: Some introductory remarks. *Curriculum Perspectives* 17 (1), 57–61.

Kenway, J., Watkins, P. and Tregenza, K. (1997) New vocational agendas in schooling: Boys at risk? *Curriculum Perspectives* 17 (1), 73–78.

Kenway, J., Willis, S., Blackmore, J. and Rennie, L. (1997) Are boys victims of feminism in schools? Some answers from Australia. *International Journal of Inclusive Education* 1 (1), 19–35.

Lloyd, B. and Duveen, G. (1992) *Gender identities and education: The impact of starting school.* New York: Harvester.

Lloyd, T. and Wood, T. (eds) (1996) *What next for men?* London: Working with Men.

Lorber, J. (1994) *Paradoxes of gender.* New Haven: Yale University Press.

Lorber, J. and Farrell, S.A. (1991) (eds) *The social construction of gender.* (pp. 1–5). London: Sage.

May, L., Strikwerda, R. and Hopkins, P.D. (eds) (1996) (2nd ed.) *Rethinking masculinity: Philosophical explorations in light of feminism.* Lanham: Rowman & Littlefield.

Mclean, C. (1997) Engaging with boys' experiences of masculinity: Implications for gender reform in schools. *Curriculum Perspectives* 17 (1), 61–64.

New South Wales Government Advisory Committee on Education, Training and Tourism (1994) *Challenges and opportunities: A discussion paper.* A report to the Minister for Education, Training and Youth affairs on the Inquiry into boys' education. Sydney.

Pallotta-Chiarolli, M. (1997) We want to address boys' education but . . . *Curriculum Perspectives* 17 (1), 65–69.

Silin, J. (1997) The pervert in the classroom. In J. Tobin (ed.) *Making a place for pleasure in early childhood education.* (pp. 214–234). New Haven: Yale.

Volosinov, V. (1986) *Marxism and the philosophy of language.* (L. Matejka and I.R. Titunik, trans.). Cambridge, MA: Harvard University Press.

Weedon, C. (1987) *Feminist practice and poststructuralist theory.* Oxford: Basil Blackwell.

West, C. and Zimmerman, D.H. (1991) Doing gender. In J. Lorber and S.A. Farrell (eds) *The social construction of gender.* (pp. 13–37). London: Sage.

Part I

Family, community and society

Chapter 2

Constructing the gendered infant[1]

Susan Grieshaber

This chapter reports data from a study involving twenty couples, many of whom are first-time parents. It uses a feminist post-structuralist approach to show how the process of gendering can begin from the early stages of life and indicates how parental dispositions and beliefs influence ways in which parents establish environments for, and interact with, girl and boy infants. Because the ongoing process of gendering occurs within institutional and cultural contexts such as families, investigating relationships of power within these settings is an integral part of understanding gendering. Exploration of daily domestic routines and practices shows ways in which the gendered social relations of lived experience are enacted. Although the construction of gender produces multiple forms of femininity and masculinity, many of these infants are learning about gender through being immersed in cultural meaning systems that are saturated with hegemonic (dominant) forms of masculinity in everyday life.

INTRODUCTION

Medical technology such as ultrasound has enabled the identification of sexual difference well before the moment of birth. Where the sex of the foetus is known, the construction of such difference can now be extended to life in the womb. Parents can then actively construct the foetus as a gendered identity. This occurs through choosing gender appropriate names, discussing and purchasing gender appropriate clothing (such as pink clothes for girl babies), and by ascribing specific attributes (such as a 'tiny little girl baby') to the foetus according to the sex. Knowledge of the sex of a foetus therefore extends possibilities for ways in which mothers and fathers begin constructing gendered realities about their offspring. If everyday life is understood as 'an arena of gender politics' (Connell, 1995, 3), then these realities constructed from the early stages of life in the womb, or from birth onward, mean susceptibility to particular understandings of gender relations, values and social power. Specific understandings are drawn from the existing structure of social institutions such as the family, school and the media.

FAMILY, GENDER AND CULTURAL MEANING SYSTEMS

As members of society who have successfully negotiated the enculturation process, parents have been the object of

> lessons about the social world which are variously reinforced by the discourses and pedagogies of home and school . . . Together these discourses provide cultural meaning systems of concepts such as 'childhood', 'family', 'femininity', 'masculinity', 'race' and so forth.
> (Luke, 1996, 167)

These cultural meaning systems are part of the social structures and processes through which institutions and practices such as the family are organised. As specific sites where gender relations are enacted, the everyday life of families is inscribed with practices where identity (subjectivity) is defined and differentiated through the category of gender. Existing social discourses and patterns of family interaction are therefore likely to work to position foetuses, where the sex is known, and infants in particular gendered ways. Adopting a feminist post-structuralist approach is one way of understanding how this happens.

A feminist post-structuralist approach uses principles of poststructuralism and aspects of feminism (Weedon, 1987). Post-structuralism provides an awareness of how power relations within society operate in particular ways (Foucault, 1977). When combined with the aspect of gender, a feminist post-structuralist approach seeks understanding of how power relations in society are gendered, that is 'how gender power relations are constituted, reproduced and contested' (Kamler, Maclean, Reid and Simpson, 1994, 15). For Weedon (1987, 40–41), feminist poststructuralism also involves the 'identification of areas and strategies for change'. Foucault's (1979) work enables an exploration of how power is constituted in the social relationships of gender within families (at the micro level), while at the same time locating links between families and social and cultural institutions (at the macro level). This analysis examines the micro relations of mother–father–infant relationships within families and the macro links between familial relationships and the social structure. It also discusses ways in which the micro and macro levels shape, constrain and constitute each other. Some of the terms used to show how this happens include 'discourse', 'subjectivity' and 'positioning'. These are now explained.

Discourses offer ways of living everyday life. People can adopt or select from the range of positions available, but on some occasions are themselves positioned by particular discourses. According to Gee,

> [D]iscourses are ways of behaving, interacting, valuing, thinking, believing, speaking, and often reading and writing that are accepted as instantiations of particular roles by *specific groups of people*, whether

> families of a certain sort, lawyers of a certain sort, bikers of a certain sort, business people of a certain sort, churches of a certain sort. . . . They are always and everywhere *social*.
>
> (Gee, 1990, xix)

At any one time, then, each person participates in many different discourses. Each discourse has its own preferred way of doing things, which is often a taken-for-granted understanding of what is normal and counts as 'the "right" ways to think, feel and behave' (Gee, 1990, xx). Because different discourses propose a variety of ways to think, feel and behave, what they offer can be contradictory and in competition with other ways of doing things, or other discourse positions. Some discourses can also be more influential than others and assume significance for particular groups.

One example of influential discourses pertinent to gendering is the concept of hegemonic masculinity (Connell, 1995, 1996; Davies, 1996). In this understanding, dominant discourses of masculinity are used to position men more powerfully than women and girls. Connell (1996, 209) has indicated that other forms of masculinity exist alongside the culturally dominant form, but that the latter is 'an expression of the *privilege* men collectively have over women'.

Competing ways of doing things means that discourses are also sites of conflict and struggle. Subject positions, or ways of being an individual (Weedon, 1987, 3), are positions selected from available discourses. Like discourses, subject positions can also be sites of conflict, resistance and struggle. According to Weedon, language is a significant factor in sites of struggle:

> The meaning of the existing structure of social institutions, as much as the structures themselves and the subject positions which they offer their subjects, is a site of political struggle waged mainly, though not exclusively, in *language*.
>
> (Weedon, 1987, 37–38)

Gee (1990, 175) has pointed out that all persons are the '*subject* of our Discourses in at least three ways'. These include, first, being an individual actor within discourses and, second, being 'subject-ed' to the limitations imposed by the discourses in which we participate. Third, Gee (1990, 175) has argued that all discourses involve understandings about 'what counts as normal (and deviant) sorts of human beings, as well as what counts as normal (and deviant) relationships between them'.

Butler's (1990) idea of gender as performance includes the significance of what counts as normal and what is seen as aberrant. However, Butler argues that gender is an effect, a creation that has established itself as a 'truth' that is always in the process of being re-created:

> The substantive effect of gender is performatively produced and compelled by the regulatory practices of gender coherence . . . gender proves to be performative – that is, constituting the identity it is purported to be. In this sense gender is always a doing.
>
> (Butler, 1990, 24–25)

Deviations from the accepted ways of doing things count as transgressions, and such violations pose a threat to the continued effect of gender. For authoritative versions of gendering to maintain an ongoing status of truth, it is important that such breaches are infrequent, or rectified, lest gender be exposed for the illusion it is. However, it is deviations from the norm that also create opportunities for alternative ways of gendering to occur.

Because post-structuralism theorises 'subjectivity as a site of disunity and conflict' (Weedon, 1987, 21), opportunities arise for gendering to occur in alternative ways. Weedon (1987, 21) explains such opportunities as 'central to the process of political change', while at the same time responsible for 'preserving the status quo'. Feminist post-structuralist writers reject the idea of a unitary identity where, for example, the feminine or masculine can be reduced to a singular essential understanding of what it is to be female or male. Rejecting the notion of identity as an essential, single or unitary construct permits an understanding of the subject constructed through different discourses and subject positions. Scope exists, then, for examining ways in which gender is made a pertinent distinction in the social relations of families and ways in which such relations are constructed, resisted and reconstructed.

Mothers, fathers and infants are constituted as multiple identities according to specific contexts. Gender is one of the multiplicity of identities around which subjectivity is constructed, often simultaneously. For example, mothers may also be sisters, daughters, friends, workers, tennis players, etc., and are therefore constituted, and constitute themselves, differently according to variables such as time and place. This means that although a female tennis player can be a sister, wife, mother, daughter, etc., as a tennis player, she is positioned and positions herself differently from the ways in which she enacts mothering.

Challenging concepts and statements about the subject offers the opportunity for reconceptualisation, rearticulation and deployment of alternative discourses and practices of subjectivity (Foucault, 1979). This means potentially moving beyond commonsense or taken-for-granted conceptions of gender to the creation of alternative ways of doing and understanding gendering.

FAMILIES AS POLITICAL SITES

Wearing (1996, ix) has argued that in late twentieth-century Australia, difference between the genders 'is obvious at all levels of society from individual perceptions to macrosocial structures', and that men and women 'construct different realities in their everyday lives concerning their clothing, their families, their jobs, their ambitions, even their definition of happiness.' Like different forms of femininity and masculinity, there are also multiple ways of being a family, being a mother, being a father, etc., some of which are more socially acceptable (culturally dominant) than others. Families can be located in particular discursive fields (different ways of being a family), and these discursive fields 'consist of competing ways of giving meaning to the world. They offer the individual a range of modes of subjectivity' (Weedon, 1987, 35). Investigating the discursive positioning of parents therefore enables identification of ways in which parents give meaning to the world through adoption of specific subject positions and through particular routines and practices.

Meanings are always limited by the structure of social relations operating at a particular time and place and are represented through a variety of discourses. By identifying discourse forms, as well as routines and practices in which family members engage on a regular basis, it is possible to understand how discourses constitute and organise social relations in institutions such as the family. The concept of contradictory subjectivity, where particular realities can be constructed in one context and not in another, because different subject positions are adopted, facilitates the idea that gendering in the course of daily domesticity can be context dependent. Thorne (1993) has shown that young children in schools can adopt gendered identities consistent with the immediate context.

The cultural meaning systems through which families are organised make them sites of complex interactions. In addition, families are viewed as political institutions:

> Families are political in that certain members review, judge, formulate codes of conduct, make decisions and impose sanctions that evaluate and impact the actions, conditions, thoughts and feelings of other members. Such administration of power is characteristic of families everywhere and may occur whenever family members interact.
>
> (Ochs and Taylor, 1992, 301)

Families are therefore seen as political sites and as continually engaged in the construction and control of discourses, meaning and subjectivities. This includes the construction of familiar codes, styles and conventions associated with commonsense conceptions of families, along with established routines and continuity of habits that are involved in domesticity. Rituals such as eating, cleaning, mothering and fathering inscribe the institution of the family. Subject positions adopted by particular family members as part of their daily practices can be identified through the examination of such routines. Because family members may adopt different subject positions, or be positioned by more powerful discourses, the potential for disagreement arises. By implication, then, the family is also a site of potential struggle, where the relational nature of power (Foucault, 1979) offers opportunities for resistance, negotiation and change over time. The potential for altering ways in which gender relationships are constituted is therefore upheld.

In seeking an understanding of the events and interactions in daily family life that constitute gendering, views about becoming parents are explored as ways in which these families are organised. Through unpacking everyday, taken-for-granted assumptions that surround family members and their lived experiences, it is possible to make visible household relationships (including relationships of gender) that operate within the family. This process of laying bare and unmasking events and assumptions focuses on explaining practices and meanings associated with understanding everyday life. For example, unravelling taken-for-granted meanings associated with parental beliefs entails the deconstruction of commonsense meanings that have become accepted as natural, normal and unquestioned ways of understanding and explaining the phenomena of gendering.

THE FAMILIES

Twenty couples were recruited primarily through media (newspaper and radio) coverage of the intended project. Advertisements placed in suburban newspapers provided the largest number of participants, as it was not possible to involve respondents living any distance from this Australian capital city. With the exception of two men who had children from previous relationships, all were first-time parents. At the time of recruitment, all participants were employed in either a part- or full-time capacity in a range of occupations. Parental ages ranged from 25 to 43 years. Of the twenty babies born, thirteen were girls and seven were boys.

Unstructured interviews (Oakley, 1981; Taylor and Bogden, 1984) were used to gather data by interviewing each parent at home three times. The first interview occurred before the birth of the baby. (Two babies were born prematurely, which prevented the first interview with the respective parents taking place before the birth.) The second interview was conducted during the second or third month following the baby's birth. The third interview occurred when babies were between 5 and 7 months of age. Interviews lasted one to two hours, and the time increased with each interview as participants and researchers became more familiar with each other and had more to discuss.

In the first interview, parents were asked about parental and extended family expectations concerning the gender of the infant, preparations for the arrival of the infant, and how they envisioned interacting with the infant. Participants were also asked about responsibilities for household tasks prior to pregnancy. During the second interview, each parent was asked to comment on the birth experience, lifestyle changes and views on parenting. Similar to the second interview, the third interview focused on the home environment, parent–infant interactions and changes in daily family life. During these interviews, the researcher's emphasis was to listen to parents' responses to open-ended questions.

As everyday life is understood as an arena of gender politics (Connell, 1995), it was felt that conversation about changes in daily life brought about by the impending birth would reveal ways in which social relations in daily domesticity are gendered. The unstructured interviews provided a wealth of information about all the families. Parents were supplied with transcripts of each interview and invited to make any alterations to the transcripts that they felt necessary (see Lather, 1986, 1991), which some did. One mother indicated in the first interview that she held no particular preference for a daughter or son. Yet, after reading the transcript, she requested that her preference be noted for a daughter.

PARENTAL RESPONSES

Responses from the parents revealed a complex matrix of beliefs, values and lived experiences about gendering and family relationships. Three issues related to these insights are discussed. First, the decision about whether to know the sex of the infant before birth is discussed. Second, parental preferences for a girl or boy are considered. Finally, imagined and actual interactions with infants are considered. For the most part, data are drawn from the first and second interviews.

To know or not to know?

The desire to know or not know appeared to have been influenced by the availability of medical technology. Such information is usually obtainable from approximately 3 months gestation age, when an ultrasound can be requested by the doctor to check foetal size and progress. For one couple, the sex of the foetus became known following an amniocentesis. Eight couples and one mother came to know the sex of the baby before birth. The remaining eleven couples and one father chose not to know the sex before the birth, although the father who decided not to know asked during the latter stages of the pregnancy and was subsequently told. Of the eleven couples who chose not to know the sex before the birth, three couples were in complete agreement and indicated that the element of surprise was very important for them. For many of the other couples, there were differences of opinion about whether or not to know.

To know

Of the eight couples and one mother choosing to know, there was a general feeling that if the technology was available, then the information may as well be accessed. Parents cited a number of specific reasons for deciding to know, including curiosity (M and F2: 1)[2] and preparation for the forthcoming event:

> Nick wanted to give it an identity (M1: 1), 'to prepare myself as in how to think of the child' (F1: 1).

> The more information that we have from an early stage the better. The surprise element will still be there, whether you know or not (M8: 1).

> . . . knowing the gender will assist in bringing me closer to my baby and start thinking about names. It will also help in buying things instead of going for yellows or whites (F14: 1).

In these three responses, the importance of knowing as preparation for the arrival of the infant is apparent. Knowing is seen as significant in order to purchase appropriately coloured items of clothing according to the sex of the foetus.

It is also important for parents to know so that they construct their unborn child as a gendered being. References are made to selection of names (which are frequently gender specific), the creation of identities for infants, as well as reasons for adding the dimension of 'closeness' to the father–foetus (child) relationship. It appears as though Nick (F1: 1) wanted to know in order to ascribe the foetus either a male or female identity and so think about the child as a girl or boy. In preparing for and thinking of the child in this way, it seems that knowing the sex of the foetus may be another way in which gender politics enter everyday life (see Connell, 1995).

The decision to know brought its own complexities. Of the nine couples who knew the gender, most did not agree completely about this decision to know. There was only one family (M and F8: 1) where a mother wanted to know but the father did not. Pauline requested the information following a scan, but did not tell Dean, as he remained hesitant about knowing. However, Dean wanted to know towards the end of the pregnancy, and Pauline was then able to share the knowledge with him. This example contrasts with those where fathers were positioned to make the decision for the couple. Here Pauline was able to use the discursive space existing outside discourses of hegemonic masculinity to construct a situation that suited both parents yet involved no compromises by either party. In situations where there was a difference of opinion, the preferences of fathers prevailed. Differences of opinion or changes in opinion about wanting to know occurred with at least six couples.

For example, although Nick and Jenny (M and F1: 1) knew, they agreed to keep it a secret from family and friends as Jenny did not want to know. Although Nick's preference for knowing prevailed, Jenny resisted by negotiating a compromise to keep it a secret. Alicia and David (M and F17: 1) also had a difference of opinion, as David wanted to know and Alicia did not. They compromised by finding out and not telling anyone, despite the fact that, according to David, 'it was the cause of some friction' (F17: 1). Alicia stated that she was, 'lying to friends that I would normally tell anything to' and indicated that, from her perspective, 'there is a real stigma attached to finding out – that it's unnatural' (M17: 1). Alicia had been able to contest David's preference and apparently continued to do so, feeling that knowing was unnatural. Having the discursive space available to resist, but then deferring to David's preference through a compromise, meant Alicia remained unhappy with the situation and continued to resist David's decision. As for Angela and Garth, Angela had indicated that she did not want to know but Garth asked the doctor after the scan and was subsequently told (M and F4: 1). These mothers did not want to know, but because their partners did, they also came to know.

For those couples choosing not to know, a similar situation existed to those who did want to know, as differences of opinion also emerged.

Not to know

In all there were eleven couples who did not know the sex of their child prior to the birth. This decision was made relatively early in the pregnancy. During the first interview, six mothers indicated that they would have either liked to know, or were tempted subsequently to find out before the birth of the baby. However, because the six fathers indicated that they did not want to know, these mothers also were not to know the sex of the infant before birth. For example, Eve and Andrew were offered the option but declined, although Eve (M6: 1) said, 'sometimes [I] thought it would be nice to know but couldn't keep a secret like that from Andrew'. Byron (F10: 1) was adamant from the beginning that there was no need to know, but Jill (M10: 1) became really curious about two weeks prior to birth, but did not find out. Les and Sue (M and F19: 1) decided not to know because, according to Les, 'it just makes it more of a surprise'. Sue admitted that, 'a few times I would have liked to know but I couldn't keep my mouth shut if I did.' In the case of Troy and Sara (M and F18: 1), Troy didn't want to know, but Sara 'could easily have caved in toward the end . . . I was dying to know.' Like many of the other couples, Jill and Byron were offered the option but declined. Jill subsequently wished she had found out, but Byron disagreed, stating that 'you should be grateful for the child you get as opposed to the sex of it' (F10: 1). None of these mothers came to know before the birth, and it was apparent that the fathers had a major influence in the decision about not knowing.

Although the responses from mothers indicated both an inclination and desire to know, they were the ones who offered reasons about why they should not know. These mothers justified not knowing on the basis of personal qualities such as an inability to 'keep my mouth shut'. This was apparently a sufficient reason given that the father did not want to know. The data revealed no major friction between couples about the decision not to know and there is no evidence that mothers challenged fathers over the issue. Mothers appeared, therefore, to be positioned to accept that fathers could be instrumental in making the decision about whether to know or not. In addition, these mothers were accepting of their self-identified 'inadequacies' as reasons for not knowing.

A girl or a boy? Parental preferences

Parental preferences for either a boy or girl, and the outcomes, can be seen in Table 2.1. Most notable is the preference by just over half the fathers (eleven) and nearly half the mothers (eight) for sons. Two fathers and five mothers listed preferences for daughters, and, as the table indicates, the numbers of fathers and mothers who recorded no particular preference were the same.

Sons

Many more mothers and fathers indicated preferences for sons than preferences for daughters. One father with two daughters from a previous relationship recorded this as a reason for preferring a son. Other reasons for fathers wanting the first child to be a son included the following:

> There's a kind of message that the first one should be a boy, because the boy should be more dominant (Nick; F1: 1).
>
> As a father I thought it would be nice to have the eldest as a boy, to look after his sisters and brothers (Andrew; F6: 1).
>
> Nerida [mother] doesn't have a preference but 'I imagine it as a boy, I think of it as being a boy' (Tom; F12: 1).
>
> Both parents wanted a boy, 'Then ideally the second child would be a girl. The older brother would then be protective towards his sister' (Peter and Tanya; F and M16: 1).

Table 2.1 Parental preferences and outcomes

Family	*Mother's preference*	*Father's preference*	*Outcome*
1. Jenny and Nick	son	son	daughter
2. Zoe and Nathan	daughter	none	daughter
3. Alison and Don	son	son	daughter
4. Angela and Garth	son	son	daughter
5. Ellen and Brad	son	son	daughter
6. Eve and Andrew	none	son	daughter
7. Yvonne and Bert	none	son	daughter
8. Pauline and Dean	daughter	daughter	daughter
9. Olivia and Nat	none	none	daughter
10. Jill and Byron	son	son	daughter
11. Karen and Richard	daughter	none	daughter
12. Nerida and Tom	daughter	none	daughter
13. June and Bill	none	none	daughter
14. Alice and Mal	none	none	son
15. Kelly and Mike	none	none	son
16. Tanya and Peter	son	son	son
17. Alicia and David	daughter	daughter	son
18. Sara and Troy	son	son	son
19. Sue and Les	son	son	son
20. Judy and Sam	none	son	son
Preferred son	8	11	7
Preferred daughter	5	2	13
No preference stated	7	7	

> Boy. Only because of the [family] name. My sister's children do not have the name – mainly for my father I would like a son (Sam; F20: 1).

These reasons for wanting a boy first are inextricably bound up with understandings of hegemonic masculinity. For example, Nick (F1) indicated that the boy should be more dominant. This can be read as an implicit contrast with the positioning of girls as passive, and as boys being more important than girls (because boys should come first). A similar idea is expressed by Andrew (F6) as well as Tanya and Peter (M and F16), where the eldest son is constructed as responsible for younger children, specifically as being protective toward his younger sisters. Understanding boys as dominant and capable of responsibility, and girls as requiring the protection of older brothers, is a social construction that implies that girls need to be safeguarded. The irony is that such safeguarding could also require adoption of dominant discourses of masculinity. Although parental perceptions may change, it is difficult to see that such perspectives would not become part of daily life in these families. Sons would be constructed as being more independent than daughters and as responsible for the protection and well being of their sisters. Such understandings indicate a binary, where sons are active and dominant and daughters are constituted as passive and deferential to brothers and perhaps fathers.

The idea of a son continuing the family name is again consistent with hegemonic masculinity. It is constructed as something significant that female children are unable to do. This parental expectation has significant implications for the males of the family over a period of time (lineage), and sits comfortably with functional conceptions of the middle-class nuclear family (see Parsons and Bales, 1955). Within this understanding of functional sociology, the family is responsible for the socialisation of female children to be nurturing and caring, and male children to be autonomous, independent and able to successfully shed anything associated with the (inferior) feminine (Parsons and Bales, 1955). Although the legal system in the state of Queensland has made it difficult (but not impossible) for infant girls to retain their mother's name, it has been common practice for mothers and infants to take the father's name. A more recent trend utilises a combination of both parents' surnames and provides evidence of ways in which the dominance of hegemonic masculinity is being contested. These more recent developments do not appear to be important to Sam, as his concern is the way in which he can assure continuation of his lineage by fathering a son (for his father).

Eight mothers indicated that they would have preferred sons. There is some evidence to suggest that these mothers wanted sons because the fathers had indicated such a preference:

> I didn't care either way, but I knew Troy would have liked a boy . . . his male idea of having a son first. It was in the back of my mind all the stereotypical things, I've got big brothers, the big brother syndrome . . . I guess for Troy, in a sense, I wanted a boy (M18: 1).

The ways in which some mothers were positioned to want sons because of the father's desire for sons requires further consideration. Not surprisingly, there are few direct responses by mothers about how their preferences may have been influenced by those of the father. Yet the table of preferences shows that eight mothers preferred to have sons.

It could be that mother's preferences for sons were influenced by the preferences by fathers for sons. Partial explanation of the apparent inconsistency between the mothers' preferences and the lack of explanatory data about those preferences may be found perhaps in the origins of involvement in the project. Nineteen mothers and one father responded to the advertisements for participants in this research project. It is possible that many of the fathers had little or no choice in their involvement, having been volunteered by their partners. The desire by mothers to include fathers in the project may itself be an example of hegemonic masculinity in operation, where mothers have had to work hard to ensure that fathers participated. Nevertheless, the silence of mothers about this issue lingers.

Reasons for preferences

Some parents drew on their own family structures for preferring particular family patterns. In the following excerpts, two mothers indicate distinct preferences because of their own family structure. The first mother, Jill, wanted a continuation of the birth order that she had experienced in her family as a child:

> I've got an older brother so it's a normal thing for me, so this child should be a boy. The first child should be a boy because that's what it is in my family (M10: 1).

The second mother, Zoe, who is the youngest of five children, saw the birth of a daughter as the younger sister that she always wanted but didn't have. 'I've always wanted a little sister but for a first child it's not important' (M2: 1). Although indicating desire for a 'little sister', Zoe played down the significance of her desire. She hesitantly dared to state a preference (Zoe looked cautiously at her husband while making this statement), and then immediately discounted it by stating that it was not important whether the first child was a girl. Here, Zoe appeared uneasy in identifying a preference, an indication of the way in which she was positioned, or the position she adopted in the relationship with her husband.

In some instances, parental preferences for either a boy or girl were influenced by perceived social conditions and the position of women and girls in society. Boys and men were deemed by the parents as able to protect themselves, whilst infant girls and women were a different story. The safety of girls and women was again prefaced on the understanding that their vulnerable social status was of concern. The following comments by two fathers indicate the nature of this concern:

> There's so many idiots out there. Guys seem to be able to handle it better, more able to defend themselves, or whatever, it's not a really good place for young women now-a-days, I don't think (F4: 1).

> . . . with the whole gender thing, girls to me would seem to be more vulnerable than boys when growing up. I'd worry a little bit less if it was a boy (F11: 1).

In the first transcription excerpt, field notes indicate that the term 'idiots' refers to males. Implied in both statements is the necessity of certain categories of men (such as fathers and brothers) to ensure the safety of women and girls. This assumption is based on socially constructed understandings of the fragility of women and girls and their inability to protect and defend themselves. There is no indication of what it is that women and girls need to be protected against. This silence suggests a commonsense assumption that 'everybody knows' why women and girls need protection. No such concerns were raised for boys, as boys were constructed as being able to defend themselves as well as girls.

In a similar vein, some respondents expressed particular beliefs about mothering girls as opposed to mothering boys. For example, Alicia (M17: 1) said she wanted a girl because she doesn't like adolescent boys. This preference is based on Alicia's understanding of how having a son will affect her long-term situation as a mother. It is also bound up with socially constructed commonsense assumptions that the behaviour and characteristics of some adolescent boys are undesirable. Being female, Alicia felt that she would be better able to understand another girl: 'I just thought I would be better with a girl than with a boy'. Nerida, however, stated that she would prefer to have a girl first:

> because they are cute and you can dress them up and it's the same gender [as me] so it's more familiar to me than having to do stuff with a little boy that I wouldn't know how to do, like teaching him to go to the toilet (M12: 1).

Nerida's preference is based on her construction of infant girls being familiar territory because of her own gender. Additional assumptions include doing things with girls that you can't with boys (like dressing them up); that girls can be described in particular ways (cute) that boys can't be; and that she would have to teach her son how to manage toileting. Here Nerida has not included in her discussion her view of the father in child rearing practices. This perception of undertaking toileting routines herself indicates an understanding of her own socially constructed position of mothering as being all-encompassing.

Fathers and daughters

Although eight fathers expressed no specific preference and ten wanted sons, only two fathers held preferences for daughters. Of the fathers who preferred a daughter, one had a son from a previous relationship and for this reason would have liked a daughter. Of significance is the disappointment fathers showed when they found from the scan that they were fathering daughters and not sons. Perhaps this disappointment can be connected to some of the unexplained reasons for mothers expressing preferences for sons. Fathers asserted their disappointment in the following terms:

> I guess I was a little disappointed as I was hoping for a boy because I can identify, I can understand them, I had brothers . . . and I thought a little girl, what do they need? (F1: 1).
>
> . . . and I wanted a boy . . . [I] was disappointed when I found out (F3: 1).

... wanted a boy ... I saw my younger brothers take care of my younger sister ... I still see that as a good thing ... I had this moment of disappointment (F4: 1).

Bert (F7: 1) had a strong preference for a son and felt he would rather not know because, 'I'll either be really disappointed or really elated'. If people asked about his preferences, he said he wanted a boy. Even though he wasn't close to his own father, Bert liked the idea of having a son, 'it was an illogical preference' (F7: 1). Likewise, Brad said, 'I could have been disappointed at the birth instead of being disappointed now [at the ultrasound]' (because he wanted a boy) (F5: 1).

The frankness of these fathers in openly admitting their disappointment was in complete contrast to the mothers. Mothers with particular preferences did not express such disappointment when told whether the foetus was a girl or a boy. Instead, mothers usually rationalised their preferences in some way, were more accepting and made it seem less important than those fathers who registered such disappointment.

Having discussed the decision to know or not know, parental preferences, and responses to the identified sex, the discussion now moves to the imagined and actual interactions of parents with their infants following birth.

Imagined and actual interactions with infants

During the first interview (before the birth), fathers were asked to think about the images they had of themselves interacting with their babies. Responses revealed images of interacting with the children not as infants, but at a time in the future when the children were several years of age. Images held by nearly all of the fathers reflected some sort of recreational or sporting involvement with an older child, and, for the most part, that child was assumed to be male. For example, Nick could only imagine what it would be like

with a little boy ... more difficult with a little girl. I told myself, there's no reason why I can't take a girl camping, fishing and sporting things (F1: 1).

Other fathers indicated similar positions:

because I'm sporty oriented person most of my images have been sporty with my son, but my mum is one of the sportiest creatures on earth (this comment was made after this father found out they were having a girl. He was initially disappointed about having a girl instead of a boy) (F3: 1).

[Garth] wanted to take him [the infant] out and teach him how to play golf (F4: 1).

> [Nat thought in terms of his own childhood] . . . mechanical things you do with your dad, out to the shed or down to the horses; playing golf, doing something together (F9: 1).

> I imagine myself being with a son in more special ways than I would with a daughter (F11: 1).

For Bert, the images of interacting with an older child (son) also prevailed:

> I guess I could picture myself with the ten year old son doing things, outdoor things such as bush walking, going fishing (even though I hate fishing), but that type of activity (F7: 1).

Although knowing they were having a girl, Mike said he would

> take her to the football . . . they'll [the baby] have to like camping though. Our friends and family go camping a lot . . . sport is very important (F15: 1).

Sam said that he'd make a

> conscious effort if it is a girl to include her in as many male things as possible because I'm a real supporter of the equity movement, like fishing, golf (F20: 1).

Other fathers who weren't as oriented to the outdoors tended also to hold images of doing things with older children. Tom imagined debating with the infant when older: 'when they are older, when they have opinions and they can argue with you' (F12: 1). Nathan (French nationality) indicated he wanted the baby to speak French and would introduce it to good food (F2: 1).

On the whole, first interviews showed that fathers were not positioned to discuss their involvement in nurturing infants. The majority of fathers could imagine themselves interacting with their child only when the child was older. In fact, the closest that any of the twenty fathers came to talking about nurturing was one who mentioned holding the baby, and two who mentioned that they would be washing diapers. However, the second round of interviews revealed that, despite the images, daily life was different. Many fathers were calming babies when they were upset and were involved in tasks such as bathing the infants when they arrived home from work. For example, Nathan played the guitar as, 'it settles her [the baby] most of the time' (F2: 2). Don stated that he was 'quite good at calming her [the infant] down' (F3: 2). Andrew was responsible for all care of the baby, including bottle feeding, as 'Eve [mother] was sick for a while' (F6: 2). References by fathers to cuddling infants were frequent and emerged as a part of their daily interactions:

> I hold and cuddle her a lot (F11: 2)

> I'm a fairly tactile person, when burping the baby I always give lots of cuddles (F12: 2)
> Sometimes I cuddle him to sleep talking about what he's done during the day and what he'll be doing tomorrow (F19: 2).

Despite this involvement in nurturing, images of what fathers might do when the children were older continued to dominate responses to questions asked after the birth. Garth, one of two professional sports people involved in the project, indicated that, 'She can play whatever she wants . . . I'll just sway her if I can' (F4: 2). Brad was looking forward to Sonya fishing and worming (F5: 2), and Byron perceived his daughter to be very bright and hoped, 'she will finish uni at fifteen and be doing her Masters at Oxford by seventeen' (F10: 2). Richard revealed that he often 'wonders what she will be and talk[s] about one day when she is a . . . lawyer, artist, Olympic athlete, whatever is in my head' (F11: 2). Les had the cricket pitch ready in the back yard and said that he

> put the rattle in the baby's right hand so he won't be a left-handed bowler. . . . It has always felt very natural raving on to him. That is, playing cricket, the tennis, how he's going to bring Monica Seles home one day (F19: 2).

The pervasiveness of such images indicated pleasurable things to come in the future, which were to be shared between father and child. This orientation towards the future, rather than a concern with the present, may be indicative of fathers' perceptions of making what appears to them to be a more tangible contribution when children are older.

Talking about fathering differs from actually doing it. Fathers did hold, placate and nurture their infants, but they did not often speak about it. By far the dominant images, both before and after the birth, were those about good times in the future, with fathers constructing their children as involved with them in preferred sporting or leisure activities. Here, Butler's (1990) notion of gender as performance is illuminating. Using her account, these sporting and leisure images of the future represent preferred gender norms for fathering, so that speaking about nurturing infants may pose a threat to these preferred norms. Butler (1990, 33) understands gender as the 'repeated stylisation of the body, a set of repeated acts . . . that congeal over time to produce the appearance of a substance, of a natural sort of being'. Speaking about nurturing could threaten or disrupt the illusion that makes gender seem a reality or natural part of everyday life. Going beyond the boundary of preferred norms by speaking about nurturing poses the threat of exposing gender as an effect that preserves its own reconstruction. Holding, placating and nurturing infants could be seen as a violation of the norms of fatherhood. However, the performance of such duties within the private sphere of the home is less risky than a public performance. This may be the reason that some fathers spoke about ways in which they were involved in nurturing their infants. Nevertheless, this remains a site of competing and contested discourses.

In stark contrast to fathers, mothers' images discussed in the first interviews were immediate and concerned with how they would manage the birth and subsequent feeding, bathing and other routines that they understood needed to be established. There was little discussion concerning these routines as mothers generally expected that they would bear prime responsibility for them, although with support of fathers. Mothers showed varying degrees of comfort about this situation and feelings ranged from eagerness to apprehension. For example, Olivia said, 'I haven't been particularly excited about having a child but maybe I needed more enthusiasm from Nat' (M9: 1). Olivia had never pictured herself with children and was worried that she hadn't 'felt maternal at all' throughout the pregnancy. She was hoping it (feeling maternal) was 'going to kick in sooner or later' and perceived Nat to be much more comfortable with children than herself (M9: 1).

Like Olivia, other mothers also talked about the anticipated role of the father as they imagined their own interactions with the infant. For example, Zoe stated that she wanted her husband to 'have as much involvement in it as I do', and to 'know how to do everything' (M2: 1). Angela indicated that it would be her husband

> guiding me the whole way, he's the one with experience [from his large family]. To start with, I'd like him around a week or so after the birth to help me settle in and figure out how to do everything (M4: 1).

Support from fathers and the desire for father involvement with the infant was valued highly by mothers and was seen as essential for establishing the baby comfortably in the home environment.

CONCLUSION

Throughout the data collection process, parents raised a number of questions. Several parents asked questions indicating that they perceived the study to be about parenting and not specifically about the gendering process. Additionally, a small number of unsolicited parental responses substantiated some commonsense assumptions about gendering based on visible physical attributes. After reading their transcripts, other parents stated that what they had discussed bore little relation to gender. In contrast to these parental understandings, those working on the project (a research assistant and myself) found the data an abundant source of ways in which cultural meaning systems are saturated with versions of everyday gendered life: an 'arena of gender politics', as Connell (1995, 3) has indicated. Parental perceptions of enacting gender on a daily basis seem to be based on understandings connected with visible physical attributes (such as dressing infant girls in pink clothing) that are frequently used and understood as signals of gender identity. Awareness of how more subtle forms of gendering and gendered practices (such as hegemonic masculinity) occur in daily domestic interaction and practice was not apparent.

Several issues that emerged from the data confirm aspects of hegemonic masculinity operating in the course of daily domesticity in these families. The position adopted by many mothers to defer to fathers' preferences about knowing or not knowing the sex of the foetus showed that few women were constituted to resist or challenge this aspect of hegemonic masculinity. Despite indicating that they wanted to know, many mothers accepted their personal 'inadequacies' as reason enough not to know. Such actions could therefore establish a precedent for future situations, as discursive spaces are not available for mothers' decisions to prevail in cases of differences of opinion. For many, discursive spaces would certainly appear available to voice a difference of opinion, but few had little hope of more than this if fathers were positioned (and positioned themselves) within frames of hegemonic masculinity. Alicia, who deferred to David's preference to know but continued to resist her own acquiescence, continued throughout the pregnancy to struggle with the way in which she and David were positioned. For other mothers, no discursive spaces were available for resistance or contestation about whether to know or not.

Restriction or limitation of discursive spaces through adoption of forms of hegemonic masculinity has the potential to create silences. The predominance of fathers' responses occurred because some fathers adopted the more powerful position of hegemonic masculinity, which had the effect of silencing some mothers. Mothers were able to adopt more powerful positions in the interviews when issues of domestic routines with infants such as feeding and bathing were discussed. However, data overall show a predominance of responses by fathers (fathers tended to talk more than mothers) and a tendency for mothers to want to provide opportunities for fathers to respond (mothers offered fathers the chance to speak before they did). The possibility exists that for some of the mothers in this study, a hegemonic form of masculinity is a regular part of daily life. In such circumstances, mothers may find themselves with severely restricted discursive spaces in which to operate. For other couples in the interviews, mothers were positioned to offer the opportunity to fathers to respond first. Both interviewers detected a strong sense that mothers wanted fathers to be fully involved in the whole process of becoming and being a family. In the interview situation, this meant that mothers actively attempted to involve fathers by making eye contact, gesturing or suggesting that they respond first.

Responses showed fathers talked about their (mostly imagined male) infants only in terms of the distant future. This, combined with the relative silence of fathers about nurturing in the short term, shows some of the specific ways in which these men take up positions as fathers. It appears that they are reluctant, or perhaps are not discursively constituted, to discuss caring behaviour in which they may engage following the birth of the baby. These same fathers made significantly more references to the caring behaviour in which they actually engaged after the birth; however, these references are not numerous. Futuristic perceptions of fathers enjoying leisure or sporting activities with their older, often male children dominated the images that these fathers offered in their talk. These images, combined with concerns about the vulnerability of women and girls and the importance of men and boys being dominant and protective towards women and girls, confirm several representations in which aspects of hegemonic masculinity prevail. The challenge with such stereotyped commonsense assumptions is that they, 'resist correction through the testimony of science or rational argument because they reflect not the absence of accurate information so much as fundamental ways of interpreting experience' (Silin, 1997, 230). Although a formidable task, providing alternative ways of interpreting experience creates opportunities to push aside meanings that have become accepted as natural and unquestioned ways of understanding and explaining the phenomena of gendering in family contexts.

NOTES

1 This project was funded by a Queensland University of Technology, Faculty of Education Research Grant and a Queensland University of Technology New Researcher Grant.
2 (M and F2: 1) can be read as mother and father number 2 (of the twenty couples in the study). This statement was made during the first interview (designated by the 1). Pseudonyms have been used.

REFERENCES

Butler, J. (1990) *Gender trouble: Feminism and the subversion of identity*. Routledge: New York.
Connell, R. W. (1995) *Masculinities*. St Leonards, NSW: Allen & Unwin.
Connell, R. W. (1996) Teaching the boys: New research on masculinity, and gender strategies for schools. *Teachers College Record* 98 (2) 206–235.
Davies, B. (1989) *Frogs and snails and feminist tales: Preschool children and gender*. Sydney: Allen & Unwin.
Davies, B. (1996) Power knowledge desire: Changing school organisation and management practices. Canberra, ACT. DEETYA.
Foucault, M. (1977) *Discipline and punish: The birth of the prison*. (A. Sheridan, trans.). Harmondsworth: Penguin.
Foucault, M. (1979) *The history of sexuality 1: An introduction*. London: Allen Lane.

Gee, J. P. (1990) *Social linguistics and literacies: Ideology in discourses.* London: Falmer.
Kamler, B., Maclean, R., Reid, J. and Simpson, A. (1994) *Shaping up nicely: The formation of schoolgirls and schoolboys in the first month of school.* A report to the gender equity and curriculum reform project. DEET. Canberra.
Lather, P. (1986) Research as praxis. *Harvard Educational Review* 56 (3), 257–277.
Lather, P. (1991) *Getting smart: Feminist research and pedagogy with/in the postmodern.* New York: Routledge.
Luke, C. (1996) Childhood and parenting in children's popular culture and childcare magazines. In C. Luke (ed.) *Feminisms and pedagogies of everyday life.* 167–187. Albany NY: State University of New York Press.
Oakley, A. (1981) *Interviewing women: A contradiction in terms.* In H. Roberts (ed.) Doing feminist research. 30–61. London: Routledge & Kegan Paul.
Ochs, E. and Taylor, C. (1992) Family narrative as political discourse. *Discourse and Society* 30 (3) 301–340.
Parsons, T., Bales, R. F., in collaboration with Olds, J., Zelditch, M. and Slater, P. E. (1955) *Family: Socialisation and interaction process.* New York: Free Press.
Silin, J. (1997) The pervert in the classroom. In J. Tobin (ed.) *Making a place for pleasure in early childhood education.* 214–234. New Haven: Yale.
Taylor, S. J. and Bogden, R. (1984) *Introduction to qualitative research methods: The search for meanings.* (2nd edn) New York: John Wiley.
Thorne, B. (1993) *Gender play: Boys and girls in school.* Buckingham: The Open University Press.
Wearing, B. (1996) *Gender: The pain and pleasure of difference.* Melbourne: Longman.
Weedon, C. (1987) *Feminist practice and poststructuralist theory.* Oxford: Blackwell.

Chapter 3

Boys and girls with disabilities

Maternal expectations of gender behaviour and independence

Anna Bower

INTRODUCTION

This chapter describes mothers' perceptions, beliefs and ideas about issues of gender and independence in their child with a disability. While studies focusing on disability issues have compared and contrasted male and female children, few studies have examined mothers' perceptions and expectations for male and female children with a disability. This chapter describes how mothers articulated their expectations for gender development and considers the hopes and expectations they have for their children in the future. Issues of independence are linked to employment, self-care issues and personal autonomy for both male and female children. Most significantly, mothers link independence with their hopes and expectations for happiness and personal autonomy of their children. While mothers don't appear to differentiate between boys and girls in their hopes for their children, the mothers who have a child with intellectual disability, either female or male, appear most concerned about this issue.

THE DILEMMA OF BLUE VERSUS PINK

Studies of child gender have traditionally been linked with mothers, who are perceived to have the first significant influence on children's gender development. Mothers' child rearing behaviours tend to be closely examined and attributed to children's subsequent perceptions of female and male behaviours (Woollett, Phoenix and Lloyd, 1992). Yet it cannot be denied that the relationship is reciprocal: mothers don't merely influence gender appropriate behaviour of their children, their children's behaviours similarly influence the experiences of mothering. In general, a child's gender is attributed considerable importance in Western societies (McGuire, 1991). Specific expectations are placed on female and male members of society and these expectations shape children's perceptions and anticipations very early in life. Traditional adherence to gender difference in child rearing practices has been much criticised by the post-modern feminist movement (e.g. Davies, 1988; Everingham, 1994), proposing the notion that female children are encouraged through parenting practices, education and societal expectations to become more dependent than their male counterparts (e.g. Dunn and Morgan, 1987; Honig, 1983; McGuire, 1991; Mac Naughton, 1992, 1993). Such practices continue to be demonstrated in the different expectations societies have of young male and female children. While it appears acceptable for a girl to show her dependence through crying, the boy who cries past a very young age continues to be reprimanded, indeed ridiculed, by peers and society at large and encouraged to show his personal independence by 'being tough'.

It appears, then, that children today receive many conflicting messages. On the one hand they are expected to exhibit stereotyped gender behaviour, whilst on the other they are told that gender differences do not exist, that girls can be the same as boys in their needs, likes and behaviours and have equal opportunity in today's world. While some parents consciously make an effort to avoid stereotypical expectations and behaviours from their sons and daughters, other parents continue to find security in parenting practices that closely resemble their own childhood experiences in terms of being male or female. Yet, although parents tend to have separate expectations for their female and male children, they appear to be acutely aware of the need for individual independence for their children in a highly competitive world.

THE SOURCES OF MOTHERS' IDEAS ABOUT GENDER

Research has shown that mothers have a tendency to draw on their own backgrounds and possibly on their own childhood experiences when they describe their perceptions and ideas about gender roles. Their views are shaped by a wide range of rich personal experiences as well as by the influence of the media. Goodnow and Collins (1990) identify a range of sources for the development of ideas about gender. Frequently parents' views of gender roles tend to be influenced by their views about the future. Parents also consider biological and environmental factors as influencing the development of gender differences and identity. A study by Antill (1987) explored parents' views and beliefs in terms of same-sex and cross-sex behaviours and concluded that fathers, particularly fathers of sons, discouraged cross-sex activities more than mothers. Stereotyped ideas continue to be strongly linked to gender differences, with 61 per cent of parents desiring that their sons demonstrate masculine and their daughters feminine behaviours (Palacios, 1986). In a study that examined the effects of children's physical appearance on parents' responses, Zebrowitz-McArthur and Kendall-Tackett (1989) report that parents tended to be more favourably disposed towards baby-faced children of the opposite gender and proposed more severe punishment for mature faced children of the same sex as the parent. Furthermore, many parents continue to adhere to category based gender judgement. For example, the notion that boys are naturally more talented in mathematics, in contrast to girls who have to make a greater effort, may result in the expectations for girls being lowered, while the ability of boys may be overestimated (Goodnow and Collins, 1990).

While such views and beliefs and their associated restricting effects on child development are reported for parents of children without disability, they similarly appear to influence the personal development of children with disability, although possibly in more subtle ways. The presence of any type of disability is linked to a degree of loss of personal independence. It is, however, the intellectual and multiple disabilities that tend to result in significant loss or absence of independence.

THE SIGNIFICANCE OF PERSONAL INDEPENDENCE

In most societies, expectations of personal independence tend to be influenced by gender. Traditionally, male members of society had greater expectations of independence placed on them than females. This is most vividly illustrated by the prevailing practices earlier this century, when it was largely considered a waste of resources for girls to become educated. Girls were expected to continue in their traditional female roles as nurturers, which generally involved the dependency on male members of the family. The growing proliferation of feminist principles, however, has gradually resulted in the recognition for equality and equal opportunity for personal independence.

Western societies place much value on the development of individual independence and personal autonomy. Children in contemporary Western societies are unlikely to remain living with their parents past their years of schooling, training or studying. As a result, parents tend to prepare their offsprings for personal independence and independent living from a very early age. Personal independence is characterised by a range of behaviours, which may include the ability to:

- make decisions (*intellectual*)
- take care of own needs (*social*)
- gain and maintain employment (*social*)
- form relationships (*emotional*)
- accept citizenship responsibilities (*social, communitarianism*)

(Bower, 1996, p. 35)

It is anticipated, and indeed expected, that independent adults will be fully able to care for themselves in every aspect of life, thereby releasing parents from their responsibility of care. Ultimately, however, the ageing process of the parents may result in a role reversal, where offspring may need to take increasing responsibility of care for ageing, dependent parents in later life. Such social patterns result in the increased awareness of the importance of personal independence for children in our societies.

While the need for personal independence is today recognised as being of equal importance for female and male children in Australian society, gender issues have been and continue to be researched and debated by a wide range of social scientists. The issue of the development of personal independence related to gender tends to be of a less explicit nature. While gender equity issues have addressed the social standing of women by dramatically improving their opportunities, contemporary women continue to experience a degree of dependency when they become mothers. This dependency is implicitly communicated to children and transmits powerful messages, particularly to female children, who intuitively model themselves on the roles of their mother.

INDEPENDENCE, GENDER AND DISABILITY

Mothers who have a child with a disability are specifically aware of the need for independence. Significant disability tends to result in exceptional developmental patterns for children, many of them directly influencing the reaching of personal independence. In many instances, it has been noted that the degree of disability appears to influence directly the level of independence of a person. Moderate to severe intellectual disability almost certainly ensues in a significantly decreased level of independence for intellectual, social and emotional aspects of living. Physical disability affects the physical independence and mobility. Unless physical disability is associated with intellectual disability, these individuals enjoy increasingly improved opportunities to live relatively independent lives (Stieler, 1994). While it is acknowledged that intellectual and physical disability represent only two of a wide range of disabilities, a study of their impact on the ways in which mothers perceive these disabilities may influence the development of independence of their child and serves as a useful framework for discussion.

Mothers' perceptions, ideas and beliefs are best related in their own words, and what follows is a description of a study that focused on mothers' beliefs and ideas about gender related issues and in particular those of independence for their children who have a disability. While mothers continue to be children's major carers during the early years, in the case of a child with an intellectual disability, they tend to remain the major carers when the children become adolescents and later young adults. It therefore seems appropriate to examine the ideas, beliefs and expectations that these mothers hold for their child with a disability. The research examines the similarities and differences of mothers' gender related expectations of their children for two separate disabilities: mothers who have a child with an intellectual disability, Down's syndrome, and mothers who have a child with a physical disability, spina bifida. The aim of the study was to determine whether those mothers who have a child with an intellectual disability share similar expectations for their children's development of personal independence with those mothers who have a child with a physical disability. Furthermore, the study explored whether gender is an influential factor related to mothers' expectations of independence.

BACKGROUND TO THE STUDY

The findings of this study are extracted from a larger and more comprehensive qualitative study of mothers' ideas and beliefs about their family in families with a disabled child. The participants in this study were twenty mothers who have a child with Down's syndrome and fifteen mothers who have a child with spina bifida. Mothers talked candidly about issues of gender and independence and perceived these issues to be of major importance. The mothers largely volunteered their stories about gender and independence in the context of talking about family dynamics, experiences and views of sibling relationships, and gender relationships appear to be an important aspect of family dynamics.

The first section describes mothers' ideas and beliefs about general gender issues in the family and include statements from mothers of the two groups, Down's syndrome (intellectual disability) and spina bifida (physical disability). The second section focuses more specifically on mothers' ideas and beliefs about issues of independence of their male and female children. Each mother is identified by a substituted name, followed by an indicator of the child's specific disability, e.g. DS (child with Down's Syndrome) SB (child with spina bifida).

MOTHERS' PERCEIVED IDEAS AND BEHAVIOURAL DIFFERENCES BETWEEN GIRLS AND BOYS

The statements that follow in the next sections are verbatim responses made in personal interviews by some mothers in this study. Although the study occurred in the past, mothers' responses, as well as some author's comments, are presented in the present tense, which reflects more sensitively the ambience of the moment and the subtleties of their meaning.

The following examples describe how mothers perceive the behavioural gender differences between their sons and daughters and simultaneously suggest that the mothers expected gender behaviours. The mothers illustrated their perceptions of gender differences in a variety of ways. Many of their responses indicate that ideas about gender roles remain anchored in socially well-established beliefs, despite considerable coverage by the media and contemporary literature highlighting the limitations of the traditional approaches to gender socialisation. The notion of 'girls are made of sugar and spice and all things nice, and boys are made of slugs and snails and puppy dogs tails' (old English folklore) appears to remain a thriving ideology, supported by a series of statements made by mothers in this study who said: 'boys do so many dangerous things' or 'boys are total grubs' or 'I want her to be a real little lady, it will make life easier for her'. Mothers' ideas of gender appropriate behaviours are aptly illustrated in the following examples. They create distinct lines between male and female gender roles.

> Andrea (DS):
> they are different sexes, and uhm . . . but I do think that makes a difference, because as much as we are supposed to be living in an equal society . . . (laughter) . . . there are vast differences between girls and boys and they do want to do different things, and they do head in different directions.

Later, Andrea made the following reference to her daughter who has Down's syndrome:

> I am trying to raise her like a real little lady . . . I consider her manners and her good behaviour to be her major assets in life. If the first thing she walks in the door and she's accepted she is a long way through that door. It's been a major thing for me from the time she was a little girl, the way she sits, her manners, the correct way of doing things, even to the point of being a little old world about it, but it suits Hillary to a 't'.

> Margaret (DS):
> all boys should have their genes genetically engineered you know . . . because as soon as they learn to ride a bike . . . even him . . . he has got to try . . . he sort of . . . as soon as he could ride the 2-wheeler bike, straight away he wanted to go down that steep hill on the cement you know. Girls are . . . uhm . . . different.

> Maria (SB):
> I mean . . . again . . . he is a boy . . . and no matter what you think of . . . you know . . . wanting him to be a responsible boy rather than uhm . . . you know . . . you worry emotionally . . . his concerns and I mean . . . Actually it worries me that I see it differently because he is a boy and not a girl . . . I'm thinking, well there you are . . . (self-conscious laughter).

Although the mothers in this section differentiate between the ways in which boys and girls act, Maria focuses on the gender specific emotional development of her child who has a physical disability. Clearly there appear to be some similarities between the two groups of mothers in the way they perceive their children's gender, yet their ideas indicate that they distinctly differentiate between male and female gender related behaviour. Some mothers suggested an awareness of what may be termed an 'ideological correctness' relating to gender attitudes and ideas held by a contemporary society, as is illustrated by the following statement by one mother who has a son with Down's syndrome:

> I know you are no longer supposed to say these things . . . you know . . . but I think boys need to be treated differently to girls . . . you know? They are so different you just have to.

Ideas about children's gender inappropriate behaviour

Children's gender inappropriate play behaviour tends to become a concern as children enter the middle childhood stage of development. Prior to this, play activities socially attributed to either male or female gender tend to be accepted for girls and boys. While fathers tend to be less tolerant of boys engaging in what they perceive to be 'girls' activities', it has been found that mothers show much greater acceptance of such differences (Goodnow and Collins, 1990). In addition, Goodnow and Collins (1990) report that 'fathers are more concerned than are mothers with conformity to gender stereotypes for both sons and daughters, and especially so for sons' (p. 20). Mothers in this study reported that fathers tend to show increased concerns about sons' female play behaviours, such as playing with dolls, but are less interested in the play behaviours of their daughters, thus supporting the literature.

Mothers who have a child with a disability do not appear to show concern for gender atypical behaviour of their child. Individual achievements of the child who has a disability are of such importance to parents, that the nature of these achievements becomes secondary to the progress in development. Thus mothers tend to focus less on the appropriateness of gender based games and play than they do on the child's developmental gains. While mothers showed some evidence of valuing typical female or 'lady-like' behaviour in their daughters, particularly those who have a child with an intellectual disability, they perceived such behaviour as promoting the social acceptance of the child. Among those mothers who have a male child with an intellectual disability, non-masculine gender behaviour emerged as a concern, as this is perceived as important to the social acceptance of the male child in the community. This is evident in the following examples:

> Rose (DS):
> you know he is a bit of a 'couch potato' doesn't like boys games much,

mind you he hasn't got many friends, but I keep encouraging him to play the boys' games. He is now swimming . . . this is his second full year of swimming training and now he is . . . because his fitness has increased, and the coach is actually strict with him now, treats him like a man now.

Ailsa (DS):
He's a real sook of a boy, you know . . . he likes it indoors, does not like to play rough with the others. He's always around me, wanting to cook and so on. He says:' I love you Mum, I want to stay with you.' It is not so bad for me but Wayne (husband) really hates it.

A mother who has a child with a physical disability expressed relief that her son shows typical male behaviour, despite his physically disabling condition, when she said:

Moira (SB):
He loves being outdoors you know, in the garden. He is always collecting lizards and bugs and things, he moves through the bushes on his bum and he gets real filthy you wouldn't know how, he's a real boy that one . . . he is.

While Moira, who has a son with a physical disability, clearly emphasises her preference for masculine behaviours, she also indicates her relief at his appropriate 'boy type behaviour'. Rose and Alison, the two mothers who both have a son with Down's syndrome, seem accepting of the gender inappropriate behaviours of their male children, although Rose aims to ameliorate this situation by involving her son in sports activities, which for boys is socially very appropriate. It appears then that atypical gender behaviours result in a degree of vulnerability for mothers in terms of increasing the level of dependence of the child on the parent.

Gender and position in the family

It has been argued that family configuration of siblings influences mothers' expectations of their male and female children (Dunn and Plomin, 1990; Goodnow and Collins, 1990). It is well documented that the eldest daughter tends to be expected to adopt a leadership role in terms of assisting the mother in mothering tasks (e.g. McGuire, 1991). Alternatively, the eldest son tends to be conferred a degree of power over the younger siblings. In families who have a child with a disability, the roles siblings take in terms of their position in the family become less distinct (Kazak, 1986). In families without a child with a disability, mothers' expectations for their children's roles remain relatively stable throughout their development. This sibling role stability, determined by the age and position in the family, also tends to occur in families who have a child with a physical disability, provided there is no associated intellectual disability present. Sibling role stability does not occur in families who have a child with intellectual disability, because the intellectual development of such a child occurs at a much slower rate. This appears to have a significant impact on mothers' expectations and hopes for the independence of their child who has an intellectual disability.

DISABILITY AND INDEPENDENCE

As previously argued, it is a basic social norm of Western societies that expects mothers to value and anticipate that their children will acquire personal autonomy and independence on reaching adulthood. These values are implicitly or explicitly formulated and stated as long term goals and are present from the birth of the child, and the progression towards this goal is taken more or less for granted. Mothers who have a child with a disability tend to perceive independence in different contexts. From the very beginning the child's, and indeed the family's, future is tainted with additional uncertainties and anxiety. Yet the goal of independence is of such importance, that most mothers who have a child with a disability focus on personal independence consistently and aim for their child to reach at least partial independence on reaching adulthood. A number of mothers in this study previously cited (Bower, 1996) indicated that they believed total independence was difficult, if not impossible, to achieve for their child. Characteristically, these mothers belong to the group who have a child with an intellectual disability. The level of intellectual disability associated with Down's syndrome is characterised by significantly delayed cognitive development, which results in these children remaining intellectually dependent on others for a major part of their lives, depending on the degree of disability. Some expectations, ideas and beliefs these mothers have for their child are presented below.

The first group of mothers have a female child with Down's syndrome, and their expectations range from being optimistic to being realistic and pessimistic about the prospect of their child reaching a significant degree of independence; and their verbatim responses are presented with this in mind.

> Meg (DS):
> I hope that Susie will be able to live on her own and do her own thing. She's very practical. She's very . . . if she were here now and I am talking to you and if I pause for a minute she'll fill in. So she will say what I was going to say. Her language is wonderful . . . too good sometimes (*laughter*). But she really has a very good vocabulary. She has no trouble expressing her point of view.

Similarly, Andrea has high expectations for the level of independence her daughter should achieve when she says:

> Andrea (DS):
> our aims, consciously in the back of our mind is independence for Charlotte as much as she can gain. You realise that's not tending towards independence when you are just catering for every whim of that person. For Charlotte it's always to achieve the highest level of independence that we possibly can. We would like to think that she can live . . . uhm . . . apart from us when she is an adult. We are not sure what situation, may be a group situation, or uhm . . . I don't discount the fact that she could uhm . . . find a relationship for herself as she gets older. I'm sure there is a possibility there as time goes on, but uhm . . . we don't really envisage her living with us to the end of our days, mainly because we don't really think that would be good for her. And also socially for Charlotte, I would like to think that she could achieve a circle of friends that could be close friends, and that she can participate in a lot of things. I personally like the Ballet and she has been taken. She really enjoys it, she loves going to the theatre. She likes the whole aspect of dressing nicely and supper afterwards. She likes that and I would really like to think that she can have a situation where she could do things like that. Hopefully she would also have some friends and people she is involved with in whatever sphere she is in . . . may be a work situation or whatever.

Interestingly, this mother includes herself in the process of her child becoming independent, when she says: 'for Charlotte it's always to achieve the highest level of independence that we can'. Andrea is also clearly influenced by the female gender of her child when she links her expectations for social independence with expectations of appropriate female behaviour, has ambiguous hopes for future employment for her child and is the only mother in this study with a daughter with Down's syndrome who raised this issue.

Marion has realistic expectations for her daughter. She remarks on the sheltered life she lives at the moment but hopes that eventually she will make a few friends, be more independent and be able to go out with them.

> Marion (DS):
> she's really happier within herself, because she is going out and just sort of being a bit more independent and doing a few things that she wants to do on her own. She hasn't got me hanging around her all the time.

Anita seems particularly concerned about social acceptance of their daughter, as she perceives this to be an important aspect of developing the chances of independent living arrangements. Yet this mother appears to be only too aware of the limitations regarding the personal independence of a person with intellectual disability, as she points out the dangers and her fears associated with this. Anita is deeply concerned about her child's vulnerability as a result of such partial independence, and fears for her child's personal security. She expresses these fears as follows:

> Anita (DS):
> the most important issue is for Libbie, my daughter who has Down's syndrome, and her sister to have their own independence, both be socially acceptable, and I mean Lois as well as Libbie. I guess it will always be like that, I always want Libbie to be socially acceptable. It goes a long way towards independence when you are socially accepted by everyone. As long as she is happy and can stand on her own feet, I'd like to know that she can cook and dress and look after herself and all that sort of thing, uhm . . . the same as Lois. But then there is always this fear, hopefully nobody will take Libbie down and take advantage of her and what-have-you.

The remaining mothers who talked about independence of their child appeared to have more limited expectations for the future independence of their daughters, characteristically related to the lower level of intellectual functioning of these children. Ruth talks more in terms of dependence and the need for protection than independence. Clearly, these mothers, who have to come to terms with dependence related issues associated with intellectual disability, place lower priority on gender issues. Ruth associates independence with the prospect of possible employment when she says:

> Ruth (DS):
> yeh . . . probably . . . well, and as far as Eve goes, I guess I worry about the future. In a way the age that she is at is really great, because she is at school, and so she is occupied for the day. But at the same time she is still a very little girl, very loving and very easy and you know . . . uhm . . . I guess I worry about her growing up and being in danger, you know . . . being molested and all that . . . all kinds of things. Or what will happen to her job wise or what she'll do in the future when we are not here. But then you can't look that far ahead I think.

Joy's daughter is severely intellectually disabled, but Joy never the less aims to achieve the highest possible level of independence for her child.

> Joy (DS):
> well, for me, a lot of people tend to . . . uhm . . . you know want to do things for her, whereas I want to try and encourage her to be a bit more independent. And the things that I know she can try to do, I mean it is hard at home, she makes a huge mess and it is a lot more work, but I think the outcome is going to be a lot better. I hope she will be able to be

self sufficient, you know . . . her life will have a bit of worth. I do not expect her to go to school and learn and become academic, I mean you have to be realistic.

Clearly, independence is very important for Joy and although she holds realistic expectations on the one hand, she hopes for an almost unachievable level of independence for her child on the other.

Linda sees the prospect of personal independence for her daughter in terms of living skills and self-care skills. She fully anticipates for her daughter to live in a home as an adult when she says:

Linda (DS):
I'll put her in a home so she can look after herself . . . and for her sister to check on her from time to time and have her for social times and things like that. Not aspects of holding down a job or anything spectacular, it is too early to tell, we don't know how good she is going to be or how bad she is going to be. But as long as she can live independenfly, that's my main aim.

Finally, Alice contrasts the expectations she holds for her daughter with Down's syndrome and her brother. She looks realistically into the future when she says:

Alice (DS):
I can't really see now what will happen. I suppose he (brother) will go on his course of life. She will probably become more a home girl and have me to look after her. And he will become more and more independent. But I think I would like for both of them to reach their full potential and enjoy life . . . basically.

The analysis of these mothers' stories suggests that for children who have an intellectual disability, the expected attainment of personal independence far outweighs emphasis on issues of gender development. Gender appears to be of importance to mothers, but it becomes noticeably inconsequential once physical or mental health issues need to be considered.

The following sequence of mothers' statements relates to male children who have an intellectual disability. Interestingly, all mothers of boys raise the issue of future employment in a variety of contexts, compared with only a few mothers of girls who raised employment as an important aspect of independence. It appears that, for these parents, the notion of employment is linked to masculinity and its related perception of independence, and that these mothers appear to strive towards this socially well-accepted paradigm.

Roslyn, who has a son with Down's syndrome, appears to work actively towards a level of independence that may include employment when she says:

Roslyn (DS):
I want him to be independent. I am working towards that, and I hope that a job is not out of the question for him. This is one of the reasons why we bought the cleaning business so that he may be able to work with Bill down the track. Work is important you know . . . it is all about self esteem and that, you know. May be as parents of special children we tend to mollycoddle and make excuses and I try to never do that with Freddy. I try not to interfere too much, I'm hoping that I am stepping back.

Gayle also appears to have high expectations for her son, all based on his improving self-help skills.

Gayle (DS):
Tim is pretty good, he can get himself dressed and things and when he was away on camp I noticed . . . not because he is my child . . . how much more independent he was than a lot of other kids. I don't think a job of some kind is out of the question, you know . . . in the morning he gets up and he is getting himself dressed. Now we are making the bed . . . uhm . . . we are coming out, we say what we want for breakfast. If I'm busy he will make the toast, he will put the kettle on, and when I come up some mornings tea is made and he will say 'Mum I put some toast on for you', so you know . . . I mean he's going to be all right.

Nola has expectations for independence for all her children and bases her hopes for her son who has Down's syndrome on her observations of improvement. She says:

Nola (DS):
I think independence is the big thing, not over, not too independent, now that Adam is growing up, just so that he is starting to get a bit of responsibility, so when he will be an adult he will not rely on us all the time. He likes to think that he is independent and that he can do his own thing. He is growing up socially and is willing to learn. So mainly just for his independence and to be able to get along in life and stand up for himself and take care of himself.

Margaret appears to have some conflicting expectations for her son. On the one hand, she says that she does not expect a high level of independence for her son, but on the other, she is anticipating him acquiring basic academic skills and possibly employment.

Margaret (DS):
He will always be pretty dependent on us I think, but my hopes are that both of them, more Anthony than her (daughter), he will be able to read and write and so he . . . you know . . . get a manual job or whatever.

Fiona realistically recognises the ongoing dependence of her son when she says:

> Fiona (DS):
> You know as it is starting to get easier now, independence is painfully slow as I watch him tie his shoelaces and want to get in and do it myself. But I don't and he is doing more for himself, but I think I'll always be there for him.

Cathy seems to be confident that her son will be able to get some sort of employment later, and she is prepared to move to a country town to do this. She says:

> Cathy (DS):
> You know as for being independent, uhm . . . I see for Edward . . . I can not see why he can not do a job, even . . . even if I'm prepared to go back out west. I can see myself going out, doing something to enable him, then do whatever independently.

And finally Pauline, whose son is severely intellectually disabled, also places self-help and basic living skills high on her list of priorities when she says:

> Pauline (DS):
> He is getting more independent on a lot of things, but you know . . . even getting dressed for school, this morning he wanted to get dressed in bed, and he gets side tracked, but he'll at least make an attempt, that is progress. And bathroom skills, he seems to know that now, he seems to know the routine. When he is hungry in the morning, he gets out the cereal and gets out the bowl and the milk, and he'll fix himself a bowl of cereal, no big deal, but he can do it. A little sign of independence . . . at last!

This group of mothers paints a clear picture of the importance of personal independence for their children with an intellectual disability. It appears that mothers who have a male child with an intellectual disability may have slightly higher expectations of independence for their child, as revealed by the stories of Margaret, Cathy, Fiona and Pauline in the above transcripts. Interestingly, employment was raised more frequently by mothers of male children than those who have a female child with Down's syndrome. This could be taken to indicate that self-sufficiency may perhaps be regarded as more important for male than female children, and having to care for a female offspring as an adolescent and adult may be less inappropriate than it is for a male. Within the group of mothers who have a male child with Down's syndrome, employment was raised consistently as a possibility, even by those mothers whose child has relatively low functioning skills.

The group of mothers in this study who have a child with a physical but not intellectual disability appear to have a lesser focus in personal independence than the previous group. The presence of average intellectual ability ultimately assures those children who have spina bifida intellectual, if not physical, independence. The availability of increasingly adaptive facilities, such as electric wheelchairs or specifically modified cars, integral to the enhancement of personal autonomy for this group of people. Again, the following statements from mothers of both male and female children who have spina bifida suggest expectations for independence for their children in terms of life style and, in the case of Mary, in terms of future employment.

> Silvia (SB):
> That's what we, we've always aimed at Julian to be, independent. You know he can dress himself, he can do his own toilet business all himself, and he has the last three years. Now he doesn't need us, and that's what we want. Yes you see, now Julian is capable of living his life by himself. At the moment, you know, he doesn't need me all the time. He should be able to get some sort of work we hope, but that's a long way off.

> Kaye (SB):
> Well I just hope, I guess . . . uhm that Simon for instance can just cope happily with life in that he is independent and able to feel happy in himself in what he does, even if it is not a good solid job . . . that he can find some way of dealing with his time productively and feel that he is contributing somehow, he is useful somehow, and even if it is staying at home and making something. As long as he is happy, and uhm . . . if he does achieve beyond that, that's fine, but I don't like putting unrealistic expectations on him.

Mary also emphasises the importance of the possibility of employment and links this to her children's future independence in terms of becoming independent and responsible citizens. Interestingly, she has the same expectations for her son with spina bifida as she holds for her other son without a disability.

> Mary (SB):
> Well, you know, I mean . . . I work full time and they have to be . . . they are responsible children. They have to get themselves ready for school, and uhm . . . and help around the place. They're not expected to be loafers, like they have chores to do. They get pocket money for that. They have cows to look after and chooks to look after. With that, you know I think it's important, that they learn to do a job, and they learn to do it well. You know to me that's important, if I die tomorrow they could look after themselves the way that I taught them. Well, I hope

that they can get themselves a job and have a happy family life . . . uhm . . . I'm not exactly sure what the dynamics of that are going to be, but to me it's important that when they leave home they know how to work and do a job properly, and if they do that they should be able to stand on their own feet.

Once again, the above statements from mothers confirm that in the case of a child having a disability, gender issues appear to be of less importance and significance than the ability to achieve personal independence and therefore achieve independent citizen status. Maria links her expectations for her son's independence with his need for an operation when she says:

Maria (SB):
His sister pushed him occasionally, but not often, he is very independent in his chair. It frightens everybody at school, you know . . . he flies down the ramp. He needs an operation on his legs, it's something that has got to be done, you know . . . it is just something to make him a bit more independent from everything. In every other way he is independent, so it would be good you know . . . it will help him to live a normal life . . . get a job and all that.

When mothers who have a male child with spina bifida are contrasted with mothers who have a female child with this disability, a subtle gender difference emerges. Interestingly, the concerns of the second group tend to centre more on physical independence, with a strong emphasis on toileting and health issues rather than the possibility of future employment.

Susan (SB):
She can do all her own toileting but we still can't manage the clothing and I don't know where to go with that. Because if you pull the knickers down . . . and you've had an accident . . . and you pull the pad at the same time . . . you're in a mess. So, well, I've been talking with the Spina Bifida Association, I actually went two weeks ago, and I brought home two different pairs of pants that they trialled. But I haven't got any further, I must admit I am slack when it comes to get her to do things on her own.

Yvette (SB):
She's been told to fend for herself ever since she was a tiny little puppy, and she does fend for herself. But there is the toileting, it is definitely an issue, I worry about that when she is older, it will always be an issue for her, but we'll see.

Kirsten (SB):
And outside the classroom she uses a wheelchair. She does not like to be pushed and gets around by herself, at school this is, not at home. At

> home it is different, she wants us to do it all for her. Anyway she needs to be catheterised four hourly, which amounts to only once a day at school. For bowels, we make sure she also goes to the toilet the second lunch break. She does it all herself now, we have promoted that she has to look after herself. Irrespective of the problem you create for yourself by doing too much for her, I mean the priority is the problem for her, her future life . . . that she has to be independent. So that's when you pull back.

At least one mother in this study expressed her concerns for normal sexual functioning of her daughter.

> Laurel (SB):
> I worry about what happens when she is an adult and she wants to have sexual relations. We don't know, there are some problems but . . . you see . . . I hope that she can have a normal life in that way, you know.

There appear to be subtle differences in this sample of mothers' expectations for independence for their male and female children who have spina bifida. In families without a child with a disability, the gradual achievement of children's independence is largely taken for granted, and parents therefore do not raise this issue specifically. For those mothers who have a child with a disability, the issue of eventual independence appears to be influencing their expectations from birth. Furthermore, the gender of the child appears to influence mothers' expectations, with mothers holding higher expectations for employment for their male child with either a physical or an intellectual disability. For their daughters, the concern for social acceptability in terms of managing their own personal lives has been shown to be of primary importance.

CONCLUSION

Differences in parents' expectations for their children's gender development is widely documented in the literature (e.g. Everingham, 1994; Goodnow and Collins, 1990; McGuire, 1991; Woollett *et al.*, 1992), although few studies have focused specifically on families who have a child with a disability. This paucity of research has been largely influenced by the difficulties of considering and examining the diversity of disabilities, and further complicated by the range of degree of disability affecting the lives of children and their families.

This chapter has reported the findings of a study that examined mothers' perceptions and ideas about gender differences of their children who have a physical or intellectual disability. The responses from the group of mothers in this study provides a relatively stereotypical picture of the social expectations mothers hold for the future of their children.

While significant changes have occurred over the past decades in terms of women's participation rates in pursuing careers and employment, it continues to be more likely for women to interrupt their careers to have children and/or adjust to the career demands of their partners.

Interestingly, gender differences in mothers' expectations can be observed for children with disabilities both in terms of employment and personal independence. It appears that gender issues and social norms are pervasive, and that mothers who have a child with a disability, although aware of their child's decreased intellectual or physical abilities, tend to adopt the accepted social norms as benchmarks for their expectations. The wide acceptance of normalisation and social integration has contributed significantly to the expectations mothers hold for their child with a disability. Yet these expectations continue to reflect the established and socially accepted gender differences that appear to be in place for society at large.

IMPLICATIONS FOR EARLY SPECIAL EDUCATION

Educators have an important part to play in the shaping of mothers' expectations for their children. In accepting that both male and female children today are being exposed to similar social situations, they have the responsibility to promote independence for all children. In the case where the parents want their child with a disability to remain at home and continue in a situation of dependence, educators have the opportunity to influence the thinking and future planning for the child, not only by promoting the highest possible level of independence for each child, but also by giving parents the courage to let the child have independent experiences and possibly some supervised employment opportunities in the future. Personal autonomy and independence for children with a disability is a gradually occurring process, but needs to be considered from birth and instigated no later than during the early childhood stage of development. While many parents actively strive for such goals, it appears more likely that this is the case for mothers with male children. In their role of supporting the development of all children, educators have a responsibility to advocate strongly for children, irrespective of race, gender, social class and disability, so that they may enjoy similar life experiences and personal autonomy, according to their individual ability.

ACKNOWLEDGEMENT

I wish to thank the mothers who have contributed to this study by providing their rich and insightful beliefs and ideas, and have given me the permission to use their verbatim responses.

REFERENCES

Antill, J.K. (1987). Parents' beliefs and values about sex roles, sex differences and sexuality. Their sources and implications. In P. Shaver and C. Hendrick (eds), *Sex and gender: Review of personality and social psychology*, 7, pp. 294–328. Beverley Hills, CA: Sage.

Bower, A.M. (1996). *A comparative study of mothers' beliefs and ideas about mothering in families with and without disability.* Unpublished doctoral dissertation, The University of Queensland, Brisbane, Australia.

Davies, B. (1988). *Gender equity and early childhood.* Commonwealth Schools Commission, Canberra.

Dunn, J. and Plomin, R. (1990). *Separate lives: Why siblings are so different.* New York: Basic Books.

Dunn, S. and Morgan, V. (1987). Nursery and infant school play patterns: sex-related differences. *British Educational Research Journal*, 13, pp. 271–28l.

Everingham, C. (1994). *Motherhood and modernity.* Sydney: Allen & Unwin.

Goodnow, J.J. and Collins, W.A. (1990). *Development according to parents: The nature, sources and consequences of parents' ideas.* Hillsdale, NJ: Erlbaum.

Honig, A. (1983). Sex role socialisation in early childhood. *Young Children.* September, pp. 57–70.

Kazak, A.E. (1986). Families with physically handicapped children: Social ecology and family systems. *Family Process*, 25, pp. 265–281.

McGuire, J. (1991). Sons and daughters. In A. Phoenix, A. Woollett and E. Lloyd (eds), *Motherhood, meanings, practices and ideologies* (pp. 143–161). London: Sage.

Mac Naughton, G. (1992). Equity challenges for the early childhood curriculum. *Children & Society*, 6, pp. 225–240.

Mac Naughton, G. (1993). *Equal play, equal work.* Office of Preschool and Childcare, Melbourne.

Palacios, J. (1986). *Parents' ideas about child development and education.* Manuscript, University of Seville.

Stieler, S. (1994). Children with physical disabilities. In A. Ashman and J. Elkins (eds), *Educating children with special needs* (2nd edn) (pp. 491–544). Sydney: Prentice-Hall.

Woollett, A. and Phoenix, A. (1991). Psychology and ideology. In A. Phoenix, A. Woollett and E. Lloyd (eds), *Motherhood: Meanings, Practices and Ideologies* (pp. 28–46). London: Sage.

Woollett, A., Phoenix, A. and Lloyd, E. (1991). *Motherhood: Meanings, Practices and Ideologies.* London: Sage.

Zebrowitz-McArthur, L.A. and Kendall-Tackett, K.A. (1989). *Parental reactions to transgressions by baby-faced and mature-faced 4 and 11 year old children.* Paper presented at meetings of the Society for Research in Child Development, Kansas City, April, 1989.

Chapter 4

The body, young children and popular culture

Keith Gilbert

INTRODUCTION

There is no doubt that researchers have spent little time studying young children's conceptualisations of the body. This is surprising, as the child's social world is saturated with cultural images of the body, viewed through the media of television, film, fashion and sports promotion industries. Indeed, a review of the literature that exists about the body reveals a lack of research pertaining to young children and their conceptualisations of popular images and perceptions derived from their social world. Collins (1979: 22) believed that the lack of information might be due to the fact that children 'are unable to comprehend the connections' and 'have a rudimentary knowledge of the inter-relations of images' portrayed to them through the media, thus making research difficult. Later, Greenfield (1984: 9) supported this premise by reminding us that 'children do not always understand film or television the same way adults do' and 'they do not always view images of the body from the same perspective'. However, Greenfield (1984: 17) also recognised that 'television literacy', which includes developing understanding and meanings about concepts through exposure to television, 'makes it possible to use television to transmit knowledge to the young child'. Thus, it is possible that television and other forms of media enable the child to aquire knowledge about the social context of their world and to recall those 'lived experiences'. Consequently, the messages that children receive from persuasive elements, such as television, make it increasingly more important for educators to discover the implications of such external forces on children's perceptions or ideas about the world. The social place of the body and the ways in which children conceptualise themselves (Morgan and Scott, 1993) have become increasingly important in situating the individual in cultural organisational contexts (Pugsley *et al.* 1996: 143) such as schools. The gendering of the body thus becomes closely linked to the processes of popular culture and highlighted through the schooling process.

With these issues in mind, this chapter will present and discuss points brought to the fore by children themselves as they consider and are confronted by various images of the body that are portrayed in the media and in the fashion and sports industries. Furthermore, it considers the ways in which children perceive themselves and the role of cultural factors in shaping their gender roles. It interweaves issues that are, for the most part, never discussed in everyday interactions between children, adults and the societal 'norms' that have been created through the discourse of consumerism, and our fascination with cultural icons portrayed via television, sports, fashion and film. Finally, it will explore the social dimensions that affect the gendered perceptions of children regarding their bodies, thereby providing a rich source of information that can be utilised by teachers in the classroom setting. This is important because it illustrates how, as teachers, we often take children's ideas for granted, and rarely question how society influences one of the single most important aspects of young children's lives, that is their gendered bodies.

METHODOLOGY

The data in this study were collected in order to support a larger study that involves researching the conceptualisations that individuals have developed about the social context of the body over time. The analyses presented in this chapter are derived from data gathered over a period of eight weeks in two primary schools in Queensland, Australia. Eighty Year 2 (5 and 6-year-old children) took part in the study which was principally qualitative in nature. The research methodology consisted of interviews by student teachers who acted as research assistants in the study. All interviews were audio taped and transcribed. The tape recorded interviews were analysed by creating transcripts of the tapes in order that we could clearly identify the major issues that relate to young children's perceptions of themselves and each other. In other words, we attempted to identify the meanings that the children made about their own bodies, those of other children and the influence that societal factors play on their perceptions. In analysing the data, a 'grounded theory' approach, as highlighted by Glaser and Strauss (1967), was undertaken and rigorous examination of the data was supported by a questionnaire where each child's answers to questions were written onto a recording sheet for easy access during data analysis. This supported the interactionist structure of the research which was of paramount importance throughout the study. Children were also asked to draw and colour a picture of what they thought they looked like. This was completed in order for the researchers to have some ideas of whether the image of the children fitted their personal perception and as a starting point for discussion with the children; later on pictures of film, TV, sports stars and people involved in popular culture were shown to the children in order to elicit differing responses. Children were also observed in the playground situation which assisted us in the identification of those who were active and those who were sedentary, so that we might better understand them as active, moving young bodies. What follows is a description that interlinks children's responses with literature in the area, to provide ideas about the relationship between the influences of popular culture on children and the perceptions of their bodies.

INFLUENCE OF THE TELEVISION INDUSTRY

Perhaps the biggest influence on children over the past forty-five years has been that of television. When referring to children's viewing habits in the USA, Levin (1994: 14) comments that, 'TV has become a central force in children's lives, many children now spend more time infront of a screen than in your classroom'. Levin continues by further informing us that in the US 'children now average 35 hours per week watching TV and playing video games and by age 18 children will have spent at least 7 years watching TV'.

Children's television viewing in Australia also appears to be having an increasingly powerful effect upon the way in which children perceive their world, their surroundings, their own place in the world and, more importantly for this study, their bodies and how their bodies fit into their world. When the children in this study were asked what they liked doing best, they often cited watching TV as a popular pastime. They were well aware of the influence of TV on their lives, as the following three comments suggest:

> Cartoons are cool mate. I watch TV everyday but my mum turns it off when she thinks that I watch too much. She says that I have square eyes.
>
> (Amy age 5)

> I kinda like TV but my favourite programme is on when I'm in bed so mummy videos it for me. My favourite programme is Baywatch.
>
> (John age 6)

> I watch it in the morning, and after school and after tea. I like cartoons and sports, like cricket.
>
> (William age 5)

Comments such as these were common and refer specifically to the importance and enjoyment of television in the children's lives.

Interestingly, the programmes that the children cited are littered with images of the body in various shapes and forms. It would seem that the body images portrayed to them must in some way influence the perceptions they have of their own bodies and the society in which they live. As Goffman (1976: 1) remarks, 'If one examines the details of social life with a highly conscious eye, one learns – deeply – who and what one is in the socially organised world.' In the same way, the children in this study were able to articulate the relationship between TV images and themselves. Images from their favourite programmes were recalled by the children when linking themselves to people whom they described as heroes and heroines. Mostly these were actors and sports stars who displayed both good looks and finely tuned bodies. These particular images gave them a feeling of self-worth as they imagined themselves in the roles of the movie actor or sports person. Indeed, some of the children were observed in play situations imagining themselves as their favourite character/hero in make believe games during lunch breaks and free time. However, there was also a 'downside' relating to such perceptions. For example, more often than not, the images portrayed on the television screen in children's programmes are surreal in nature and far removed from the world in which they actually live. These images frequently show likenesses of the distorted body in the form of cartoon images, like Donald Duck, which are capable of changing from quite normal visual perceptions to wild-eyed cataclysmic creatures which cause children to have skewed perspectives of the body. As Edwards and Gilbert (1997: 8) remark, 'television becomes a genetic code which controls the mutation of the real into the hyper-real'. These conditions of visual overload or technopoly (Postman, 1993) that ushered in the post-modern era have caused viewing to be dominated by simulated visual models that dictate and define children's viewing experience and challenge visual perceptions of what the body is, what the body can do and where it is in space. Kirk (1993: 2) supports this statement when referring to TV by commenting that: 'Children become frightened by the often trans-cultural identity of the figures which are portrayed to them via the television screen.' In this study I am suggesting that children as young as 6 have been subjected to images of body distortions that have influenced the perceptions that they have of themselves and others. Indeed, many of the children were quick to point out their favourite cartoon characters when asked the question, whom they most resembled. Surprisingly, the answers did not include their parents, siblings or peers. Comments like the following were common:

> I think Mickey Mouse is great and Minnie.
>
> (Megan age 5)

> Ren and Stimpy are my favourite because they are funny and make me laugh.
>
> (Ralph age 6)

> My mum tells me I look like Donald Duck (he's a famous duck) and sound like him too!
>
> (Mathew age 5)

As mentioned previously, these images portray the 'human like figures' in cartoons often as grossly misshapen and in surreal contexts. Indeed, Goffman (1976: 15) suggests that, 'pictures that are covertly doctored or covertly rigged (as suggested by the cartoon figure) display scenes that can't be read in the same way that uncontrived ones routinely can'. Thus, it would appear that children are receiving a distorted view of the real world and imagine that there is a relationship or some connectivity between their bodies and cartoons. This supports the previous statements of Greenfield (1984), that children who are not yet fully developed cognitively are not processing images in the same way that older individuals are. For example, cartoons, which change shape and images and portray the body in unusually distorted positions, display characters structured on the human form that can complete amazing feats. These are but fabrications, yet many were perceived by children in this study as real, so that reality became blurred, causing the children who constantly watch cartoons to have a surreal understanding of the human body and its shape and form. The 'commercial syncretism' or figures in their make believe world influence children to the extent that many understand the cartoon character as a living body, or almost an immortal body that changes shape to suit the situation. Even when pounded by bombs, guns, hammers or explosives, the cartoon characters manage to pull themselves together and survive until the next round of disasters. Consequently, the children in this study were beginning to think that they were also indestructable. For example, John noted that he was 'Superman and could fly at supersonic speed' and Janet wanted to be like the Wolf in the Road Runner ' 'cos he always comes back for more smashing'.

There were other television images of the human body that also influenced the children. For example, scenes that appear on the nightly news are often sensationalised and very graphic in nature. Children, by the age of 6, have become accustomed to visualising the effects of war, poverty and destruction on the human form on a regular basis. Grossly malformed dead bodies are portrayed to the public on the news and serve to define the cultural identity of the body that children have grown used to. Thus, the normal functioning human form (whatever that might be) is shown to be something other than normal. Indeed some groups (Shilling, 1993a) have even suggested that some scenes from the news are so disturbing and complex for young children that the timeslots should be changed or the programme should be given a different rating, warning parents about the graphic nature of the content. What sorts of messages are these graphically highlighted pictures giving to our young children? Overall, in this study the messages given to the children from the news were negative. For example, several children were disturbed by the sight of bloodied and misshapen bodies, as they placed themselves in situations other than what they see in their everyday lives. The following comments were commonplace and highlighted the effect of the over-exposure of the disturbing images to young children and their concerns about their own bodies.

> I don't like the News programme. I don't like dead people. I hate all those bodies.
>
> (Simon age 5)

> I . . . I saw a man get shot and it was bad.
>
> (Wendy age 6)

Of course, the responsibility of children being exposed to violence on television is not the sole duty of the television executives. Parents must also be educated to take more of a role in the ethical and moral aspects of their children's lives. Until this occurs, children will continue to be negatively affected by unsuitable programmes.

In summary, serious questions need to be asked of television companies that have control over the forms of messages that children receive because, as this study suggests, they are often responsible for influencing children's perceptions of their own shape and form by highlighting extremes of perfection and imperfection. Many of the comments highlighted the infallibility of the human body for the children who were, by the age of 6, already conditioned to seeing cartoon images in fantasy contexts and confronted by images of human suffering and horror on the news. These messages are contradictory in nature and thus confusing for young children. The issues and graphics created by the television producers had a strong effect on the children's perception of their bodies. Of related interest is the fact that most of the cartoon characters were depictions of the male gender and most of the news items displayed horrific scenes characterised by male domination. Consequently, there appears to be a dichotomy existing between cartoon (make believe) and news (stark reality) that has allowed the media, in particular the television stations, to become the 'final site of moral arbitration in the post-modern world' (Denzin 1996: 215). Indeed, although we 'pride ourselves in being a culture of substance' (Burke, 1996: 163) the substance of the 'twentieth century male orientated culture' portrayed through the television screen is an important factor in children's understanding of their own being and the place of the male and female body and its appearance in the world in which they live. Problems arise when girls are continually confronted by images of male domination. Images depicting men and boys in strong positions and women and girls in situations that are weak and defenceless are common. Popular TV culture thus enhances the ascendancy of the male body in society and the subordination of the female role and promotes the ideals of a girl's body being weak and subordinate to that of a boy. We need to start giving children positive images. This study suggests that the misleading and violent images are disturbing for young children, in particular young girls.

THE INFLUENCE OF THE FILM INDUSTRY

In this study children indicated that they enjoyed going to the movies and were interested in most aspects of the film industry. However, as one would expect, they were unaware of the financial motives or moguls that drive it. Such individuals are responsible for developing many of the heroes and heroines of our young children. Indeed, they are the people responsible for promoting actors and actresses as icons, which children come to idolise. The idols usually represent the most physically attractive individuals in our society, who are often seen clad in little clothing to highlight the socially acceptable body form. After talking with the children, we found that it appears as though film makers have developed a set of cultural norms, which they back up with advertising, emphasising youth, health, fitness and beauty as important ideals for our society. The children's preferences seemed to be greatly influenced by the images portrayed to them. For example, the comments by Melinda suggest that she was enamoured by Arnold Schwarzenegger:

Melinda: Arnold Schwarzenegger is my favourite actor.
Keith: Why do you like him?
Melinda: Oh 'cos he has ... um ... big muscles (giggles) and can do everything.
Keith: What do you mean?
Melinda: He's awesome. I saw him shoot six or seven men in one movie.
Keith: You liked him because he shot people?
Melinda: No not really I just like him. He's big and all that. You know if you're big and strong you can do anything.

(Transcript: Melinda age 6)

This is despite the fact that Schwarzenegger films are not usually considered as suitable entertainment for 6 and 7 year olds. Furthermore, many children will never look like the gods and goddesses of the silver screen and few will be 'big and strong'. Indeed, film can be said to contribute to young children's fabrications of the human body, since techniques employed to distort reality, such as airbrushing, costume and make-up, serve to confuse the audience, and blur the line between what is real and what is not. Goffman (1976: 27) remarked, 'behind these artful efforts one may be able to discern how mutually present bodies, along with non human materials, can be shaped into expression'. In this study it was evident that there were pressures on girls to look older and conform to the norms that were driven by the images they saw on the movie screen. The children were influenced by film stars, actors and actresses who make films that permeate our culture and which 'conventionalize our conventions, stylize what is already stylization' and 'make frivolous use of what is already something considerably cut off from contextual controls' (Goffman 1976: 84). In this way bodies, which are often stylised, like those in popular films such as *Clueless* and *Baywatch* (the movie), become accepted in our society as the ideal. Children, from a very young age, become influenced by these images of our popular culture. Beauty is thus a prominent feature of the bodies portrayed on the screen. There are very few portrayals of ugly children in films, suggesting that 'beauty is not in the eye of the beholder' but presented to children through the minds-eye of the producers and directors. When asked about her favourite film star, Rachel (age 6) responded 'I like Pamela Anderson. So does my dad and my brother. She has the most enormous boobs and my dad says they can't be real!' It was apparent that the children were rarely subjected to images of unattractive people on screen. Indeed, most children indicated that they were conditioned to the celluloid portrayal of the human form, choosing the attractive film stars above others in the series of pictures we asked them to review. By and large, the pictures were a source of children's amusement as they recalled a scene or a film. Interestingly, because the children in this study had been exposed to the famous icons through the medium of film, they had almost total recall of actors who had been over-exposed in the press and magazines, indicating the power of the film industry in shaping children's perceptions of the body. This is so much the case that, like other forms of media, film makers have the final say over how the actors are depicted and over the images that influence youth in their final profit making venture. In this way, capitalism can direct young children towards pre-packaged images, thereby moulding their perceptions of the body through the medium of film.

THE INFLUENCE OF THE SPORTS INDUSTRY

Undoubtedly, sports are firmly ingrained in the Australian psyche (Gilbert, 1996: 12), and to be fit and healthy is a desired outcome of many young people. This study provided some graphic examples of how children are influenced by the sports images that are portrayed through various media. Sports stars, whose main occupation in life is to be athletic and who spend most of their waking hours exercising and training for special events, were viewed by most of the children as being different and possessing extraordinary, often superhuman, bodies and powers. When asked who they would most like to look like, nearly every child quoted the name of a successful sports person, as highlighted by the remarks of the following children:

> Michael Jordan. (Basketball)
>
> (Mark age 5)

> I think I look like Willie Carne. (Football)
>
> (Sam age 6)

> I think I would like to look like Jeff Fenech. (Boxing)
>
> (Troy age 6)

> Alan Border is my hero. (Cricket)
>
> (Wison age 5)

> I like, what's his name . . . mmmm . . . something Little. (Jason Little, Rugby Union)
>
> (Sam age 5)

It was interesting to observe the girls' responses, as they included several sporting figures who were male and who were high profile figures in the press and sporting community. Girls also frequently cited Michael Jordan as a person who they would like to be. However, girls also named some favourite sports stars who were female:

> I like Cathy Freeman. (Olympic Athlete)
>
> (Sally age 6)

> Don't really know. Can't think of any. Oh ya Susie O'Neill she's good. (Swimming)
>
> (Linda age 6)

> I would like to look like Samantha Riley the famous swimmer.
>
> (Robin age 5)

> I think I look like Vicki Wilson. (Netball)
>
> (Alison age 6)

> Lisa Curry Kenny she's always on TV and does good things with kids. (Swimming)
>
> (Monica age 5)

It was also evident that context and recent events influenced the children's choices of who they would like to be. The interviews in this study took place just after the Olympic Games had been televised and many children chose Kieran Perkins, the world champion 1,500 metre swimmer who had just received great publicity in Australia and a gold medal at the Games. The children in this study thus equated sport with success and, by association, swimming with success. Since being successful in sport means having an athletic body, then the children were watching and choosing individuals who looked good and who fitted the mythical image of Australian popular culture: the 'bronzed Aussie'.

The introduction of the hyper-real world of instant replay, zoom camera, overhead camera, slow 'mo', split screen, car 'cam' and helmet 'cam' has introduced new and different dimensions of the body to children. In short, the pictures transmitted to the children via the hyper-real world transports the child into the heart of the action so that the spatial and temporal dimensions of the body are changed. The children thus identify with the hyper-reality of the situation and become enchanted with the bodies of elite athletes. For example, in this study the person that many boys wanted to look like was Michael Jordan, a black American athlete who bore little resemblance to most of them or individuals in their family. The phenomenon of Michael Jordan has obviously reached the young of today by clever sports marketing which appears principally through television advertisements designed to make MJ the most widely recognised athlete in the world. Interestingly, the images of Michael Jordan portrayed in the media are of a fit athletic and attractive figure who can do just about anything. In fact the advertising campaign urges the normal person to 'just do it', as if it were the most simple thing to do. This is interesting because in the USA only 1 per cent of the population achieve success in the sport of basketball (Frey, 1996: 214) and yet at an early age children become infatuated with sporting prowess. This sporting prowess is rarely viewed live but is promoted on the 'silver screen' by clever advertising and is reinforced by males in the family setting who idolise sports stars and persuade their children to follow the family team or sport. The Jordan phenomenon has been explained further by Denzin (1996: 320) who poignantly reminds us that 'Black personalities like Michael Jordan, Spike Lee, Arsenio Hall, Oprah Winfrey, and Bill Cosby focus, organise and translate Blackness into commodifiable representations and desires.'

In this study these desires were obvious in young children of all colour and gender, suggesting that images that are viewed on the television screen are powerful change agents that can influence young children's perceptions of the body. Indeed, the phenomenon of Michael Jordan could be described in technological terms as promoting the body itself (Edwards and Gilbert, 1997: 16).

Interestingly, this study found that the children's worship of sports stars was a very personal matter, as they related their self and their own body to the sporting hero or heroine. This is important, as Radner (1995: 143) argues, because 'In a sense the construction of the "modern" body is the production of a public body, specific to a class, a gender and a historical period which eventually becomes the body politic, the body of the citizen. ' If Radner's argument is accepted, then it would seem to be a natural progression to assume that children are greatly influenced by public sports heroes. They were influenced to the extent that many of them had strong impressions of their own physical abilities when observed acting out scenarios from last weekend's games in the playground by emulating sports stars and their particular actions. It would be interesting to investigate to what extent this form of cultural identity influences the children's perceptions of their body.

Several Australian sporting idols were mentioned as favoured persons that the children would most like to look like. The boys' choices included Guy Leach, a famous Australian surf star, who is regularly shown on the TV wearing only a bathing costume, various rugby union and league stars who have been depicted in yearly calendars and even an obscure athlete who is not well known but starred in a television ad campaign selling men's shampoo. Mostly the girls chose women who were sports stars and Olympic athletes such as Samantha Riley and Susie O'Neil, swimmers who are regularly viewed on the TV. They also chose other stars such as women basketball players from the successful Australian team, who were required to wear one piece Lycra suits rather than the normal uniform of loose shorts and shirt in order to enhance their appeal to a television audience during the sixteen day period of the Olympic Games. Other athletes mentioned by the girls obviously included those with the highest media profiles like Cathy Freeman and Jane Fleming, both stars who have excelled in track and field. Jane Fleming is also famous for her yearly sports girls calendar. One girl even mentioned that she used a particular athlete's name because her dad thought that she was pretty. Generally, throughout the study it was concluded that there was a definite gender orientation towards male athletes by both girls and boys, suggesting that TV images of our athletes and sports stars are mostly of the male gender and that the girls really have fewer role models strongly promoted by the media. Interestingly, only the attractive women in Australian sport were highlighted by the children in this study.

It was evident from the responses that children gave that sports personalities exerted a powerful influence on their selection of role models. Furthermore, the images of the body portrayed by their heroes influenced the ways in which they desired their body to look. The commodification of the body by the sports industry and the marketing of sport related items had a profound impact on the way in which this group of children viewed their world.

THE INFLUENCE OF THE FASHION INDUSTRY

Kirk (1993) was quick to point out the fact that the fashion industry has been one of the most debilitating factors, causing problems for youth fitness, health and wellness. The images portrayed by the fashion industry undoubtedly influence the very basis of our society, as young girls, in particular, follow the fashion industry and the powerful statements that it makes through the medium of magazines and television programmes that vilify the young, slim and athletic bodies. Indeed, the process of the influence of a media led fashion industry was clearly developed by the work of Naomi Wolf (1990) in her book *The Beauty Myth*. In this book she pointed out the influence of the beauty industry on individuals' perceptions of self and claimed that women were being seduced by the industry in order to look good and to feel valued as a member of society. It is interesting to note that the 'norms' of the fashion industry have been established in a climate dominated by males. Children in this study indicated that they are already reading fashion magazines. This meant that they were exposed to the cultural norms of western society and greatly influenced by the fashion industry in which the notion of being slim is fundamental. Throughout the study there was no doubt that girls' desire for a slim body was influenced by the Australian and international fashion industry. For example:

> I want to look skinny like Elle MacPherson.
>
> (Wendy age 6)

> Mummy says that I have to go on a diet before we go to Lucy's wedding (sister). I am going to be a flower girl and mummy wants me to look good for the photographs.
>
> (Louise age 6)

> I hate fat kids, they smell funny.
>
> (Mary age 5)

Furthermore, there were also comments made by boys to indicate that they too had contempt for overweight peers. This was evident when Brian (age 5 years) said: 'Richard is a fatty, we all call him names he hates it.' These comments were chosen out of many that were similar and reflect the idea that being overweight or unfit is socially unacceptable for children of both genders. They also reflect the images that young children are absorbing through different types of media. It was clear from other comments that the children were very much influenced by fashion magazines, and many could name popular brand names of products and fashion labels that were regularly promoted in the magazines.

With these thoughts in mind, it is easy to understand that, when shown pictures of individuals who were regularly presented to the children in fashion magazines, there was a general consensus that slimmer, more attractive individuals (both male and female) were more pleasing to the children. All children tended to identify themselves with these images rather than the images of overweight individuals who were deemed less than perfect in their eyes. This indicates that there is a form of cultural leadership and symbolism associated with the fashion industry that has an extensive effect on society. Indeed, all children chose well-known individuals who conformed with Australian cultural norms. Such images are promoted via the beauty and health industry in magazines, posters and television advertising.

The children could name many of the cultural icons of the fashion industry. Of interest, for example, was the fact that all the children were aware of Elle MacPherson and that she was a famous Australian model who modelled swimsuits, underwear and starred in films. This is also relevant because her nickname is 'The Body', which tends to suggest that she has the ultimate shape to which individuals in society should aspire. Not surprisingly, then, when asked which person they knew most about in the fashion industry, all of the children responded with Elle MacPherson. This indicates that the Elle MacPherson publicity machine has been very successful, at least in Australia. The scenario has been well calculated by the fashion industry.

Many girls in this study indicated that they wanted their body to be like that of the 'super models' in advertisements and, more significantly, were able to remember the fashion label or product that they represented by associating the form, shape or notoriety of the body with a particular brand of product. Another example of this form of body worship can be seen from the various videos that are produced to enhance the fitness of our youth. The famous example is, of course, the 'Jane Fonda' fitness video, which has become a cultural icon in the fitness industry. MacPherson, like Fonda, has become an idol, and when referring to such public idols LeFebre (1984: 175) remarks:

> an idol's outstanding advantage is that they are perfectly unremarkable (neither too ugly nor too beautiful, too vulgar nor too refined, neither too gifted nor without gifts), that they lead the same 'everyday' life as anyone else and that they present to everyone an image of this 'everyday' life transfigured by the fact that it is not his but that of another (an Idol, therefore rich and famous).

The children were not aware of the *status* of the idol in society. They seemed to be concerned with the fact that the models were attractive and represented fashion. Exposure of the models in the media meant that it was not surprising that some girls, in this study, saw themselves becoming clones of their idols. This was evident in the following comments, for example:

> I want to look like Elle she is fantastic and fit. My mum tells me that I could be a model when I grow up.
>
> (Naomi age 6)

> We have already been interviewed by a modelling agency and my

mum and dad take me and my sister to have our picture taken. I was in the Myer Christmas show.

(Francine age 6)

My older sister is a model and travels everywhere and wears nice clothes all the time.

(May age 5)

These comments are interesting because, in the modelling industry, the child's body is represented as a commodity. In addition to representing the body in a form of display, the modelling industry encourages the transition between young child and youth to occur prematurely. A recent example of this form of idolatry gone wrong has been the case of Jon-Benet Ramsey, a USA beauty queen who was murdered at 6 years old. The television pictures of this young girl, who was made up by her parents to look many years older, were both condemned by and abhorrent to American society, and were claimed by the press to have hidden sexual meaning. As Pugsley *et al.* (1996: 141) remarked, 'the body is not only physical, it is also sexual' and there are some situations in which the 'body is available for watching and violating (either physically or symbolically)'. Coming to terms with this concept is difficult unless you have been involved in the scene yourself. There were three children in this study who were involved in the Queensland children's fashion industry and their comments about the process were insightful:

I work sometimes late at night. I was in the big Myer parade in the city in the City Hall. I remember lots of lights and having to change quickly.

(Jonathan age 6)

I have had my pictures taken for an agency in togs (bathing costume) and I like making those funny poses. It was fun.

(Amanda age 6)

we are going to be in a show next week. I always come first or second behind Dianne .... its fun playing dressups.

(Tasha age 5)

The three children were interesting and, compared with the other children, were more confident, outgoing and talkative. Perhaps Cybill Shepherd (1986: 388) summed up the model's dilemma when she noted that 'as with everything else, you start with the body'. The body is thus the central focus of modelling and the children in this study were significantly influenced by the images of the bodies of others. Indeed, whether we like it or not, every child is subject to judgement because of the shape of their body and the sum of the parts: the face, height, hair or muscle mass and tone. The fashion industry attempts to 'cash in' on this phenomenon by introducing the children, through the various media, to constant reminders that they are not perfect, but because the goal posts of fashion are constantly changing, children have mixed messages about what shape is 'trendy' and what the norms of society really are.

CONCLUSION

This chapter has highlighted the ways in which popular culture has impacted on children's conceptualisations of their body and body image. It is evident from the comments made by the children that the media, fashion and sports industries have influenced the ways in which children perceive themselves and how they want to be regarded in the world. It is clear that children are constantly concerned about how they look, what they wear, and what others think of them. In short, children as young as 6 and 7 are already concerned with the image that they portray to others in everyday interactions. These perceptions are driven by external forces that shape our culture and set norms where capitalist world views are strongly developed and promoted. To argue that we all have different opinions of what we look like is essential to the cultural meaning of the body and manifested in the relationships that each of us has regarding our own body. There is no doubt, then, that the image that we wish to portray to the rest of the world about what we are, as a person, is often viewed through the eyes of others, and how we feel about the image that we portray is the most important aspect of the way in which we live in our body. Furthermore, this study has shown that children who live and interact with others in a western culture are likely to have been subjected to western icons depicted in the television, film, video and sports industries, who they then wish to emulate. There is a link between these desires and the way in which we enact our lives in society, as most of us wish to conform to societal norms. The perceptions that children have of the body are therefore strongly influenced by cultural icons that suggest and determine how the body should be presented in a certain way. Of import here is the notion that there were definite gender differences related to such perceptions in this study. For example, the girls appeared to be more influenced by the fashion industry than the boys. Indeed, it could be argued that the fashion industry pressures young girls to conform to their perceptions of what the body should look like and how it should be dressed. There were few sporting role models for the girls, but many for the boys, with both sexes being highly influenced by role models from the USA. Consequently, what is needed are educational contexts that ensure that children are provided with the opportunity to gain balanced viewpoints of the world in which they live and the relationship of their bodies to that world. As Shilling (1993b: 57) argues, 'education is of crucial importance in forming, among pupils, particular orientations to their bodies'. Finally, as Pugsley *et al.* (1996: 144) succinctly point out, 'Growing up is not only social and emotional, it is also physical and concerned with bodily things.' Young children who are becoming aware of their own bodies, and other people's bodies, should be afforded the opportunity to discuss issues surrounding their conceptualisations that are non-threatening and gender neutral.

The media (television and film), fashion and sports industries play an important role in young children's understanding of their world, and in particular how their bodies fit into the social perspective of life. An understanding of the impact of the issues of popular culture and the effect that it has on young children's perceptions of the body must be of concern to the educators of the young.

REFERENCES

Burke, P. (1996). *Gender Shock: Exploding the Myths of Male and Female.* London: Cambridge University Press.

Collins, W.A. (1979). Cognitive processes in television viewing. In D. Pearl, L. Bouthilet and J. Lazar (eds) *Television and Behaviour: Ten Years of Scientific Progress and Implications for the Eighties. Vol. 2 Technical Reviews.* Rockville, Md: National Institute of Mental Health.

Connolly, M. (1995). Phenomenology, physical education, and special populations. *Human Studies*, 18, 25–40.

Denzin, N.K. (1991). *Images of Postmodern Society*. London: Sage.

Denzin, N.K. (1996). More rare air: Michael Jordan on Michael Jordan. *Sociology of Sport Journal*, 13, 319–324.

Edwards, A. (1997). *Power in Professional Sports Franchise.* Unpublished manuscript.

Edwards, A. and Gilbert, K. (1997). *Postmodernism, Sport and Television Viewing.* Unpublished manuscript.

Frank, A.W. (1990). Bringing bodies back in: A decade review. *Theory Culture and Society*, 7(1) 131–162.

Frey, D. (1996). *The Last Shot: City Streets, Basketball Dreams.* New York: Simon & Schuster.

Gilbert, K. (1996). *Sport in the Australian Context*. Unpublished manuscript.

Glaser, B.G. and Strauss, A.L. (1967). *The Discovery of Grounded Theory: Strategies for Qualitative Research.* Chicago: Aldine.

Goffman, E. (1976). *Gender Advertisements*. Cambridge: Harper Torchbooks.

Greenfield, P.M. (1984). *Mind and Media: The Effects of Television, Video Games, and Computers.* Cambridge, Massachusetts: Harvard University Press,

Kirk, D. (1993). *The Body, Schooling and Culture.* Geelong: Deakin University Press.

LeFebre, H. (1984). *Everyday Life in the Modern World.* New Brunswick, NJ: Transaction Books.

Levin, D.E. (1994). *Teaching Young Children in Violent Times: Building a Peacable Classroom.* Boston, Mass: ESR.

Morgan, D. and Scott, D. (1993). Bodies in a social landscape. In S. Scott and D. Morgan (eds) *Body Matters.* London: Falmer.

Postman, N. (1993). *Technopoly.* New York: Alfred Knopf.

Pugsley, L., Coffey, A. and Delamont, S. (1996). Daps, dykes and five mile hikes: Physical education in pupil's folklore. *Sport, Education and Society*, 1(2) October.

Radner, H. (1995). Shopping around: Feminine culture and the pursuit of pleasure. London: Routledge.
Schmidt-Millard, T. (1995). Body awareness – new task of physical education or return of an ideology. In J. Mester (eds) *Images of Sport in the World.* Proceedings of the 75th Anniversary of the German Sport University, Koln. Nov. 1–5.
Shepherd, C. (1986). Shepherd's philosophy. *Harpers Bazaar Magazine,* 388–391
Shilling, C. (1993a). *The body and Social Theory.* London: Sage.
Shilling, C. (1993b). The body, class and social inequalities. In J. Evans (eds) *Equality, Education and Physical Education.* London: Falmer.
Sparkes, A.C. (1997). The fatal flaw: A narrative of the fragile body/self. In A. Sparkes (ed.) *Qualitative Teachers, Genders and Careers.* Lewes: Falmer Press.
Turner, B.S. (1993). *The Body and Society.* Oxford: Blackwell.
Wolf, N. (1990). *The Beauty Myth: How Images of Beauty are used against Women.* London: Vintage.

Chapter 5

Toward a most thorough understanding of the world

Sexual orientation and early childhood education[1]

Virginia Casper, Harriet K. Cuffaro, Steven Schultz, Jonathan G. Silin, and Elaine Wickens

Written collaboratively by five educators from the Bank Street College of Education, this chapter focuses on sexual orientation and early childhood education, an issue that is often overlooked. The authors describe research projects they have undertaken to explore elementary school teachers' thoughts and attitudes about sexual orientation in relation to children's sexuality and parents' sexual orientation. Building from there, they examine the connections between teachers' reflections of their own childhood experience and their current attitudes towards sexual orientation. They then move from exploring adult conceptions of family to examining those of children. Finally, the authors describe the process of transformation at Bank Street College as the institution struggles to include gay and lesbian lives in the early childhood and graduate school curriculum. Throughout the chapter, the authors continually connect their proactive stance for inclusion around sexual orientation with their larger vision of a more just and equitable society.

In 1989, an informal hallway conversation just outside the cafeteria at Bank Street College led to the formation of a lesbian and gay research group. It was not total happenstance that brought three of us (Virginia Casper, Steve Schultz, and Elaine Wickens) together in the hallway that day. Nor is it happenstance that two other faculty members (Harriet Cuffaro and Jonathan Silin) joined our group in 1994. Although there are many differences among us – we are women and men, straight and gay, parents and teachers, from working-class and middle-class families, from urban and rural environments – we have all chosen to work in a unique institution with a particular history and specific location in the educational landscape. Founded as the Bureau of Educational Experiments in 1916 by Lucy Sprague Mitchell, Bank Street College is part of the progressive tradition that sees schools as both a route to social change and a context in which to study the development of children (Antler, 1987; Biber, 1984; Shapiro and Nager, 1995). It remains a small, informal, and nonhierarchical community by contemporary standards.

Perhaps we found ourselves working collaboratively at Bank Street because it is a place where hallway conversations such as ours are frequently intense and impassioned, where the tension between what is and what might be is not forgotten, and where stories about children and questions from graduate students are placed in a political context. While it is now possible for faculty at Bank Street to be out as lesbian or gay in their classrooms, to advocate for curriculum about lesbian and gay families, and to participate openly in gay politics, this has not always been the case, nor is it true for everyone in every facet of the institution.

Brought together because of our belief that schools can help to create a more just society through fostering democratic processes and principles, we five also came together as friends and colleagues, some of us with shared histories going back to the 1960s. Although we had a common educational vocabulary, talking about sexual orientation presented new challenges. For example, one straight member of the group was uncomfortable with words such as "dyke" that occurred easily in the talk of gay members. She did not even want to refer to the sexual orientation of lesbian and gay people because she felt that this might have a negative connotation for them, as if they would read it as an accusation. Gay members of the group pointed out that they see such labeling as defining their identity and as a source of pride. In turn, when we have discussed the interviews we have done with teachers, there have been moments when gay members of the group heard only homophobia in the responses of participants, whereas straight members identified different complexities of thinking and the possibility for dialogue contained therein.

The word "collaboration" comes from the Latin *collaborare*, to labor together. As contemporary educators, we are well versed in the literature on collaborative research and cooperative learning. We have also read the postmodern theorists on the significance of difference, the end of grand narratives, and the disappearance of the coherent subject. They remind us that no one is objective, and that an attempt to create a seamless narrative would belie the counterpoint of our ongoing conversations. However, when we are faced with the hard task of writing an engaging essay that reflects many voices, these postmodern reminders do not seem especially helpful. While we enjoy a common interest in qualitative methodologies – in-depth interviews, classroom ethnography, and textual analysis – each of us brings a unique perspective. By alternating between the first-person singular and first-person plural, we have sought to honor our differences and to recognize the mutual influence and shared understandings that have emerged over the last six years. Our knowledge of lesbian and gay issues in schools is constantly being constructed and reconstructed, which is a distinct outcome of our laboring together.

Within a month of coming together, the initial members of our group wrote a position paper identifying the need for research on improving communication between lesbian/gay parents and the schools. During the following year we conducted our first interviews with parents, teachers, and administrators as we sought to clarify how each group saw the others. This chapter briefly summarizes our research since that time and describes the changes in the visibility and salience of lesbian/gay issues that occurred throughout the college community as a result of our work (Casper, Schultz, and Wickens, 1992; Casper and Schultz, 1995; Wickens, 1993, 1994; Wickens and Schultz, 1994).

Our work brings together several new pieces of research that we have conducted in public and private schools in inner-city and rural settings among people from diverse ethnic, racial, religious, and class backgrounds. In the first section, Elaine Wickens describes how our research has grown out of concerns raised by our graduate students; in the second, Steven Schultz explores the ways that adult attitudes about sexual orientation are shaped by their early experience. In the third section, Virginia Casper makes us reconsider the role of experience in children's conception of family, and in the fourth, Harriet Cuffaro returns to the adult perspective, now in terms of the issue of institutional change and the cumulative impact of our research on teacher education at Bank Street College. Jonathan Silin, who has coordinated the writing of this piece, concludes by highlighting our shared commitment to creating a more equitable society.

PARENTS' QUESTIONS AND TEACHERS' RESPONSES

Two projects of the lesbian and gay research group grew out of questions asked by graduate students. Since findings from the first project on lesbian and gay parents have been presented elsewhere (Casper *et al.*, 1992; Wickens, 1993), in this section I (Elaine Wickens) focus on the second project, an exploration of how teachers might respond to parental concerns about the perceived sexual orientation of a six-year-old boy. While some of the teachers we interviewed saw homosexuality as "not normal," we also found that participants were ready to talk about the issue and that they recognized the need to work effectively with gay/lesbian parents and children.

When some of my colleagues first learned that I had become involved in anti-bias research centering on gay and lesbian issues, inevitably they asked me how and why I had begun this work. Simply put, I was in the right place at the right time to act. And for those who wanted to know more, to listen to where my memory took me, to share past times, there was this to tell.

I grew up in a small town in West Virginia in the 1930s, prior to desegregation. Political activism and concerns about social equity were a part of my childhood. My father supported the miners when they struck, and my older brother was an organizer for Henry Wallace during the 1948 Presidential campaign. I remember sitting on top of the mountain we called the Devil's Teatable, which overlooks the Kanawaha River. I used to look down on the polluted river and wish it could be cleaned up so that everyone would swim in it and the world would be sweet. That river seemed the only place that was free in a world of segregated pools, schools, movie houses, and restaurants. I can also remember that sometime before I was in first grade, there was a man in our neighborhood who did odd jobs and delivered ice. People made fun of him, called him "sweet lips." In retrospect, I wonder if the jokesters were laughing at him because they thought he was gay, but they aren't around to ask. In high school, I took part in a walkout when the principal of our school told dialect jokes in the assembly. I did not plan to be part of the walkout, but I was there and chose to act.

I chose to act too when the president of Bank Street College called for a faculty group to plan residence and day-care center for homeless families. The project was to be a collaboration between the College and the Salvation Army, an agency that had a policy barring the employment of lesbian and gay teachers. Bank Street's own hiring policy explicitly prohibits discrimination based on sexual orientation. Working with the Salvation Army, I argued, would clearly compromise our principles and policies. After much discussion, the College decided not to pursue this project.

One day in the midst of the heated college-wide debate about the Salvation Army, Penny, a former student who is now working as an elementary school teacher, stood in my office doorway. She asked, "What do you know about having two moms as parents in a classroom? My principal told me to get ready for a five-year-old boy with two moms who would be in my classroom in the fall." I told Penny that I had never thought about this situation before and would see what I could find out.

I met with Steve Schultz later that day to talk about Penny's question. I told him I was surprised that I had never thought about gay- and lesbian-headed families entering the school culture. After further conversations with Virginia Casper, the three of us decided to explore Penny's question in a more systematic manner by interviewing gay/lesbian parents, early childhood teachers, and administrators (Casper *et al.*, 1992; Wickens, 1993). Our goal was to learn what lesbian and gay parents wanted the school to know about their families, and what they in turn wanted to know about the school. With the gay and lesbian parents' permission, we also interviewed their children's teachers and school administrators to find out what school personnel wanted to know about gay- and lesbian-headed families and what they felt the families should know about the school.

Through these interviews, we learned to place the issue of gay and lesbian parents within the context of an inclusive, broadly defined multicultural education. Since young children's curriculum frequently focuses on the meaning of family, the inclusion of gay- and lesbian-headed families has special salience to the early childhood classroom. Most parents must make difficult decisions about the disclosure of personal information when their children first enter school, and these concerns are heightened for gay and lesbian parents. Our interviews provided important insights into the ways that specific educational settings invite or discourage disclosure of sexual orientation. They also revealed confusions amongst gender identity, gender role, and sexual orientation. Many school personnel shared questions: Would children growing up with two parents of the same sex have access to what they considered to be "appropriate gender role models"? Do girls need to have a male parent in order to recognize their own femininity? Do boys need a father in order to exhibit masculine behaviors? Do boys need a mother in order to recognize their own masculinity? Confusion about gender and sexual orientation led teachers to wonder whether children raised in gay or lesbian families would grow up to be gay or lesbian themselves. In general, most lesbian and gay parents did not have these concerns. They simply wanted both male and female adults – relatives, friends, and teachers – in their children's lives who represented diverse cultures, careers, and sexual orientations.

Two years after Penny appeared at my office door, another graduate student, Josephine, raised an even more provocative question. She was standing in the school yard early one morning when a mother of a six-year-old in her class approached her with a discomforting remark. She said, "I, we, think our son is gay. He dresses in my clothes all the time." Taken aback, Josephine responded, "He does play with girls a lot."

Josephine brought this incident to her conference group, which was composed of five other graduate students and myself, her advisor. Conference group is a place where students regularly bring events from their practice teaching for discussion and peer feedback. At the time, I naively assumed that Josephine was motivated by a desire to give a more complete response to these concerned parents, one that was accepting of the possibility that their child might be gay. This assumption framed my work with the group that day. It was two years later that Josephine told me she had only recently become more comfortable talking about lesbian and gay issues, and that at the time of her participation in the conference group she had actually disapproved of lesbian and gay lives. In this situation, I think that my own enthusiasm and research commitment had blinded me to the reality of Josephine's attitude. She had taught me an important lesson.

Just as Penny's question helped to initiate our research, Josephine's concern served to enlarge our perspective. Now we realized that teachers not only had to get ready to talk about gay- and lesbian-headed families, but also to address questions about children's sexual orientation. In order to learn how other teachers would respond in Josephine's situation, we interviewed thirteen informants. During 1993, my own life circumstances allowed me to conduct interviews in the rural southwest, as well as in New York City. I chose experienced teachers from diverse backgrounds – Anglos, Latinos, Native Americans – who had worked in either public or private early childhood (K-2) settings. The children in these settings reflected diverse racial, religious, and socioeconomic histories. I began each interview by describing the situation in which Josephine had found herself that morning in the school yard and asked the teachers how they would have responded to the mother's comment. I also asked whether they had found themselves in similar situations and, if so, what they had done. These simple questions led to interviews that lasted from thirty minutes to an hour. The interviews were tape recorded and transcribed. All members of the research group reviewed the transcripts and discussed their responses together.

We learned that several of the teachers had already been queried by parents of children as young as three and four years of age about their child's sexual orientation. When asked what they would say to parents of a six-year-old, half of them gave replies such as, "I guess I would say it's normal for children to experiment with different roles. I would try to put it in a range of normal behavior for that age."

Several of the teachers had never thought about the question, and one could not even imagine herself in Josephine's place. The interview itself caused other teachers to explore the issue of sexual orientation for the first time, and we were able to observe their thinking as it evolved. For example, at the beginning of one interview, a teacher who taught second grade in a public school announced that while she believed all children capable of learning, she also thought a child who might be gay belonged in a special education class. But at the end of the interview, just as I was leaving, she called after me, "Let me know what you find out. I might have to get ready for this." The teacher's initial assumption that anyone can learn expresses her hopefulness about all children, while her designation of a special education classroom indicates her view that being gay is a problem requiring expert management. As a teacher educator, my own hopefulness is buoyed by the teacher's final comment, an acknowledgment that she may need to learn more about sexual orientation and young children.

Our informants asked many questions themselves. What was really known about the origins of sexual orientation? At what age could a young child be said to be gay? The majority of teachers tended to agree with the teacher who said:

> The notion that a child is doing or being anything just doesn't make sense. . . . There's no way of knowing that a six- or seven- or eight-[year-old child is gay]. I just don't think that anybody could possibly know that.

Is this kind of comment an indication of hidden homophobia? We don't know. It might also be read as a lack of information about sexuality in young children. In fact, there is little scholarly literature and even less easily accessible literature that examines the formation of sexual identity in an unbiased way (Chodorow, 1992; Green, 1987). Additionally, because many teachers understand early childhood as a time of rapid changes, experimentation, and play, they are reluctant to fit children into rigid categories.

Teachers frequently wanted additional information from parents who felt their child might be gay. They wanted to place the specific behaviors parents described into a larger context; for example, what else was going on at home? This effort to contextualize behavior, to avoid judgments based on a single incident of any kind, is common practice in early childhood education. It is a strategy teachers often employ when confronted by overwrought parents who are overly anxious about a child's behavior. Teachers, in turn, are practiced at giving multiple concrete examples of behaviors that concern them.

Teachers often wanted time to reflect on the situation being presented by parents and to search for unarticulated questions lying beneath the surface. What were parental attitudes toward homosexuality and the possibility that a child might be lesbian or gay? What did they do or say when they found their child dressing up in the clothing of the other gender? One teacher explained her response this way:

> I would ask the parent to say more about why this is a concern for them. I would try to help them with a lot of support to address these concerns. I would want to see if there is homophobia on the part of the parent. I suppose you could be truly concerned about your child and not be homophobic. . . . If the child has been dressing up in both parents' clothes all along or just playing dress-up in his or her own room, then I would try to help the parent see this as part of a continuing and very normal part of childhood.

The need to reassure parents that dressing up in clothing of the other gender was within the range of normal behavior reverberated throughout our conversations. Although most teachers used the idea of normal behavior with the best intentions to reassure parents, we found it could convey a hidden and less than positive message about homosexuality. If it is normal for a six-year-old boy to dress in clothing of the other gender then he is okay, he is not gay. But, if he continues with this behavior in later years, then when is he no longer okay? When is it no longer normal? Do we imply by our language that being gay is abnormal? Do we also confuse questions of dressing in clothing of the other gender with questions of sexual orientation?

Words such as "normal" are a reflection of many professionals' traditional reliance on the literature of child development, and this normative language is embedded in many accepted standards of practice (Bredekamp, 1987). In recent years, however, this reliance has come increasingly into question, along with its implicit beliefs in normal development (Kessler and Swadener, 1992; Silin, 1995).

When we began our research, we wondered if other educators would be interested in our work. When we presented our project at the 1993 conference of the National Association for the Education of Young Children, two hundred people attended the session. Queried as to whether they had been asked about a child's sexual orientation, half of the attendees raised their hands. We were especially impressed by how one teacher responded to a mother's concern that her son might be gay because he liked to wear jewelry. Her words capture the direct and unbiased manner that we feel best addresses the question of sexual orientation:

> First we talked about seven-year-olds and their general interest in dressing up, fantasy play, and fidgeting with little plastic junk like toys, rings, hair barrettes, etc. I told her Ben was right on target in that area. Then I mentioned that wearing jewelry didn't mean that he was gay, but that one in ten people is gay, so it was likely that three children in our class are gay! She was a bit shocked. But if Ben is gay, she should start enjoying that fact ASAP!

When I went back to West Virginia a few years after the schools had been integrated, I found children of different races pushing each other on the swings and riding on the backs of each others' bikes. I asked a teacher who had taught me many years earlier how this had come about. She said, "We knew [integration] was coming and we didn't want any child to get hurt." The tone of her voice reminds me of the informant who at the end of our interview said, "Let me know what you find out [in your research]." Respecting the complexities of social change, we think there's a tone of openness in this comment. For us as researcher-activists, it also sounds a note of obligation to talk together with teachers, teacher educators, and parents about sexual orientation as a matter of equity. In the following section we explore the roots of educators' own attitudes about sexual orientation in order to understand better how they may influence these conversations.

GAY AND LESBIAN PARENTS IN THE CLASSROOM

In this section, I (Steven Shultz) examine some of my own experiences and those of the educators in our first study (Casper *et al.*, 1992), in order to understand the ways individuals come to accept lesbian and gay parents in their schools.

One educator we interviewed, Ms. Frankel, a public school principal, made certain connections between her early experiences and her present-day attitudes:

> I think one has to work backwards from one's current philosophy, which isn't only an educational one but a political one. It seems to me that all my adult life I've been involved in areas where that is exactly what we were trying to do, be inclusive. I think the civil rights movement had a very big impact on me – successes and its failures. I think probably my childhood, which included very strong feelings about unions, and also a pair of aunts who were Communists in the thirties, and who were closer to my age than to my mother's age, and whom I spent a great deal of time with, they taught me a lot about people being different, that that's the way life was, and that everybody deserved a break.[2]

The common features in Ms. Frankel's story, and in many others we collected, were the connections among feeling different, of translating that feeling into a broad respect for diversity in general, and the fact that the way people experience, think, and talk about the world changes over time.

For me, how I received the world and what I expressed in it was changed by my son the moment I became a parent, then changed again after I became ill, and again when my companion died from AIDS. All of these people and events affected me deeply. They turned the kaleidoscope through which I received the world, and they altered the range, pitch, or tone of my voice as they suggested new vocabulary to describe my new experiences. A slice of the world not previously noticed can suddenly become visible. Mr. D'Angelo, a public school principal, describes how the work of his brother served as a catalyst for Mr. D'Angelo's own greater awareness, which may in turn have created a shift in his thinking about sexual orientation and gay people in general:

> I don't even remember thinking about [gay people], to be quite honest with you. No, I don't think I ever really thought about it . . . I have a brother who's a lawyer, who at one point was representing gay people. He had a very strong point of view with respect to their needs being incorporated into all aspects of our society and had a strong opinion about what was going on.

Perspectives can be personal and idiosyncratic, and at the same time be shaped by cultural and social dynamics. This conspires to make the deconstruction of one's view anything but a simple matter. Certainly self-reflexive analysis involves autobiography, remembering and connecting the stories of the people and events that make up one's life. Both Mr. D'Angelo and Ms. Frankel responded to questions related to their attitudes about diversity and their knowledge of gay people by citing autobiographical stories. These stories give substance to their more generally sketched beliefs, and they do so with a flavor that is unique to their authors' own lives. And once voiced, as many of our informants confided to us, they understood their *own* attitudes better than they did prior to the interview.

Philip Jackson, in his book *Untaught lessons* (1992), writes that our early experiences and subsequent memories may affect our present-day selves in ways that often seem mysterious. The mystery comes in the difficulty and sometimes impossibility of putting our finger on the particular event or interaction behind our actions, thinking, and understandings. Jackson, for instance, affectionately remembers that his high school math teacher, Mrs. Henzi, had a definite and powerful influence on him, but he cannot identify why or how. Given the deep roots that influence how we see and interpret our experiences and, at the same time, the always-present possibility of change, we wanted to explore the stories teachers shared with us about how their attitudes towards lesbian and gay people were shaped: What did they recall? What connections did they make? Some of the educators who learned that they had children with lesbian, gay, or bisexual parents were also dealing with the issue of sexual orientation for the first time in their own lives, and were struggling to fit it into their current worldview.

Father Stephen, a school administrator, combines life experiences with his interpretations of church teachings. He asserts that he would be "against bias of any kind . . . on the basis of gender, religion, sex, or whatever," but his strong convictions and life experiences lead him to view homosexuality – particularly lesbian and gay parents – as dangerous:

> What I view as an effort – a continuing and increasingly strong effort – to have homosexuality accepted popularly as an equally viable lifestyle. I would not want to be part of such an effort. I think that so much of the problems of our time is the breakup and deterioration of the average, normal family . . . I had an uncle who was rather severely retarded. But he became a carpenter, a sanitation worker. But he was able to survive because of being embedded in this family context, and he did not wind up on the street. He did not wind up in an institution, but he was able to be supported. And I think a great deal of the problems today with homelessness stem from that deterioration of the family structure. And, I think that some of the advocates of homosexual equality with heterosexual equality would encourage a kind of diminution of the value of the heterosexual family.

Father Stephen's remarks make clear the powerful ways that personal experience is employed to attempt to justify a point of view. Yet this justification and the connections individuals make to explain them are sometimes not only personal, but also mysterious. Father Stephen's story is less an example of the clear connections between one's personal stories and current beliefs than it is of the lengths individuals may go to interpret a personal story to defend their attitudes. Except for the importance of family both in Father Stephen's story and in lesbians and gays having children, deeper, more explanatory connections seem absent. His story reminds us that the *ways* people interpret and use their own experiences are individualistic. Father Stephen's anecdote warns us that personal stories remembered and shared are not always as complete as the associations individuals make and feel about them. A close reading of his story suggests that the ideas of a group – in this case a religious one – can serve as powerful "regulators" of our beliefs, providing illogical justifications for them if logical ones are absent.

This varied use of experience is illustrated by the ways that Fred, a kindergarten teacher, and Sol, a first-grade teacher, interpreted somewhat similar experiences. Fred related his experiences of growing up without a father to the life of Dan, a child in his class who has lesbian parents:

> My father died when I was fifteen. You go through everything then . . . It's only been in the last five years that I can sort it out, that it's become clear. That reflection, I think, comes with time. The same thing with the situation with Dan. [Dan's parents] can set up as much as he can handle, but there are some things that you're just not going to be able to foresee. With the father gone, the fact that he doesn't see his father anymore, it's a big break. I went through that. It causes a lot of pain, and you have to deal with it, because it's not going to change. But the more I think about it, the more I think there's some [thing] unconscious that may play a part at some time, as in a need or something that's not even voiced. He is a bright boy, but he knows he's different.

Fred's perspective contrasts with that of Sol, a first-grade teacher whose father also died when he was a child. Both adults use their similar early experiences to interpret the needs of children with lesbian and gay parents in their classrooms, but they do so in markedly different ways. Sol commented:

> Where I'm coming from is that my father died when I was nine and a lot of the adult men really moved in to fill the gap. I appreciated it and even then I understood that my mother was alone and a lot of people were supporting us and it was important. [But] without being able to verbalize it, I understood from that age that this was really offensive. The assumption wasn't that I had lost a specific human being who could not be replaced, but that I had lost the man that has to be in a boy's life and I was offended by the whole idea of big brothers. So whether I was gay or straight I would have this perspective that it is

> absurd to say you need a male or a female role model. You need at least one caring adult caretaker, period.

Stories that appear similar in nature or theme clearly are not experienced in the same way by the individuals who figure in them. And although it is the facts of the stories alone that make up our experiences, our previous life stories, our individual temperaments, our historical milieus, and the cultural, economic, and social contexts in which we find ourselves are all influential in shaping the way we read the data of our life experiences. Fred and Sol offer examples of different ways in which similar data can be read, and of how they can then be used to interpret the events occurring in the lives of children in their classrooms.

Through examining some of the stated attitudes and stories of educators regarding lesbian and gay people, this section has attempted to show the effect of early events and interactions on individual attitudes and how they are frequently drawn upon to explain new twists and turns encountered in one's world. Yet, a note of caution is required here. Simply because points of view can draw from deeply personal events in one's life does not make all perspectives equally justifiable or true. And, in fact, it is this deeply personal element that can most powerfully warp our own ideas and attitudes. Without stepping back and looking at any charged issue with a more disciplined eye, the closeness of personal memories *can* have the potential to cloud our vision. It is with honest reflection on these raw materials of our own biography – a kind of checking in with the outside world like that encouraged in the discussions of the children in the following section – that we can best clarify and direct our own practice.

THE ROLE OF EXPERIENCE IN CHILDREN'S CONCEPTION OF FAMILY

> Louis told Jake he couldn't have two mothers, that you need a dad to have a baby. Jake answered immediately, "I have two mothers. My mom went to a doctor and got some seed and that's how I got started."
>
> Six-year-olds, New York City Public School

Although we were concentrating on listening to adults in our initial research, reports of children's comments, such as the one above relayed to us by a teacher (P. Stafford, personal communication, 1990), came to me (Virginia Casper) from parents, students, and colleagues.

Messages appeared regularly on our voice mail, and little scraps of paper with intriguing anecdotes began to pile up in our mail boxes. Inadvertently, our research served as an invitation to others to think about these issues with us, which helped us refocus our work with children.

The image of young children sharing and playing out their evolving concepts of family during the course of a school day is a familiar one to early childhood educators. As family forms are becoming more varied and more visible, children who have been raised by gay and lesbian parents join with other children to enlarge the already diverse family constellations talked about by children in classrooms. My growing awareness of what children know about families was shaped by my ongoing observations of young children as a teacher educator. As a parent I was acculturated to the assumptions children have about each other's families, but as a lesbian mother I was particularly attuned to the subtle comparisons that children make. I recall a walk home from school as a group of first and second graders analyzed the different meanings of "father," "daddy," and "papi.". I knew such conversations were not rare and that children's direct and indirect experiences with a broad range of family forms were affecting their thinking about what constitutes a family.

Trained as a developmental psychologist, I became curious about what the literature had to say about children's conceptions of the family. Twenty-five years of research claims that children's experiences with family have a minimal impact on how they define a family and which groupings of people they determine to be examples of a family (Newman, Roberts, and Syre, 1993; Pederson and Gilby, 1986). The gold standard in this research is Piaget's (1928/1965) original study of a child's increasing ability to reason about kin and family relations. Piaget's premise was that without more mature cognitive structures, a young child's experience of being a brother, for example, did not bring that child closer to understanding the inherent reciprocity of that relationship. Using traditional methodology of standardized individual child assessments, the research following Piaget shows that neither family-related curricula (Watson and Amgott-Kwan, 1984) nor the very direct experience of living in a particular family form appears to have any effect on children's definition of a family or their validation of those situations as family (Brodzinsky, Schechter, and Brodzinsky, 1986; Newman *et al.*, 1993; Pederson and Gilby, 1986; Powell, Wilcher, Wedemeyer, and Claypool, 1981.) Investigators of children's family concepts have failed to incorporate post-Piagetian research on the ability of young children to decenter, take the perspective of another, and utilize non-egocentric thinking (Borke, 1975; Hart and Goldin-Meadow, 1984; Shatz and Gelman, 1973). These abilities appear to surface more when children are presented with tasks that make "human sense" (Donaldson, 1978). And with notable exceptions (Newman *et al.*, 1993; Bernstein, 1988), efforts to integrate children's affective expressions about family with their cognitive understandings have been minimal. Finally, while increased family diversity is almost always cited as a rationale for such work, only a handful of studies actually include diverse samples. It is these few studies alone, however, that suggest that experience does play a role. The experience of living in a divorced family, for example, makes children more likely to accept a single-parent family as an example of family (Camera, 1979; Moore, Bickhard, and Cooper, 1977; Wedemeyer, Bickard, and Cooper, 1989). While there have been studies that look at the effects of being raised by gay parents (Patterson, 1992), studies that look at the role of experience in children's conceptions of family do not include children from lesbian and gay families.

I was stunned by these data and perceived them to be counter-intuitive. As a teacher educator I found them at odds with my own observations of young children in group settings. As the idea of doing more structured observations began to gel, Steven Schultz and I looked to theory in order to ground our study. Given our commitment to ethnographic methodologies, we sought to generate or extend theory rather than test it (Casper, 1996.) As we began to conceptualize a study, we utilized both Vygotsky (1934/1962) and Piaget (1928/1965). Piaget separated young children's early-absorption and direct use of adult language from their later, more conscious understanding of a concept based on their developing cognitive structures and direct experience. Thus, he believed that a young child's definition of family comes less from actual experience and more from direct adult transmission. Vygotsky never studied children's thinking about family to the same extent as Piaget. Nevertheless, his juxtaposition of spontaneous (everyday) and formal (scientific) concepts became a pivotal point for our thinking. Vygotsky emphasizes the interactive connection between what we know (spontaneous/everyday) but cannot yet express, and concepts we have learned (formal/scientific) but for which we do not yet have significant experience to bring richness of meaning.

In order to explore how children think about families as part of our ongoing collaborative exploration, a research team was established during the 1992–1993 academic year, consisting of two graduate faculty members (myself and Steven Schultz) and two classroom teachers from an urban, private, progressive school for children ages three to thirteen. A mini-grant allowed us to pilot an ethnographically based study. We decided to begin by observing and videotaping in five classrooms, including children from a first grade, two second grades, one fourth and one eighth grade.

In this school, daily classroom meetings that often open with questions to prompt a discussion are an ongoing part of the curriculum. As we began to listen to family-related discussions across this broad age span, the differences in issues between the younger versus the older children, combined with our own limited resources, directed us to focus on the younger children.

Rather than representing a group of people in the global sense, ethnographic work is known for its ability to represent what Robin Leavitt (1994) calls "a dramatic instance." In this vein, it is important to acknowledge some of the unique aspects of this school community. Children in the classes had known each other and their families for at least a few years, and some since the age of two. In each class we visited, many family structures were represented, and some children appeared to know of gay- and lesbian-headed families even if they were not actually represented in the group. Each class already included family study as a part of its naturally evolving curriculum. Teachers informed us when particular discussions would take place, and we also planned some sessions jointly in our collaborative meetings. While perhaps not "typical," we view this environment as rich in family-related experiences. Following are brief excerpts of discussions in three of the classrooms.

The continent of love

Michael, a K-1 classroom teacher, overheard some children in his class wonder aloud about marriage. A few children wanted to know if boys could marry boys, or girls could marry girls. The children arrived one morning to see that Michael had put these questions on the chart for discussion: Can a man marry a man? Can a woman marry a woman?

Early in the conversation, one child introduced the idea of love between members of the same sex, saying, "My cousin has two moms. They got divorced from their husbands. They started to love each other and asked each other, 'Do you want to live together?' They said yes." This child's comment reflects both her direct experience of her aunts and a repetition of a relative's account of their family story. This cogent statement was ignored and the rest of the children went on to discuss what is allowed and what is not. The children said such things as:

Sam: In some countries a man and a man, and a woman and a woman marry. But they can't here. It would be breaking the law . . . My mom told me.
Emily: A law is like a big rule . . .
Tanya: This is not a country. It's a city.
Sam: Different parts of the world are called countries.
Rachel: This isn't one of them.

Here we see that children's main source of evidence tends to be what they see and what they've been told. What is reported is direct and raw. "I know," "I saw," or "My mom told me."

Mid-way through the conversation, Michael helped the children clarify concepts with two questions: What's the difference between living together and getting married? What's getting married?

The discussion jumped between the requisite objects and place for marriage and what constitutes love:

Sam: You don't have to like . . . you have to *love* to get married. Loving means more than liking.

Emily: You have to wear fancy clothes. There's something called a wedding dress.
Tanya: I know another name for a country. It's a continent.
Glora: I don't think the United States is a continent. A continent is something up in space.

The next week, Michael posed the following question to the group: What is a family? The group got right to the issue of babies: who can and can't have them, what you "need" to have children. In passing, the meaning of divorce also became clear: "It's when you don't like each other anymore." At this point the following exchange occurred:

Adam: You can have two dads or two moms.
Michael: How do you know?
Adam: I forgot the word.
Michael: Just describe it.
Adam: I can't.
Jason: A step-dad?
Adam: No.
Sandra: I know what a boy and a boy is when they get married . . . (*She speaks loudly and distinctly*) Gay.
Michael: (*to Adam*) Is that what you're talking about?
Adam: (*nodding*) Yes.
Michael: Uh huh.

These children in Michael's class were not being "taught" about gay and lesbian families, but rather encouraged to struggle with definition. They all drew upon their spontaneous/everyday (Vygotsky, 1934/1962) experiences with family in their efforts to make sense of love, marriage, divorce, and relationships. Through discussion, the children were also using more formal/scientific (Vygotsky, 1934/1962) language, helping each other to enrich their everyday concepts of family. In the next section, we see children who are entering middle childhood and are already beginning to measure their own experiences against more firmly internalized societal norms.

Fitting families to the city or the city to families? Six- and seven-year-olds make crate cities

In two first/second-grade classrooms, the students conducted a year-long study of the city, which culminated in building a "crate city." Constructed from discarded wine crates and figures, made to scale of wood and cardboard, the city included private houses, apartment buildings, libraries, schools, shops, etc. Children worked as a group to decide who would live in the city, what relationships the residents would have, how the buildings would look, and what kinds of jobs would be necessary to make the city function well. Along with this work, the children spent a good part of the year discussing the nature of family.

In mid-spring, one of the teachers, Judy, expressed her surprise and dismay to us at the conventional nature of the families her children had made up and placed within the city. The children's actual families represented great diversity; moreover, as a group, they had had rich discussions about family all year. When she shared her puzzlement with the children, they defended their choice of traditional nuclear families saying, "It's the usual," "There was no room [for other kinds of families]," "[Other kinds of families] wouldn't fit." In order to shift the tone and quality of the conversation, Judy asked the children to think about a boy in the other first/second grade who had two mothers. Many of the children had visited this child's home, seen his mothers at school, or met the entire family in the neighborhood. In asking them to consider their experience of his family, Judy brought to consciousness knowledge they already possessed.

The other first/second grade was a bit behind in the construction of its city. On hearing of Judy's experience, Beth, the teacher, decided to have a discussion to revisit their previous talks about different kinds of families before the children actually constructed their families. In this meeting, she asked, "Who is in your family?" Quite a few children named those in their immediate and extended family; others joined in with their feelings about family, including how they felt when grown-ups argue. Eventually, a child with two lesbian mothers described his family as "two moms and a dad," continuing, "My two moms live with me and my dad lives in Philadelphia and it's confusing." A discussion ensued in which other children tried to postulate what might be confusing about "having three parents." Not much was established beyond this point, although questions and comments were aired with the same open tone as the rest of the meeting.

When both classes finished their cities, one could see that these discussions did more than just remind the children that they all come from a wide variety of family structures. In the process of drawing and constructing people for their families in the crate city, the children experimented, commented, asked questions, and sometimes changed their family planning. In Beth's class, the children clearly profited from their additional discussion of family prior to actually creating the families for their city. Three girls initially expressed their desire to make a family with two mothers and a female child. Another family also included two fathers. When the families were actually created and the city was finished, there was one family with two mothers (not created by the child with lesbian mothers) and numerous other constellations that broadly represented the family diversity of the children in the class. And, by a unanimous vote, it was decreed: no baby-sitters allowed in this crate city!

These conversations are but moments in the long year that a class of children spend together. Yet in these moments, issues are raised about what children know of contemporary families, the persistence of stereotypes that contradict lived experience, the impact of these stereotypes on children living in diverse family structures, and the deep connections between cognition and affect.

The teachers in each of these classrooms took the lead in making lesbian and gay families salient, a natural part of the spectrum of possibilities. Evocative questions helped children reach into their own experiences and pull out what they already knew and what remained problematic. In this way, teachers helped children find and name their everyday experiences of family. Thus, each learning environment was transformed into a place where assumptions about what constitutes family were unhinged, creating a different standard than the one from which children usually take their cues. In turn, this allowed the children to venture forth with their thoughts, questions, fantasies, and feelings about family. In the next section we explore the importance of teachers, at all levels, creating classroom environments where such conversations can happen.

EXTENDING INVITATIONS: THE PROCESS OF INSTITUTIONAL CHANGE

In this section, I (Harriet Cuffaro) will highlight some of the qualitative changes that have occurred in the social atmosphere of Bank Street College in relation to more open discussions about sexual orientation. It is an account of our institutional experiences – of small and large events, of individual and group activity, of interactions and transactions, of transformations, and of events and people outside the institution that also served as catalysts for change.

As educators, we know that every classroom has a quality that can be felt by the people who enter it. That quality is partly determined by the materials provided and the way space is arranged. Equally important is the social atmosphere – something that is sensed and that determines the nature of the relationship between and among people. It also determines whether the telling of personal stories is invited or inhibited. The same can be said of institutions.

When I joined the Bank Street faculty over twenty years ago, there were gay and lesbian people throughout the institution, but theirs was an invisible, unspoken presence, known but unacknowledged. For all of our progressivism on many issues, in this area we as a community were politely mute. The social atmosphere invited silence.

The first "breaks" in the institutional silence occurred in the early 1980s in the School for Children, with the appearance of lesbian families who were open and articulate about their relationships. The impact of their presence on the institution, however, remained localized in the Children's

School. In 1987, the presence of another lesbian family in the College's Family Center for infants and toddlers did not remain local to that community. At the first parent meeting of the school year, the director of the Center welcomed all families and named the variety of families, among them gay and lesbian families. This public statement of inclusion was reinforced as pictures of each child's family were placed on the walls, and the children talked about and questioned the meaning of family. Student teachers working in the Family Center also talked and questioned, expanding the conversations about gay and lesbian families into the Graduate School. Though most often restricted to events in various parts of the institution, a qualitative shift was occurring within the whole. The words "gay" and "lesbian" now were spoken aloud, but still with some quality of distance, of tentative inclusion.

Further changes slowly began to occur within the institution at large. For example, the discussions surrounding a possible contract with the Salvation Army described in an earlier section of this article contributed to heightened awareness of gay and lesbian issues. In the Graduate School, certain events continued to bring gay and lesbian issues to the forefront. In January 1989, during intercession, the Graduate School held a series of meetings with a multicultural theme for students and faculty. At the suggestion of a lesbian faculty member, one of the organizations invited to attend was the Gay and Lesbian Teachers of New York City. Few people chose this session – only two students, myself, and two other faculty members. In the discussion that took place, one of the students underlined the invisibility I have described when she said, "We're not here. Even in the child development courses nothing is said." In exasperation she blurted, "We're not even mentioned in terms of abnormal psychology!" At our next teacher education faculty meeting, I presented the student's comments and feelings. There were surprised and mixed reactions among some faculty, but the discussion did lead to including sexual orientation as part of development in some of the Child Development courses.

It was after the publication of the 1992 *Teachers College Record* article, "Breaking the silences: Lesbian and gay parents and the schools" by Virginia, Steve, and Elaine, members of our research group, that another teacher education faculty meeting turned into an extraordinary event. While congratulating our colleagues and expressing pride in their pioneering work, veils slowly began to drop and silences were truly broken. One staff member spoke of learning that her daughter was a lesbian and asked for help in understanding this new knowledge. Another staff member "came out" at the meeting. While everyone present at the meeting did not join in the discussion, as happens at any faculty meeting, for two hours people spoke honestly of their confusions and ignorance, and there were expressions of ambivalence and uncertainty. It was a powerful, memorable, human time of caring, of vulnerability, and a sharing of personal experiences. What had been invisible to many became visible, known, familiar, and spoken. Did the recognition and acceptance of a publication contribute to priming this public conversation? Looking back, the seemingly isolated events in different divisions of Bank Street probably had more impact than we perceived. Time and events were influencing the whole institution, not just its parts. Most critically, the increasingly visible, assertive, and national presence of gay and lesbian people created a new societal context that also influenced the consciousness of the Bank Street community.

Time, acknowledgment, and the determined efforts of individuals and groups of individuals have led to a changed social atmosphere and consciousness within Bank Street College. There are public notices announcing meetings of gay and lesbian students and faculty; there are more changes in courses. In what follows, I describe the changes I have made over the past three years in the Foundations course I teach.

The first third of the course examines the history of changing educational aims in elementary and early childhood education in the United States. As a transition to the next major topic, issues of equity, the students read George Counts's (1932/1978) *Dare the schools build a new social order?* During these sessions on equity, we focus on the effects of classism, racism, and sexism on educational aims, and students are asked to write a paper on an equity issue. Frequently, students choose to write about equity issues of particular interest to them that have not been discussed in depth in class, such as disability and bilingualism. While Steve, Virginia, and Elaine were conducting their research on the experience of gay and lesbian parents in schools, my own awareness was sharpened by our conversations about their work, and I began to devote a small amount of time to sexual orientation as an issue of equity. No one chose to write about this topic, but in the final paper of the course – an educational autobiography – one student wrote of her sexual orientation and her frustration and anger in keeping this secret. Each semester, as I learned more, I gradually increased the time we spent in discussing sexual orientation as an issue of equity. While few students chose this topic for their papers, more students wrote about being lesbian or gay in a homophobic society in their educational autobiographies.

In the spring 1994 semester, I added more articles on sexual orientation and heterosexism to the readings, including the *Briefing paper on children of gay and lesbian parents* prepared for the National Association for the Education of Young Children (NAEYC) Governing Board (1993), which was sent to all NAEYC affiliates to provide research and information for discussions on inclusion. I also presented to the students the various research projects in which our group was involved, such as children's concept of family and teachers' responses to "Josephine's question" discussed elsewhere in this chapter. In that semester, I received four papers dealing with sexual orientation as an equity issue. While the perspective of each of the four papers differed in what each chose to discuss, they shared a common theme: each student spoke of the teacher's social responsibility in relation to issues of equity in a democratic society.

For one student, writing the paper was an opportunity for self-examination. She wrote:

> I cannot discuss the issue at hand without exposing my biases – biases connected to values crystallized over time by a combination of religious, family, cultural beliefs. Sometimes values can be such a part of us they become habits. We stop thinking about them critically, and simply defend them. While my exploration here will be to critically challenge my values, I recognize that changes in my feelings, attitudes, values will not be instantaneous. This paper is, for me, the beginning of a journey that I know not where it will lead.

With integrity and great honesty, she continued by posing a series of questions and answers for herself, such as "What is the rationale for letting young children know that Heather has two Moms, or Daddy has a roommate?" to which she responded,

> to foster unity within their own families; to emphasize that while families may be structured differently – whether it be grandparent and child, mother and child, foster parents and child, two Dads, and so forth, familial love is the important, sustaining criterion that makes a family special.

At another point in the paper, she asked herself, "Is there a need to talk about gay and lesbian families whether or not there are such families in her classroom?" She answered, "If we value the importance of making children aware, be[ing] understanding and compassionate to others who are different from themselves, the need exists."

For another student, the dilemma was different and acutely present. She spoke eloquently of her struggle for integrity:

> Like George Counts's call to the school, I feel very strongly about creating an environment for children that transcends the walls of the classroom and is reflective of society (while at the same time reshaping it). To this date I have been very fortunate to have worked in schools that have helped and supported me and my beliefs. Next year, however, I will be working in a school that may not be as open . . . Similar to gay and lesbian parents, I have the stressful and difficult task of deciding whether or not to disclose to my fellow teachers and administrators the information that I am a lesbian . . . The fear of personal rejection and a lack of understanding is holding me back from being open about who I

> am . . . It is here where I hear Counts's words calling me to take the power and use it. I just hope that I can surrender *security*, and grab onto some courage, so I can fulfill my responsibility to my own convictions and of those of an educator.

The reality of the classrooms we see each week as we visit our students, the questions they bring to graduate classes, along with our own increased understanding and heightened consciousness over time, have all contributed to change. As a faculty, we have become more aware of how our behavior, with both children and adults, invites or silences. We strive to listen more carefully, to pause sufficiently to offer openings, and to work consciously to create a social atmosphere that invites and recognizes everyone, and also encourages questioning the given. In a fundamental sense, we have enlarged both our concept of community and the College community and renewed our understanding of the responsibilities that come with teaching, particularly in a democratic society. And like the student in the course, we also hear Counts's words, "An education that does not strive to promote the fullest and most thorough understanding of the world is not worthy of the name" (1932/1978, p. 9).

CHOOSING A MORE EQUITABLE FUTURE

When I (Jonathan Silin) began teaching in the 1960s, homosexuality was still considered a matter of deviance, a topic perhaps appropriate only to college-level courses on psychological and social pathology. Although I was living much of my life in and through the nascent gay culture of the time, it was not possible to be out at work without risking the loss of my job, a risk I was unprepared to take. Today there are thriving national organizations, such as the Gay, Lesbian and Straight Teachers Network; local projects that advocate for gay youth, such as the Hetrick-Martin Institute in New York City; and groups that support gay and lesbian families, such as Lesbian and Gay Parents Coalition International. There is also a growing literature for children about gay and lesbian lives and curriculum materials for adults (Chapman, 1992).

There is still a long way to go. In part, this reflects the conservatism of our society and of early childhood education, a field that has depended heavily on the literature of child development as a knowledge base for curricular decision-making. Early childhood educators have relied on conceptual and empirical research that distances children from adults and from their material worlds. The study we have described here on children's conceptions of family confirms what others have also maintained; developmental psychologists have frequently underestimated children's abilities to understand complex social issues (Short, 1991). In part, the remaining distance reflects popular cultural images of young children as innocent. Unfortunately, images of childhood innocence are often linked with ideas about childhood ignorance. Teachers and parents want to protect children from knowledge of the social world that they themselves find discomforting (Silin, 1995). As adults we forget that what represents change to us does not necessarily represent change for the children. Many children have never known a world without lesbian and gay families.

As we explore children's knowledge of diverse family structures, recurring questions arise at the heart of teaching (Cuffaro, 1995). To what extent are teachers able to make choices that reflect their educational commitments and to what extent are they limited by the circumstances in which they work? Is it the teacher's role to reflect current societal attitudes or to invite discussion of taken-for-granted attitudes? In response to these questions and the inquiries of our graduate students, we have recently undertaken a study of how teachers who do *not* have children with gay or lesbian parents in their classrooms discuss this issue with children.

Our research, indeed our own individual histories, indicate two intertwined realities: the central role of early experience in shaping attitudes, and the close connection between affect and understanding. Often, the interviews we conducted with teachers provided them with their first opportunity to explore how the theme of sexual orientation affects their work with children. Although relying on accepted notions of "normal" development, teachers showed themselves to be eager for more information about sexual orientation.

As individuals, we have attitudes and perspectives, and so do classrooms and institutions. Documenting the changes in institutional attitudes at Bank Street, the context in which our work as teachers and as researchers is located – those moments and situations that may be particularly susceptible to change, to questioning, and to the possibility of shifts in perspectives – we have come to understand more deeply that change is a slow process that requires equal parts of patience and persistence. We are also aware of the way that recognition outside of the institution – publications, grants, conference presentations – legitimizes work within its walls.

We recognize that our project is inextricably linked to monumental societal changes that began in the 1950s with the burgeoning civil rights movement. We see our work in the context of the ongoing national debate about an inclusive, as opposed to a monolithic, approach to culture. This article has focused on one equity issue – sexual orientation. Our commitment to build a more equitable society tells us that questioning and acting on behalf of democratic ideals is the most authentic way to fulfill our social responsibility as educators.

ACKNOWLEDGEMENTS

We want to thank all the parents and educators interviewed in the course of our research, and most especially Robin Abeshaus, Lisa Barish, Toby Weinberger, and David Wolkenberg, who collaborated with us on the study of children's conceptions of family. Over the years, Rob Caramella, Sandra Chapman, and Kathleen Hayes have also supported our work. Edna K. Shapiro provided insightful comments on an earlier draft of this chapter. We gratefully acknowledge the financial assistance of the Paul Rapoport Foundation and the Bank Street College of Education Minigrant Program.

NOTES

1 This chapter first appeared in *Harvard Educational Review* 66 (2) Summer 1996. Copyright © by President and Fellows of Harvard College.
2 All quotes in this section are from interviews conducted as a part of a research study reported in Casper, Schultz, and Wickens (1992). In the interest of confidentiality, the names of participants have been changed.

REFERENCES

Antler, J. (1987). *Lucy Sprague Mitchell*. New Haven, CT: Yale University Press.
Bernstein, A. (1988). Unraveling the tangles: Children's understanding of stepfamily kinship. In W. R. Beer (ed.), *Relative strangers: Studies of stepfamily processes* (pp. 83–111). Totowa, NJ: Rowman & Littlefield.
Biber, B. (1984). *Early education and psychological development*. New Haven, CT: Yale University Press.
Borke, H. (1975). Piaget's mountain revisited: Changes in the egocentric landscape. *Developmental Psychology*, 11, 240–443.
Bredekamp, S. (1987). *Developmentally appropriate practices in early childhood programs from birth through age 8*. Washington, DC: National Association for the Education of Young Children.
Brodzinsky, D. M., Schechter, D., and Brodzinsky, A. B. (1986). Children's knowledge of adoption: Developmental changes and implications for development. In R. D. Ashmore and D. M. Brodzinsky (eds), *Thinking about the family: View of parents and children*. (pp. 205–232). Hillsdale, NJ: Lawrence Earlbaum.
Camera, K. A. (1979). *Children's construction of social knowledge: Concepts of family and the experience of parental divorce*. Unpublished doctoral dissertation, Stanford University. (University Microfilms, No. 80–01884)
Casper, V. (1996). Making the familiar unfamiliar and the unfamiliar familiar. *Zero to Three*, 16(3), 14–20.
Casper, V., and Schultz, S. (1995). Lesbian and gay parents encounter educators: Initiating conversations. In R. Savin-Williams and K. M. Cohen (eds), *The lives of lesbians, gays and bisexuals: Developmental, clinical and cultural issues* (pp. 305–330). Fort Worth, TX: Harcourt Brace.
Casper, V., Schultz, S., and Wickens, E. (1992). Breaking the silences: Lesbian and gay parents and the schools. *Teachers College Record* 94, 109–137.
Chapman, S. (1992). *The power of children's literature: A rationale for using books on*

gay and lesbian headed families. Unpublished masters thesis, Bank Street College of Education, New York City.

Chodorow, N. (1992). Heterosexuality as a compromise formation: Reflections on the psychoanalytic theory of sexual development. *Psychoanalysis and Contemporary Thought*, 15, 267–304.

Counts, G. S. (1978). *Dare the schools build a new social order?* Carbondale: Southern Illinois University Press. (Original work published 1932)

Cuffaro, H. K. (1995). *Experimenting with the world: John Dewey and the early childhood classroom.* New York: Teachers College Press.

Donaldson, M. (1978). *Children's minds.* New York: Norton.

Green, R. (1987). *Sissy boy syndrome and the development of homosexuality.* New Haven: Yale University Press.

Hart, L. S. and Goldin-Meadow, S. (1984). The child as non-egocentric art critic. *Child Development*, 55, 2122–2129.

Jackson, P. (1992). *Untaught lessons.* New York: Teachers College Press.

Kessler, S. and Swadener, B. B. (eds). (1992). *Reconceptualizing the early childhood curriculum.* New York: Teachers College Press.

Leavitt, R. (1994). *Power and emotion in infant-toddler daycare.* Albany: State University of New York Press.

Moore, N. V., Bickhard, M. H., and Cooper, R. G. (1977). *The child's development of the concept of family.* (ERIC Document No. ED 140,980)

National Association for the Education of Young Children. (1993). *Briefing paper on children of gay and lesbian parents* (Paper prepared for the Governing Board). Washington, DC: Author.

Newman, J. L., Roberts, L. R., and Syre, C. R. (1993). Concepts of family among children and adolescents: Effects of cognitive level, gender and familv structure. *Developmental Psychology*, 29, 951–962.

Patterson, C. J. (1992). Children of lesbian and gay parents. *Child Development*, 63, 1025–1042.

Pederson, D. R. and Gilbv, R. L. (1986). Children's concepts of the family. In R. Ashmore and D. Brodzinsky (eds), *Thinking about the family* (pp. 181–204). Hillsdale, NJ: Lawrence Erlbaum.

Piaget, J. (1965). *Judgment and reasoning in the child.* London: Routledge and Kegan Paul. (Original work published 1928)

Powell, J. A., Wilcher, B. J., Wedemeyer, N. V., and Claypool, P. L. (1981). The young child's developing concept of family. *Home Economics Research Journal*, 10(22), 137–149.

Shapiro, E. and Nager, N. (1995). *A developmental framework for education: Retrospect and prospect.* Unpublished manuscript.

Shatz, M. and Gelman, R. (1973). The development of communication skills: Modification in the speech of young children as a function of listener. *Monographs of the Society for Research in Child Development*, 38(5, No. 152).

Short, G. (1991). Children's grasp of controversial issues. In M. Woodhead, P. Light, and R. Carr (eds), *Growing up in a changing society* (pp. 333–351). New York: Routledge.

Silin, J. (1995). *Sex, death and the education of children: Our passion for ignorance in the age of AIDS.* New York: Teachers College Press.

Vygotsky, L. (1962). *Thought and Language.* Cambridge, MA: MIT Press. (Original work published 1934)

Watson, M. W. and Amgott-Kwan. T. (1984). Development of family-role concepts in school-age children. *Developmental Psychology*, 20, 953–959.

Wedemeyer, N. V., Bickhard, M. H., and Cooper, R. G. (1989). The development of

structural complexity in the child's concept of family: The effect of cognitive stage, sex and intactness. *Journal of Genetic Psychology*, 150, 341–357.
Wickens, E. (1993). Penny's question: "I will have a child in my class with two moms – What do you know about this?" *Young Children*, 48(3), 25–28.
Wickens, E. (1994). *Anna Day and the O-ring*. Boston: Alyson Press.
Wickens, E. and Schultz, S. (1994). "I will have a child in my class with two moms, two lesbians. What do you know about this?" In F. Pignatelli and S. W. Pflaum (eds), *Experiencing diversity: Toward educational equity* (pp. 96–114). Thousand Oaks, CA: Corwin Press.

Chapter 6

Gendered settings and human rights in early childhood

Ann Farrell

This chapter will review the gendering of young children and their families with respect to the current human rights agenda. It examines landmark legislation and ongoing legal reforms that have brought human rights into the public arena and into the personal lives of children and families. The human rights agenda implies that responsible and caring adults will ensure their children's survival, protection and participation in the world. The settings where such rights are enacted, however, are largely gendered settings: settings where participants in families and in early childhood services are positioned according to gender and its socially constructed meanings. These gendered settings, moreover, rumour pervasive, overarching, social oppression that arbitrarily gives voice to some people, yet marginalises and silences others. Two seemingly divergent examples of this phenomenon that are used later as part of the cultural backcloth to this chapter are the gendered treatment of women and their children in the criminal justice system and the positioning of children as gendered consumers in a materialist culture. These two examples are, moreover, symptomatic of the gendered societies in which early childhood professionals live and work. This chapter further challenges us to reflect on the human rights discourse as it applies to this field of influence and, to this end, examines Young's (1990) notion of social justice and Cox's (1995) notion of social capital in living and working with children and their families as ethical human beings.

HUMAN RIGHTS LANDMARKS

The 1990 World Summit for Children endorsing the United Nations Convention on the Rights of the Child (Convention) was a global expression of the human rights debates that had been occurring for some time in both the private and the public arenas. The early childhood community participated vigorously in this discourse with respect to children's rights to 'provision, protection and participation' (Balke, 1992; Meuwese and Rijvers, 1993). In Australia, for example, successive governments since

1992 have acknowledged the rights of children as fundamental human rights and, in 1992, Australia declared that the Convention would be made an international instrument for the purposes of the Human Rights and Equal Opportunity Commission Act 1986, thus enabling the Commission to conciliate complaints about acts or practices that breach the rights of the Convention. In addition to the rights provided under this Act, the provisions of the Convention are implemented by the federal, state and territory legislation, policies and programmes in the areas of family law, social security, health and community services, education, employment, culture and criminal and juvenile justice.

Some of the entitlements of children under the Convention are:

- a name, a nationality and family ties;
- the preservation of their identity;
- family reunification to leave any country and to enter their own in order to be reunited or to maintain the child–parent relationship and
- access to medical services, primary and preventive health care, public health education with protection from harmful traditional practices.

Abrogation of the rights to a name, identity and family reunification are particularly relevant in the case of indigenous peoples, many of whom have been dispossessed of name and identity and forcibly removed from their families.

Children under the Convention are also entitled to protection from:

- abuse and neglect;
- child labour from engaging in work that constitutes a threat to their health, education and development;
- drug abuse from the use of narcotic and psychotropic drugs and from being involved in their production or distribution;
- sexual exploitation;
- the sale, trafficking and abduction;
- torture and deprivation of liberty and
- armed conflicts.

The Convention also deals with children's access to appropriate information in the mass media. Article 17, for example, emphasises the role of the media in disseminating information to children that is consistent with the child's wellbeing and respects the child's cultural background. Article 17 states that:

> States Parties recognise the important function performed by the mass media and shall ensure that the child has access to information and material from a diversity of national and international sources,

> especially those aimed at the promotion of his or her social, spiritual and moral wellbeing and physical and mental health.
>
> (Defence for Children International, 1996)

As we shall see later in this chapter, the blatant gendering of consumers within the mass media is clearly antithetical to the human right to access to diverse material. How can identity be ensured if children are subjected to unabashed stereotyping in the mass media?

While the evolution of rights for children occurred alongside those of human rights generally, it represented a distinct shift from the earlier thinking on children's rights, because it now argued for children's rights outside of or separate from the family. Within the Convention, children have the right to be brought up by their parents, but also have the right to live and learn in settings other than those provided by the family. Moreover, children have the right to be protected from all types of abuse, including that which occurs within the family. According to Gil (1991: 393), the Convention is:

> an important symbolic event. It affirms the rights of parents with respect to children, and of children with respect to parents, in the context of the best interests of the child. The Convention promulgates standards and goals for equal rights for all children to life, liberty, dignity, and personal and cultural identity; to optimum development, health, education, care and protection; to social and economic security; to freedom from exploitation, abuse and neglect; and to civil and political rights.

There is little doubt that the Convention has changed the way in which some people think about children and has heightened an awareness of adults' responsibilities to ensure children's survival, development, protection and participation. From this perspective, children are not seen as possessions, chattels or appendages of their parents, but persons to whom human dignity is accorded. Hart and Pavlovic (1991: 345) use the term 'person status' to describe the respect for the dignity of children as human beings. In her book *Citizen child*, Australian social researcher Kathleen Funder (1996) argues that children were once considered as neatly dependent and subordinate to authority; the children's rights rhetoric challenges both these assumptions through international conventions and through legal precedents in unusual cases.

It is noteworthy here that children's rights to provision, protection and participation are enacted primarily within their families (albeit in diverse forms) and within their early childhood services. Edgar (1991: 8), former director of the Australian Institute of Family Studies, sees such settings (despite their varying configurations) as 'reality constructing' institutions, as sites for multiple realities (as sites for a mother's reality, for a child's reality or for a caregiver's or a teacher's reality of the world). While these participants, with differing roles and needs, construct their own realities, this process is conducted within the relationships of shared humanity.

Children, as human beings, in families and in early childhood services are seen to need trusted advocates who will fairly and justly speak for them when their voices are either not heard or heard as mere 'babbles'. Within the human rights rhetoric, theirs is the right to be respected as learners in reciprocal social relationships. But while they may be accorded human dignity, they are also vulnerable due to their inter-dependence with adults, especially for their early survival, care and protection; and this vulnerability is acutely evident in cases of child exploitation and abuse by powerful others. It should be noted here that the early childhood movement, from its social activism in the nineteenth century, has been at the forefront of public outrage at such violations.

Human rights debates have also foregrounded some other important discourses dealing with professional, communal and personal ethics (Preston, 1994; Purdy, 1992). Early childhood professionals have for some time championed the cause of professional ethics in relation to their work as professionals, to their colleagues, to the children and families they work with and to the communities in which they are embedded (Ashby, 1991; Stonehouse and Creaser, 1991). It has been argued that human rights are germane to human ethics and that early childhood professionals should participate in the human rights debate in order to construct and enact their roles as ethical participants with children and their families (Farrell, 1995).

This process of participation in the human rights discourse, however, faces a serious disjunction when translated into our embedded learning and living contexts or ecologies – ecologies that, among other things, are tacitly gendered.

One clear example of such gendering that is antithetical to human rights is the gendered treatment of women in the criminal justice system. The next section will consider the treatment of offending women, who are usually the primary caregivers of their children, to illustrate the proliferation of gendered policies and practices in allegedly civil societies, societies in which early childhood professionals, children and their families live and work.

GENDERING

We need only look at the history of the early colonisation of a country like Australia to see deep-rooted gendering. Robert Hughes' (1988) book *The fatal shore* graphically portrays the early transportation of female offenders, often with their children, convicted of crimes (usually for minor offences against property) from Britain in order to serve the utilitarian ends of maintaining the heterosexuality of the colony and of bearing the progeny of the new society. Paradoxically, these female offenders were used to procreate the society from which they had been forcibly removed. In her review of female prisoners in New South Wales since 1788, Johnson (1988: 126) stated:

> The female convicts were taken on board the ships of the first fleets often naked and filthy and were frequently sold to the marines during the journey from England for a tipple of rum. Both on the journey and in the colony the women were regarded as a thousand times worse than the men; difficult, unruly and beyond redemption. For any digression they could be flogged, put in prison, have their heads shaved or receive a ducking.

Ironically, these practices parallelled a lack of understanding of the inhabitants of the land that was regarded as *terra nullius.* According to Australian lawyer and Human Rights Commissioner Moira Rayner (1996: 53):

> There was no understanding of the special relationship Aboriginal people had with it, nor of what these European settlers were doing in imposing 19th century colonial ideas of ownership, possession, exclusion and assimilation of not only the land but of its people, its flora and its fauna.

Since then, Australia has been committed to a policy of incarcerating women in prisons designed by men for men; until relatively recently, inmate women in Australia were issued with male prison garb, were forced to have their heads shaved or closely cropped and were denied basic toiletries necessary for coping with childbirth and menstruation.

Although two centuries have since transpired since the first colony, there is still a distinctively gendered social fabric, and it is useful now to turn to the social construction of motherhood as an example of this phenomenon.

Social theorists such as Kereen Reiger (1995) and Betsy Wearing (1984) concur that motherhood and the role of a 'good mother' are socially constructed and learned notions that are socially reinforced, especially by the mass media. Wearing's (1984) study of Australian women described the ideological construction of motherhood as being a collection of ideas, beliefs, values and practices that legitimise men's social power and maintain women's primary responsibility for child-rearing. Mothers are expected to fulfil society's vision of women as nurturing, responsive caregivers, and any contravention of that role is seen to be unmaternal and, ultimately, unfeminine. Furthermore, according to Jocelynne Scutt (1995), the Australian feminist lawyer and author, wifehood itself is a male-constructed institution that posits women-mothers as the primary caregivers of their children and perpetuates women's dependence and oppression through institutionalisation and economic and ideological oppression.

It is noteworthy that this work does not stand in isolation; an allied body of scholarly feminist literature in the areas of law and criminology presented in the next section has also developed theoretical perspectives on the social construction of women as mothers in gendered settings (Carlen and Worrall, 1987; Carrington, 1993; Genders and Player, 1987; Mann, 1984; Scutt, 1981; Smart, 1984, 1990, 1992, 1995; Worrall, 1990).

GENDERING IN THE CRIMINAL JUSTICE SYSTEM

British criminological authors such as Carlen and Worrall (1987) and Smart (1992) have theorised the relationship between the position of women in society and their representation and treatment as gendered subjects whose womanhood is regulated in the criminal justice and penal system. This wave of scholarship acknowledges that women, and, by association, their children and families, within the criminal justice system are 'muted' (Worrall, 1990), and it is, therefore, necessary to engage in a process of 'listening to and hearing the experience of women in their diversity' (Smart, 1990: 1). Farrell's (1996) policy study of incarcerated mothers and their young children in Australia and the United Kingdom has confirmed that women's prisons, in particular, ostensibly contain and regulate the lives of offending women and of their families and severely threaten their basic human rights. Children are implicated, by association with their offending mothers, and woven into the gendered fabric of the criminal justice system.

Moreover, Scutt (1981: 17) argues that criminal laws have been drafted to perpetuate the dependence of women and to maintain the status quo.

> Where women are concerned, the law has been drawn with reference to the way in which men define women, as dependant wives with no ability to make decisions; or as wretched whores responsible for their ability to lead men into committing offences against them.

Similarly, Dalton (1995), in reviewing feminist legal thought, submits that belonging to a society where women, especially as mothers, are subordinated to men leads to socialisation into a role of dependency to men. Dalton further argues that the law exercises power in disqualifying women's experience and knowledge. This chapter is arguing for human rights that both recognise this disqualification and which purposefully give voice to this lived experience and knowledge.

For example, Scutt's (1995) most recent review of criminal domestic assault in Australia confirmed that women's economic and social inequality with men militates against their giving evidence against their husbands in male-constructed and controlled courts. Scutt (1995: 231) argues that women's rights have effectively disappeared from the canvas because the 'rights which are elevated are those of the courts that make orders which are required to be obeyed'. Furthermore, the invisibility of such crimes and the relative docility of females in relation to their male counterparts in the criminal justice system exacerbates this inequity (Farrell, 1996; Mann, 1984; Smart, 1990). We need, therefore, to interrogate those practices, be they officially sanctioned or not, that, on the one hand, negate their identity as women and mothers, and on the other hand, reduce people to mere stereotypes.

The basic tenet of this chapter, therefore, is that we need to understand the deep-seated gendering that robs individuals of their identity and undermines their capacity to contribute to a civil society. The case of blatant gendering in the criminal justice system parallels a more subtle yet highly pervasive image of children as gendered consumers. Both of these manifestations, however, give us cause to reflect on the ways in which children are perceived and treated in our society which fly in the face of the human rights. As we have seen, this applies to practices within the criminal justice system, but as we will see in the next section it also applies to practices within the materialist culture, where children are constructed as gendered consumers of goods and services.

GENDERING OF CONSUMERS

Children in materialist societies are being defined as consumers of commodities and as participants in the global economy, immersed in a popular consumer culture that increasingly requires their personalised income and expenditure. The sweep of history reveals that, like the colonial history of female offenders, children also featured in the colonial labour force. In the 1700s, children were shipped in large numbers as child labour to the colonies of the New World and were economically exploited in the factories of the Industrial Revolution. Then, in the post-industrial era, children temporarily disappeared from the economy through the efforts of the labour and child protection movements (Wintersberger, 1994). In the eighteenth and nineteenth centuries, English and colonial society began to see philanthropic and protective kindliness towards children as a virtue; and such an attitude towards children was to play a vital role in the emerging early childhood education movement. This cycle of exploitation and protection persisted, and the uneasy paradox that allows two such different attitudes to exist at the same time has been repeated many times since throughout history.

Childhood itself has come to be seen as a gendered social phenomenon. Qvortrup (1994) argues that contemporary childhood is the life-space that our culture limits it to be, in its definitions throughout the courts, the school, the family and the economy.

> Every society crystallises its own set of norms, rules and regulations which dictate its attitudes towards the category of its members defined as children. From a collective perspective, childhood should be described as that period of time in each person's life which society allocates for the process of training to become a kind of member that the society wants him or her to be.
>
> (Shamgar-Handelman, 1994: 250)

Furthermore, it can be argued that childhood is a social phenomenon insofar as the social responsibilities towards children are shared, though not always equally, between the family and the society, via a range of social institutions and filtered through the pervasive mass media. Children are not exempt from participation in mass media; rather, by virtue of their immersion in mass culture, they are seen as bona fide participants. Moreover, children in the mass media are depicted as miniature adults in their couture, idiomatic language, general interests and social mores.

This mass culture is mediated by the popular media, which promotes commodified products and services that are, in turn, packed for ease of consumption. The social theorist Susan Willis (1991: 1) maintains that everything is packaged and standardised.

> Late twentieth-century commodity production has generated a companion production of community packaging that is so much a part of the commodity form itself as to be one of the most unremarkable features of daily life. Packaging catches the consumer's eyes, even though as a phenomenon of daily life, it is all but invisible. The package is a device for hailing the consumer and cuing his or her attention, by the use of colour and design, to a particular brand-name commodity.

The standardisation created by commodification is a prime vehicle for gendering. In Willis' view, commodity consumption is a vehicle for gendering. Willis (1991: 23) argues that

> we buy into a gender in the same way we buy into a style . . . it is contrived as something fixed or frozen: a number of sexually defined attributes that denote either masculinity or femininity on the supermarket shelf of gender possibilities.

One of the strongest early influences on gender is the mass toy market, with unprecedented sexual division of toys defined by specific gender traits. The universal Barbie doll is a case in point. Australian social commentator Philip Adams (1996:2) recently mused,

> The grotesque disproportionate shape of the Barbie doll with its slender torso and endless legs is clearly a factor in encouraging anorexia and the whole underlying assumption of the barbaric approach to marketing is to have the child spend, spend, spend on her polystyrene dwarfs. Clothes, hairstyles, cosmetics, furniture, skateboard, scuba gear, you name it. Barbie's got to have it. So that by the time your child is six or seven she's programmed to spend the rest of her life as an obedient consumer. Because that's another of the ideological messages built into every Barbie. Shop till you drop.

Adams reported that, in Australia alone, there are an estimated 600 million Barbie dolls, that is, 35.29 Barbies per every Australian; 60,000 are being produced every day and if you laid them end to end they could circumnavigate the planet fifty times!

There is a cruel irony that the identification of children as gendered consumers and the employment of clever strategies to attract their spending are occurring at a time of unprecedented portrayal by the mass media of the privations experienced by many children, as they reveal the image of children as victims of adult activity. These phenomena resonate with earlier commentaries about the nature of childhood and of children in a materialist society. Neil Postman (1982) prophetically mused about the 'disappearance of childhood' and David Elkind (1981) lamented 'the hurried child'.

Contemporary western societies are currently engaged in public discourse on human rights and the 'best interests of the child', while at the same time sanctioning consumptive practices that are antithetical to human rights. How can such rights be enacted in a society that demands adherence to trenchant gendered values? And these phenomena are not limited to the criminal justice system and to the consumer culture; but, as we shall see in the next section, they are evident in the early childhood services and programmes we inhabit.

EARLY CHILDHOOD SERVICES: GENDERED CONTEXTS

Historically, early childhood professionals and services have also been constructed along gender lines. While some inroads have been made into identifying sources of oppression in the early childhood sectors, little has been achieved in reducing the social impact of inequitable working conditions and low professional status. Early childhood professionals, therefore, need to review their transactions with children and their families in settings or ecologies that may still be feeling the residual effects of oppression of one sort or another. Early childhood professionals both face gendered settings and contribute to them. That is to say, they feel the effects of the gendered ecologies in which they in fact participate. No longer can there be talk about what is going on 'out there' to children in far-off family fiefdoms. Professionals are as much a part of the gendered ecology as are the parents and children they work with.

Overall, the premier role of early childhood professionals is working with families to provide learning and living opportunities that will contribute to shared and personal learning and, ultimately, to the common good. Family and social ecologies are changing in ways that consistently challenge our professional attitudes and work practices. One of the pivots of these changing ecologies is the amalgamated role of parents as care-givers and workers. Patterns of childbearing, changing family forms, the changing ideology of parenthood, the gendered division of labour within the home and workplace, the participation of both men and women in paid employment, the changing nature of the work and the exertion of economic imperatives on families have contributed to this work-care ecology as we now experience it (Edgar, 1992; Reiger, 1991; Vanden Heuvel, 1993; Weeks and Wilson, 1995).

Early childhood professionals, along with parents, are workers with caring responsibilities, sharing with families the struggle of privileged responsibility to execute their rights to care and work. In this respect, it is a prime position to enact professional ethics and human rights within the workplace, given that it is in early childhood settings that parents' and children's experience of care and work converge. Here the notions of social justice and social capital are worth discussing.

When considering human rights in the family and in early childhood services, we are confronted not by singular issues or scenarios, but by a range of interests and participants. Notions of human rights, like those of social justice, are not singular or essential, but are embedded in divergent political discourses (Rizvi, 1993) that are historical in character and constitution. According to McNay and Ozga (1985), there is usually a complex federation of interests that are sometimes competing, but sometimes mutually supportive.

SOCIAL JUSTICE AND SOCIAL CAPITAL

In this discussion, the federated interests include the rights of both children and women to be heard, seen and affirmed in a socially just society. In this regard, the American feminist author Iris Marion Young (1990: 37) advocates two major universalist values for all persons: (a) to develop and to exercise one's capacities and to express one's experience and (b) to participate in determining one's action and the conditions of one's action. In turn, these two values correspond with the social conditions that define oppression (the institutional constraints on self-development) and domination (the institutional constraint on self-determination), evident in both the criminal justice system and in consumer culture. She theorises that the concept of justice must address the structures of domination that wrongfully pervade society. According to Young (1990: 38):

> Dominance and oppression occur in systematic institutional processes which prevent some people from learning and using satisfying and expansive skills in socially recognised settings, and domination exists in institutional conditions which inhibit or prevent people from participating in determining their actions or the conditions of their actions.

Young's concept of justice is primarily concerned not with a model of redistribution of wealth, income or other material goods, but with the degree to which a society contains and supports the institutional conditions that facilitate a good life. In the light of gendering within the criminal justice system and of the gendered commodification of childhood consumerism by the mass media within a materialist, consumer society, there needs to be a keen interrogation of policies that perpetuate both institutional oppression and human domination. This involves examination of practices and relationships that make for the common good in the families and early childhood services in which young children, their families and caregivers relate, or, as Cox (1995) argues, to pursue social capital.

According to Australian political scientist Eva Cox (1995), social capital is the reservoir of trust and mutuality that holds people together. Social capital is the social glue, the weft and warp of the social fabric that comprises the myriad interactions that make up our public and private lives. Cox argues that there has been an extensive erosion of social capital within families and communities in the rearing of children and that our sense of collective responsibility for other people's children has diminished. She emphasises that trust is essential for our social wellbeing. Trust is based on positive experiences with other people, it grows with use and leads to cooperation. Yet in consumer culture and in the criminal justice system, we find that the ethos of competition overrides the ethic of care. Without trusting the goodwill of others, we retreat into bureaucracy, rules and demands for more law and order.

Her apologetic is that we should create a culture of child-rearing that expects children to be aware of the needs of others, to be coöperative and to be able to work with others, to experience connectedness and relationship. In the family, social capital includes the presence of adults and the range of parent–child exchanges about academic, social and personal issues. In the community, social capital involves expectations for social interactions, such as an adult listening to the children of others. But there are factors that militate against this. There is an advance in individualism, wherein concern for one's own wellbeing supersedes an interest in others; and this is exemplified in the tyranny of rampant consumerism.

Nel Noddings (1992) is a key protagonist in the philosophical debate on the collective responsibilities of institutions such as schools to care for others. Noddings presents a case for schools to 'care', to care for self, to care for those in the inner circle, to care for strangers and distant others, to care for living things and to care for ideas. As participants in a socially oppressive consumer society, early childhood professionals along with children and their parents need to ask how we can enact social justice and justly use social capital for the common good.

Given the gendering experienced in so many of the worlds we inhabit, early childhood professionals need to participate in the human rights debate and to enact professional ethics with children and with families so that we can together enjoy the benefits of values and practices that reduce personal and social inequities and affirm human dignity for carers and workers, adults and children. We therefore need to legitimate and affirm the value of our work in giving and receiving care in educative early childhood communities.

> It would be rash to sweep away the legitimacy in our society of needing care and giving care. Altruistic caring and receipt of care, and rights-based publicly endorsed care, are both required. In a strong civil society people want to and need to have these bonds . . . society also needs free reign to be given to these bonds so that individuals are linked and fully incorporated into a society with the degree of cohesion required for what the French call '*solidarité*'. Legislation is always the fall back position, the sledge hammer; it can never do the fine work that is the hallmark of a civilised society.
>
> (Funder, 1996: 10)

Perhaps then we can work towards institutional conditions that, in Young's terms, make for learners determining their actions and developing their skills both within families and within early childhood services.

In this chapter, we have reviewed the gendering of young children and their families against the backdrop of the human rights debate. We found that the settings where human rights are enacted are, however, largely gendered settings, with people positioned according to gender and its socially constructed meanings. This chapter presented two examples of this phenomenon: the gendered treatment of women in the criminal justice system and the positioning of children as gendered consumers in a materialist culture. It was argued that these two examples are indicative of the wider gendered settings in which early childhood professionals live and work.

In sum, this chapter challenges us to consider our work with young children and their families as contributing to a socially just and civil society, pursuing those educative experiences and relationships that will sustain us and our children now and into the next millennium.

REFERENCES

Adams, P. (1996). Barb-aryan hordes. *The Australian*. November 2–3, 2.

Ashby, G. (1991). Professional ethics: An overview of discussion in the Australian early childhood journals 1960–1990, *Australian Journal of Early Childhood*. 16.1, 11–16.

Balke, E. (1992). Children's rights and the World Summit for Children. *International Journal of Early Childhood*. 24.1, 2–6.

Carlen, P. and Worrall, A. (eds) (1987). *Gender, crime and justice*. Milton Keynes: Open University Press.

Carrington, K. (1993). *Offending girls. Sex, youth and justice*. St. Leonards, NSW: Allen & Unwin.

Castelle, K. (1989). *In the child's best interest. A primer on the United Nations Convention on the Rights of the Child*. New York: Defence of Children International.

Cox, E. (1995). *ABC Boyer Lectures*. Sydney: Australian Broadcasting Commission.

Dalton, C. (1995). Where we stand: Observations on the situation of feminist legal thought. In F.E. Olsen (ed.), *Feminist legal theory*. Aldershot: Dartmouth.

Defence for Children International Australia (1996). *Australia's promises to children. The alternative report*. ACT: DCI.

Edgar, D. (1991). Families and the social construction of marriage and parenthood in Australia. In R. Batten, W. Weeks and J. Wilson (eds), *Issues facing Australian families. Human services respond*. Melbourne: Longman Cheshire.

Edgar, D. (1992). The changing ecology of Australian childhood. In B. Lambert (ed.), *Changing faces. The early childhood profession in Australia*. ACT: Australian Early Childhood Association.

Elkind, D. (1981). *The hurried child: Growing up too fast, too soon*. Reading, MA: Addison Wesley.

Farrell, M.A. (1995). Whose right? *Educating Young Children. Learning and Teaching in the Early Years*. 1.1, 9–10.

Farrell, M.A. (1996). *A comparative policy study of incarcerated mothers and their young children in Queensland, New South Wales, Victoria and England*. St. Lucia, Brisbane: The University of Queensland, unpublished PhD thesis.

Funder, K. (ed.) (1996). *Citizen child*. Melbourne: Australian Institute of Family Studies.

Genders, E. and Player, E. (1987). Women in prison: The treatment, the control and the experience. In P. Carlen and A. Worrall (eds), *Gender, crime and justice*. Milton Keynes: Open University Press.

Gil, D.G. (1991). Children and work: Rights to become creative and productive. *School Psychology Review*. 20.3, 389–400.

Hart, S.N. and Pavlovic, Z. (1991). Children's rights in education: An historical perspective. *School Psychology Review*. 20.3, 345–358.

Hughes, R. (1988). *The fatal shore: A history of the transportation of convicts to Australia. 1787–1986*. London: Pan Books.

Johnson, J. (1988). Women in corrections: A strategic approach. In D. Biles (ed.) *Current Australian trends in corrections*. Canberra: Federation Press.

Mann, C.R. (1984). *Female crime and delinquency*. Alabama: University of Alabama Press.

McNay, I. and Ozga, J. (1985). Perspectives on policy. In I. McNay and J. Ozga (eds), *Policy-making in education. The breakdown of consensus*. Oxford: Pergamon Press.

Meuwese, S. and Rijvers, K. (1993). *International yearbook of children's rights*. Netherlands: DCI.

Noddings, N. (1992). *The challenge to care in schools. An alternative approach to education.* New York: Teachers College Press.
Ochiltree, G. (1994). *Effects of child care on young children. Forty years of research.* Melbourne: Australian Institute of Family Studies.
Postman, N. (1982). *The disappearance of childhood.* New York: Laurel.
Preston, N. (1994). *Ethics for the public sector: Educating and training.* Leichhardt, NSW: Federation Press.
Purdy, L. (1992). *In their best interest? The case against equal rights for children.* Ithaca, NY: Cornell University Press.
Qvortrup, J. (1994). Childhood matters: An introduction. In J. Qvortrup, M. Bardy, G. Sgritta and H. Wintersberger (eds) *Childhood matters. Social theory, practice and politics.* Aldershot: Avebury.
Rayner, M. (1996). Self, self-esteem and sense of place: An Australian framework for children's rights claims in the 1990s. In K. Funder (ed.), *Citizen child.* Melbourne: Australian Institute of Family Studies.
Reiger, K. (1991). Motherhood ideology. In R. Batten, W. Weeks and J. Wilson (eds), *Issues facing Australian families. Human services respond.* Melbourne: Longman Cheshire.
Rizvi, F. (1993). Multiculturalism, social justice and the restructuring of the Australian state. In R. Lingard, J. Knight and P. Porter (eds), *Schooling reform in hard times.* London: Falmer.
Scutt, J.A. (1981). Sexism in criminal law. In S.K. Mukherjee and J.A. Scutt (eds), *Women and crime.* ACT: Australian Institute of Criminology.
Scutt, J.A. (1995). Criminal assault at home: Policy directions and implications for the future. In W. Weeks and J. Wilson (eds), *Issues facing Australian families.* Melbourne: Longman.
Shamgar-Handelman, L. (1994). To whom does childhood belong? In J. Qvortrup, M. Bardy, G. Sgritta and H. Wintersberger (eds), *Childhood matters. Social theory, practice and politics.* Aldershot: Avebury.
Smart, C. (1984). *The ties that bind. Law, marriage and the reproduction of patriarchal relations.* London: Routledge & Kegan Paul.
Smart, C. (1989). Power and the politics of child custody. In C. Smart and S. Sevenhuijsen (eds), *Child custody and the politics of gender.* London: Routledge.
Smart, C. (1990). *Feminism and the power of the law.* London: Routledge.
Smart, C. (1992). Regulating womanhood. In C. Smart (ed.), *Regulating womanhood. Historical essays on marriage, motherhood and sexuality.* London: Routledge.
Smart, C. (1995). *Law, crime and sexuality. Essays in feminism.* London: Sage Publications.
Stonehouse, A. and Creaser, B. (1991). A code of ethics for the Australian early childhood profession: Background and overview. *Australian Journal of Early Childhood.* 16.1, 7–10.
UNICEF (1990). *First call for children. World declaration and plan of action from the World Summit for Children.* New York: UNICEF.
Vanden Heuvel, A. (1993). *When roles overlap. Workers with family responsibilities.* Melbourne: Australian Institute of Family Studies.
Wearing, B. (1984). *The ideology of motherhood.* Sydney: Allen & Unwin.
Weeks, W. and Wilson, J. (eds) (1995). *Issues facing Australian families.* Melbourne: Longman.
Willis, S. (1991). *A primer for daily life.* London: Routledge.
Wintersberger, H. (1994). Costs and benefits. The economics of childhood. In J. Qvortrup, M. Bardy, G. Sgritta and H. Wintersberger (eds). *Childhood matters. Social theory, practice and politics.* Aldershot: Avebury.

Worrall, A. (1990). *Offending women. Female lawbreakers and the criminal justice system*. London: Routledge.
Young, I.M. (1990). *Justice and the politics of difference.* Princeton, NJ: Princeton University Press.

Part II

Aspects of gender in school contexts

Chapter 7

Gender equity policies and early childhood education

Lyn Martinez

INTRODUCTION

Despite the fact that research in the area of early childhood has heavily influenced policy for gender equity in education over the last ten years, for the most part early childhood, more than primary and secondary schooling, seems successfully to evade the focus of gender equity policy. A number of factors pull the attention of gender equity policy activity away from early childhood, including the traditionally isolationist cultures and philosophies of early childhood education; the impact of the economistic policies of global capitalism on education;[1] and the instrumental focus on those levels of schooling where 'streaming' along gendered lines into different subject areas is clearly relevant to different career opportunities and to the persistence of a gender segregated labour market. While the articulation between students' final years of schooling and the workplace has been the subject of a generation of gender equity programmes, the gendering of the schoolchild, or the processes through which children's learning and behaviour is regulated in the early childhood years to take on public 'student' versions of being male or female, impacting on their learning and social relations throughout schooling, has received little attention.

During the nineties, as the policies of economism have achieved meta-policy status throughout the government sector,[2] specific gender equity policy (for example, the National Policy for the Education of Girls) has been interpreted within policy environments that are dominated by the new settlements being made among business and industry, and within an era of 're-engineering' the public sector to take account of demands for a leaner, more accountable government. The liposuction that has been performed upon the education sector has resulted in a leaner, masculine torso, externally focused towards economic goals, and impatient with the more humanistic goals in which policies on equity are embedded. The accompanying processes have emphasised a greater reliance on the private sector for many of the services previously delivered by government.

This has been accompanied by a widespread renunciation by public sector management advisers of feminist agendas that seek a recognition within the public interest of those gender issues (such as equitable participation in family life) that have traditionally been considered to be of personal and private interest only.

EARLY CHILDHOOD'S PLACE IN THE ARENA OF EDUCATIONAL POLICY-MAKING FOR GENDER EQUITY

Education policy in its current phase is occurring at a global level. No aspect of education can escape the impact of the global perspective. While early childhood education may have been able to sequester its profession from the excesses of technicist and economy-driven changes to the culture of education in their particularly Australian manifestations, it cannot now isolate itself from the struggles over the purposes of education in a post-nation-state global economy. These struggles are summarised in a recently published policy text:

> As governments around the world try to come to terms with new technologies, new social movements and the politics of difference, a global economy and the postmodern condition, education policy finds itself at the centre of a major political struggle between those who see it only for its instrumental outcomes, and those who see its potential for human emancipation.[3]

In the new political economy of education – the function of education in conditioning the skills of Australians in ways that convince international capital of the worthiness of investment in this 'clever country' – the focus of education's political masters has been on the 'product' end of education – the secondary years. If post-compulsory education is understood as the 'business end' of education, then a range of factors have persistently drawn early childhood as being involved in the 'domestic end', with populations of young children presided over predominantly by women, in environments that, to the untrained eye, differ little from earlier child-care (read custodial) arrangements, preparing their young charges for life in the real world of learning.

Where leaders of business and industry (almost exclusively men) chair national and state committees on issues affecting post-compulsory education, especially in its links with training, early childhood decision-making is largely in the hands of women, even though the intensely patriarchal traditions of early childhood may dictate that their decision-making forums are chaired by men. The fact that early childhood teachers have managed to sequester early childhood from the intrusive interventions of technicist, formalised and segmentalised approaches to curriculum and teaching, which begin to develop in upper primary school and intensify in the secondary school, has also 'protected' early childhood from the gaze of policymakers in a range of areas, including gender equity.

While gender issues in early childhood were beginning to come to the fore in research that is sponsored through policy sources (e.g. the Gender Equity in Curriculum Reform project and Projects of National Significance), research from the field of early childhood is to a significant extent shaping new directions in gender equity policy. The claim that economic imperatives have had, in the mid-1990s, on the attention of policymakers, including gender equity policymakers, continually draws attention to this 'business end' of schooling, where decisions are made about differences in university entrance scores, marketable skills, and labour market transfer. It is to this level of education that the attention of politicians and senior administrators is drawn. Here differences in subject participation and achievement outcomes, transfer to tertiary education or training, and retention rates are perceived to factor into programmes for micro-economic reform, national productivity and competitiveness. It is at this end of education that information is sought to justify, in equity and other terms, the spending of education dollars.

The status of the early childhood sector has always been fragile in education systems which, even into the 1990s, retain the intensely patriarchal characteristics that have been deeply embedded in the structures of education since the establishment of public education. Men dominate the senior management staff across all education systems in Australia; men dominate principalships; and, in the teaching force, the proportion of female teachers increases dramatically towards the lower primary and early childhood end of the teaching scale. The fact that women dominate in early childhood management positions may only serve to highlight the domestic/business dualism that characterises the relationship of early childhood education to sectors at the other, 'serious', end of the educational spectrum.

The operating relations that have been established between senior schooling and business and industry, and that have driven in an almost unchallenged way by human capital theory, exist in direct contrast to the continuing 'domestic' environment of the early childhood sector. Early childhood educational philosophies have consistently valued play, intrinsic motivation, integrated multi-sensory learning, and children's 'unique' talents, where post-compulsory preoccupations of transition to work, training or tertiary education have emphasised entrepreneurialism and marketable competencies.

Another feature of the contemporary state's approach to policy-making on gender equity has been the coordination of planning and implementation of policy at centralised level. In Queensland, for example, gender equity policies in education have been incorporated into whole-of-government planning for 'Women's Policy', including its Stop Violence against Women and Economic Equality of Women policies. While this has provided some leverage for development of a comprehensive understanding of the agency of education, *vis-à-vis* other departments in enhancing gender equity across the community, it has also meant that gender equity policymakers in education have had to contend with the adult-centric perspectives evoked by the terminology of 'women's policy'. The adult-centric context of much of the policy discussions around these policies made introduction of the issues for the young girl-child problematic. These policies were also dominated by philosophies of formal liberalism, which sat uneasily with the gender relations perspectives that inform most policy on gender in education.

THE NEW POLICY ENVIRONMENT

The 'balance sheet' approach to measuring policy outcomes from electronic data-base systems has been given added impetus by the increasing pressure on the public sector for accountability, driven by control factors expressed as performance indicators or targets. While Yates and Leder (1996) have examined in detail the problems associated with measuring gender equity outcomes on the basis of Year 12 retention or achievement levels, or transference to tertiary study, there continues to be a strong demand for such data, both because it is readily quantifiable, and because it interfaces with the ways in which labour market and training gender issues are framed for the purposes of policy-making. That such data is not very useful for examining the link between education generally, let alone early childhood, and gender equity in life pathways is a point made forcefully by Yates and Leder:

> what students learn in school about themselves and each other and about their future, and not just what they achieve is relevant to their pathways beyond school. But 'hard data' are much more readily set up on the latter than on the former, which is a subtle and complex process.

While this 'end product' focus has been problematic for gender equity at all levels, early childhood is distant indeed from the discourse and preoccupations of the economist agenda. This focus, which is fed by the dependence of systems on large gender-disaggregated data-bases, similar to those used to inform labour market programmes, also sets up the gendered gaps in participation, retention and achievement rates as the *de facto* business of gender equity programmes. Eliminating the gender gaps becomes, for the busy senior administrator, the default vision and intent of gender equity in education. While girls' academic performance and retention have not been raised in gender equity position papers over the last ten years as an issue for gender equity, those who seek to contain gender equity programmes within formal equality discourses have, in recent years, been able to manipulate data-bases to claim that, on the basis of academic performance and retention, there is no gender 'problem'. This is despite the persistent patterns of girls' academic performance and retention not transferring into greater social, economic or political equality through their life pathways. This kind of use of data-bases also ignores the way in which the social and economic resources of students, which are related to their class membership, ethnicity, race and disability, influence the experience and outcomes of schooling.

However, the ease with which such data is incorporated into electronic management information systems makes it popular with senior administrators and political leaders, who are apt to rely on readily up-datable, rapidly retrievable statistical information for public relations and other exercises. Thus, data comes to be used in ways that lack analysis, but can have a strong influence on public perceptions of progress towards gender equity, with serious consequences for the way in which gender equity is understood in school cultures. One major deficiency of such data-bases is that they communicate nothing about the function of early childhood education in either producing or addressing gendered inequalities.

While early childhood educators historically have defended their realm from the excesses of instrumental education, holding strongly to the humanistic traditions of their sector, this new emphasis on the economic purposes of education holds particular challenges for early childhood educators. Clearly, they must find a place in the debates that seek to relate the cultural practices of early childhood education with those of the political economy of schooling. They must demonstrate that their practices are not only relevant to these debates, but also that, unless early childhood education is given serious consideration in these debates, much of what is intended from programmes at other levels of education will not be achieved, either in terms of the economic capital or of the social capital of the nation.

The evidence gathered through the Gender Equity and Curriculum Reform (GECR) research projects has demonstrated very clearly that attitudes about participation in paid work, the social relations of the family and the paid workforce, and attitudes about gender, race, ethnicity and class are being formed dynamically and actively in the processes of early childhood education. This research has also made it clear that, without explicit engagement with children's socially and culturally acquired knowledge at this level, gendered understandings are being implicitly endorsed and encoded as formulae for interpreting their social worlds.

The renewed focus on early childhood as a site for conditioning policies to improve the literacy and numeracy levels of Australians has brought early childhood well within the ambit of outcomes-based-management and accountability frameworks associated with new managerialism. Early childhood educators may yet be able to find resources in its humanistic traditions that can position this sector as a leader in contesting the dehumanising effects of market liberalism in education. It may yet find that this sector is well poised to insist on keeping alive critical debates: about education's role in maintaining a 'truly civil society',[4] about the kinds of communities we may want to live in, and about the kinds of practices that will enable future citizens to be able to imagine socially just futures and to have a choice in these matters. It is important for gender equity objectives, however, that this 'protection' of early childhood is not carried out in an isolationist way, but becomes part of a broader movement for socially just, emancipatory education.

In doing so, however, the early childhood sector will need to take account of factors in the policy environment that situate the relevant role of early childhood education in social justice programmes. Research in recent years has left no room for challenge to the central function of early childhood education (in partnership with other sectors of education) in achieving some of the key social changes necessary for peaceful, socially just futures. These key social changes include:

- the elimination of gendered violence;
- the achievement of a more equitable distribution of male and female labour across the paid workforce, the community and the work of private caring; and
- the development of a concept of citizenship that places value on achieving equality, democracy and human rights, not only in the paid workforce and public life, but also in the work of private caring.

Action research projects undertaken as part of the GECR project illustrate clearly that, in respect to each of these issues, early childhood practices are complicit both in 'naturalising' gendered violence in the school environment, and in endorsing dominant ideologies about 'women's place' in families, the workplace, and in public life. On the positive side, however, this action research indicates that early childhood students readily pick up the practices of social research, and become enthusiastic social critics and advocates for equity. These rich and illuminative examples of the ways in which teacher, parents and children come together to redefine their worlds in emancipatory ways have been comprehensively described in Alloway's *Foundation Stones*.[5]

Historically, early childhood educators have resisted an explicit importation of gender equity policy into this sector. The nurturant model in early childhood has emphasised teaching by example, and empowerment on an individual level. However, research in recent years in early childhood classrooms has illustrated that teachers and students in early childhood education are actively, intensively and even, at times, aggressively engaged in ensuring that the environment, interactions and behaviours of students take on 'appropriate' gender representations.[6,7] Moreover, research has demonstrated in compelling detail the way in which even very young boys use the resources of sexual harassment with versatility, to position female teachers, female students, and non-conforming boys as inferior.[8] Alloway has described the way in which boys take over the grassy ovals, and girls accommodate this gendered territory by restricting their own space needs; girls and boys both evoke their understanding of the gendered social order to monopolise particular spaces, such as construction materials or home corners; children describe adult lives and work in highly gendered terms; and both boys and girls interpret the world of children's literature within familiar gendered storylines.[9]

In the light of this evidence, it is difficult not to agree with Alloway's assertion that 'Eight's Too Late', and that the silence in early childhood on gender issues (as on other social justice issues) can be read as silent authorisation of the gendered social world. It is indeed problematic that gender equity policy has not advocated this position more strongly. It is also difficult to accept that early childhood educators can cling to notions that early childhood is innocent gender-politics-free territory, and to give themselves a virtual dispensation from the demands of gender equity policies. In Alloway's analysis:

> With the relative lack of national interest and support for the early years, early childhood teachers have often been hesitant to deal with gender for fear of politicising young children. For some, politics and young children may seem an incongruous combination. But young children's lives are immersed in the political, as they begin to know and define themselves in relation to gender, race, class, sexuality, popularity and so on. . . .
>
> Rather than dealing with the politics of gender explicitly, publicly and honestly, the process of politicising young children is achieved invisibly, in silence, by default.

The challenges are immense indeed for a group of educational professionals who have invested their lives in protecting the central principles on which early childhood has traditionally operated: the innocence and naturalness of the child, the creative processes through which 'biological' talent is allowed to flower, and a determined disinterestedness in the ways in which other sectors have been politicised by discourses of social justice and human rights. Research by Walkerdine, Alloway,[10] Davies,[11] and Clark[12] has systematically peeled back the mask of individualism and child-centred pedagogy and philosophy that early childhood practice has commonly presented to the world. Their investigations have exposed the complex factors that make up the early childhood environment – factors where race, gender, class and ethnicity intersect and provide the basis for highly differentiated experiences and learning on the part of children, as well as for variations in the way in which teachers establish and activate their relations with different children.

However, recognition of the significance of early childhood's function in the achievement of gender equity in and through schooling is arriving at the very moment when the state is going quiet on gender equity. Across Australia, the message on gender equity is that it is now time for schools to go it alone. Gender equity functions in central offices are being scaled back, and the official language is that gender equity policy has been 'mainstreamed'[13] in the processes of schooling.

MAKING GENDER POLICY

Some definition of the meaning of policy is necessary before the implications of gender equity policy on early childhood settings can be explored. This chapter takes the view that policy consists of both outcomes of political settlements, sometimes captured in official statements, sometimes captured in agreed approaches to particular issues, and as forms of practice that express particular values deemed to be important within institutional settings. Policy, therefore, can be seen to operate at a number of sites: at the level of formal statements of commitment to a particular set of values by systems (policy or guidelines); in the areas to which resources are committed to support policy implementation; in the priority accorded to the various components or targets of policy as evidenced in statements of senior system leaders in key forums, and at the level of school and classroom practice. Policy statements are frequently expressed in generic language, which is then interpreted in particular contexts. Policy may also contain statements that appear to be contradictory, being the outcomes of settlements among those who have contested for policy space for particular ideas within public statements.

It is necessary to look at a range of indicators to establish the extent to which gender equity policy has or has not addressed the factors involved in early childhood that influence the implementation and success of policy at other levels. In this context, it is also necessary to investigate the way in which policy about gender equity occurs as both gender-specific policy, and as a set of relationships between gender-specific policies and other system policies. For example, gender-specific policies are interpreted within contexts of policies on institutional reform, science curriculum and school sport. It intersects with policies on interaction with parents. These policies are not always consistent, and inconsistencies may represent degrees of institutional indifference to, or ways of challenging, gender-specific policies. As Marshall notes:

Policymakers are political creatures (a fact that too many policy

> analysts forget) in political communities where language, ideas and information are the medium of exchange.[14]

Policy is developed, interrogated, interpreted, re-made and implemented on a daily basis, in the central and district offices of systems and in schools and even homes, as a set of contests and settlements between competing discourses. This is the 'policy primeval soup'[15] in which gender equity policies for early childhood education is taken up and practised. In this context, policymakers exist throughout the lives of children. Mothers, fathers, teachers and children themselves engage with 'official' policy to determine its meaning in their own lives. However, for the most part, policymakers, for the purposes of this chapter, are those whose labour is secured at system level, for the purposes of building and implementing specific policy.

GENDER EQUITY POLICY ON EARLY CHILDHOOD: IN THE 'QUIET ROOM'

Alloway has drawn attention to the silences about early childhood in the major gender equity programmes of the 1980s and early 1990s: the fact that few projects of national significance have focused on the early childhood years; that the annual reports of state systems to the *National Policy for the Education of Girls in Australian Schools* (1987) gave little space to early childhood issues; that much of what is specifically mentioned in policy documents refers only to primary and secondary schooling. Alloway draws attention to the way in which the National Policy for the Education of Girls almost apologetically acknowledged the omission of early childhood in its Foreword, where it states:

> The Commission has concentrated on developing a process to enable concerted action by school authorities throughout Australia. It recognises, however, that for a National Policy for the Education of Girls to be effective, complementary policies for early childhood and tertiary education are also required.
>
> (p. vii)

She also noted that the *National Action Plan for the Education of Girls 1993–1997*, while advancing the need for increased recognition of the importance of early childhood experiences in shaping girls' and boys' educational outcomes, provided little focused guidance to early childhood administrators and teachers on how they were to participate in or achieve the vision of the *National Action Plan for the Education of Girls*. In her summary Alloway suggests that:

> The visible absence of early childhood from such agendas may even give credence to the false belief that gender-inequitable practices do

not occur in the more 'progressive', individually focused philosophy and pedagogy celebrated in early childhood education. By their exclusion of early childhood, documents of such national significance may imply that:

- gender issues should be addressed by teachers with older children only;
- gender equity becomes an issue only when formal curricula and more regimented, institutionalised organisational structures are imposed;
- there is no research base on which to begin to include early childhood education as a specialist field, with specialist demands for attention.

(Alloway)

Alloway's concerns have their counterpart in the frustrations of officers responsible for gender equity policy in systems, for whom the pressure is on to demonstrate the effectiveness of gender equity policies in influencing the outcomes that matter politically: those that can be demonstrated in subject participation, achievement outcomes, and transfer to post-school training options. Clearly, much of what was spoken, acted upon by policy officers, and published about girls in schools in a policy context in the period up to the late 1980s was about girls in primary and secondary schools.

However, significant attempts were made by gender equity policymakers during the 1990s to re-focus gender equity policy more holistically on the process of schooling, with an emphasis on the importance of the early childhood years. The following analyses of policy directions over the last ten years illustrates this.

The major national policy directions for gender equity in education of the last ten years have been marked by the *National Policy for the Education of Girls in Australian Schools* (1987), the *National Action Plan for the Education of Girls 1993–1997* (1993), which arose out of the evaluation of the *National Policy*, and the *Gender Equity: A Framework for Australian Schools* (1996). Each of these successive documents supplanted its predecessor, for most practical purposes of advancing gender equity policy. Each represented significant shifts in the way in which concerns about policy have been understood by systems, and interpreted into policy.

Some understanding of these shifts can be gleaned from the way in which these documents are prefaced. The prologue to the *National Policy for the Education of Girls* is titled *Being a Girl in an Australian School*, and sets out some of the experiences of discrimination that girls in different contexts have endured. The stories of girls in both primary and secondary schools are included, but the emphasis is on those experiences that show early signs of the women within being able to interpret the gendered nature of their worlds. Specific early childhood experiences are not examined. The National Policy embraced the principle that 'Gender is not a determinant of capacity to learn' (inside front cover). However, the objectives and priority areas set out in the policy strongly emphasised notions of equality in access, participation and resourcing, making possible interpretations that directed attention to the biological 'category' – girls.

The *National Action Plan for the Education of Girls* (NAPEG), by virtue of its title, enabled policy genres that focused on the needs of girls outside of a relational context to continue. However, it emerged during a stage when gender equity policy was under siege from those who considered policy-making in this area to be dominated by white, anglo feminists, and who wanted greater consideration of the class, race, ethnicity and disability dimensions of discrimination and subordination. It also emerged in the early stages of what was to become a concerted onslaught on gender policies for their alleged indifference to the educational disadvantages of boys.

The introduction to NAPEG subtly hints at the distinction that can be made between the formal indicators of gendered inequality in education and the 'progress [schools and systems] are making towards **real** gender equity' (p. vii, emphasis added). The first of the eight priority action areas in this document is 'Examining the Construction of Gender'. In a significant move away from the discourse of the National Policy, the Key Strategies and Questions for Schools set out to support the implementation of this priority action area, do not make a single separate reference to girls, but address the need for teachers, parents and both boys and girls to understand the way in which gender is constructed. It has dimensions that relate to the way in which violence and abuse of power become acceptable in gender relations. The *National Action Plan* did not depend to the extent of its predecessor, the *National Policy*, on the language of participation, access and equality in provisioning, which clearly suggested upper primary and secondary schooling contexts, where 'choices' bifurcate along gendered lines. Neither did it specifically engage with the discourses of early childhood education to make problematic the intensely and actively gendered environment of early childhood education normalised through uncritical approaches to 'child-centredness' and valuing of the 'free' expression of children's choices. In not doing so, the NAPEG probably reinforced the neglect which occurs in most generic education policy, and contributed to the marginalisation of early childhood education in debates about gender equity and policy.

The newest arrival on the national policy scene for gender equity in education is the *Gender Equity: A Framework for Australian Schools*, which opens with a statement that strongly emphasises the relational context in which gender is understood, and the need for reform to the education of both boys and girls. The primary emphasis on girls has all but disappeared from this document, and is replaced by the view that

> [T]o address the differing concerns and educational experiences of boys and girls it is necessary to acknowledge that gender is a central issue for both girls and boys.

The *Framework* represents the outcomes of debates around the needs of boys in education, and the ways in which concerns about issues such as male youth suicide, injury and death by accident rates, their literacy outcomes and needs for relational skills have been taken up within concerns to eliminate gendered violence and improve the way in which women and girls, and their interests and needs, are valued in Australian society. These concerns have shifted policy frameworks towards the way in which gender equity must be achieved through education, as well as in education. In the *Framework*, the cultural experiences and processes that prevail in schools, and the ways in which these intersect with experiences outside the school to produce asymmetrical gender relations, come under the scrutiny of policy in ways that previous statements had not been able to articulate. These concerns are also more comprehensively identified within contexts of cultural diversity of schools, the continuum of dis/abilities that exist in schools and society, different sexual orientations, the racism that permeates much of the institutional business of schools, including the curriculum, and the need for educators to have an understanding of the complex discourses through which dominant interests continue to produce new technologies through which equity issues may be sidelined.

The central pieces of national gender equity policy described here intersected with other policy sources to strengthen the focus on construction of gender in schooling. The Gender Equity in Curriculum Reform (GECR) project, which emanated from the National Strategy on Violence against Women, and other projects sponsored through Projects of National Significance and the National Professional Development Project ran a parallel course to the direction in which the major policies were moving. Policy on gender equity, then, can be seen to include those studies that have emanated from and were funded to inform the directions of emerging policy, including those projects that were carried out under the banner of the GECR project.

The GECR project established the groundwork for new perspectives in policy. This particular project resulted in a number of studies that had an influence in turning gender equity policy-making around, to move the focus of policy firmly away from egalitarian participation, retention and achievement outcomes, towards a focus on the active role of schools in construction of gender, and the need for this to be taken in account in explicit ways if girls and boys were to be prepared for the far-reaching changes to the social, economic and civil aspects of Australian and global society. At state system level, these projects, together with the new national policy directions, were enabling a new focus on early childhood education. These projects, like the new national policy directions, were heavily informed by research from the early childhood area (e.g Davies).

ANGELS TREAD . . . AND BECOME 'THOUGHT POLICE'

Two issues have cast a shadow of suspicion over gender equity policies in early childhood in more recent times: boys' literacy outcomes, and the politics of touching children. Both are deeply mired in the politics of gender, but gender equity policymakers and their constituencies have found that there is solid resistance within systems and within the community to understanding the gender dimensions of these debates.

Girls' higher average literacy outcomes have generated a popular voice that claims that gender equity has been achieved, and that, in the process, boys' needs have been ignored. The complex debates about the social construction of literacy have been largely ignored, both by system leaders and by the popular media. Even the less complex debates, which draw attention to the fact that gender differences in literacy outcomes have been a concern for decades, and that girls' purported advantage has not carried over into economic or political equality through life, have been largely ignored. The ways in which these gender effects are refracted by socio-economic circumstance, ethnicity, race and geographic location have similarly been lightly dismissed.

System responses to the literacy 'problems' in early childhood have relied overwhelmingly on responses that focus on the individual student as the problem, and have adopted literacy schemes that take little or no account of those issues raised by Alloway *et al.* in the report on the project for the Strategic Initiatives Element, National Professional Development Programme, *Boys and Literacy: Meeting the Challenge.*[16] In this project, which was mobilised in a climate of vigorous demands from the community that boys' literacy needs be addressed urgently, the authors have summarised the research on the links between language acquisition and gender in ways that should compel the attention of policy-makers and early childhood educators to issues of construction of gender. However, education systems have now had generations of experience in evading those aspects of gender equity policy that call attention to the social dimensions of masculinity and its embeddedness in educational practice.

Connections made between early literacy and gender in the DEETYA-funded *Boys and Literacy* report include the following:

> Early language patterns and practices in the home help to produce gendered language practices in children

Gender-specific play and gender-specific toys produce differential language practices with children

The language practices used in reading schemes (the first 'school' language practices children encounter) usually rely upon stereotypical constructions of 'the child', and of 'boy' and 'girl' as stereotyped, very gender-specific categories

Children's writing, reading and viewing preferences are predominantly gender-stereotyped

Children's toys and games, media texts, literature, writing and classroom tasks provide ample evidence of the pervasiveness of masculine cultural storylines as dominant patterns for boys to use in 'making sense' of the world (pp. 84–85).

The politics of touching refers to the alleged dehumanisation of learning environments where sexual harassment policies have made teachers frightened to touch students as a natural expression of praise, encouragement, restraint or comfort.

Both of these issues illustrate the fundamental challenge that gender equity policies raise for understanding how sexual politics work through the lives of children and adults, and the deep-seated reluctance of power-brokers in education systems to engage genuinely with the complexities of gendered power. Neither of these concerns will be resolved in the long term through instrumental policies, which establish either testing or intervention regimes, or which prescribe particular kinds of behaviours. Both go to the heart of the way in which gendered power is learned and understood in racialised, classed and dis/ability inflected contexts. Both point to the need for developing an understanding of what a truly culture- and gender-sensitive, diversity-valuing school might look like, and for developing positive approaches to developing violence and harassment-free school environments where students engage in all activities without risking gendered, racist, dis/ability-based or classist harassment.

Both point to the need for educators to understand the intense cultural allegiance to forms of power embedded in age, gender, race, ethnicity and ability differences, and to the need for students and teachers to become involved as researchers of their own cultures and values, to bring to conscious level the dimensions of hurt that may derive from seemingly natural practices (such as sexual 'teasing', which is in fact sexual harassment). Also, these both point to the need for recognition that, for many young children, the world is a truly frightening place, and is made more frightening when schooling does not provide students with the language, skills and space to contest the taboos and practices that oppress and silence them. The 'no-touch' debate highlights the need for gender equity policies to be grounded clearly in a compassionate justice, one that promotes a vision of gender relations that evokes responsibility at student, teacher and system level, for making the environment of the school safer and more humane, but one that is sensitive to the degrees of hurt that many children carry as a result of having experienced abuse. The 'thought police' and 'political correctness' caricatures of gender equity policymakers at all levels have set up both boys' literacy crisis and fear-of-touch issues as emanating from a male-phobic retributive feminism (the same ones that have been responsible for forcing men out of early childhood teaching). These are hardly the kinds of feminism that would ever have gained a foothold in the intensely patriarchal systems of governance that persist in education.

CONCLUSIONS

The declining faith of feminists in the capacity of the new corporate state to deliver on the unfinished business of feminism comes at a bleak time for early childhood education. As Hollingsworth has stated:

> We need more literature, more voices, more energy and more challenges to turn the tide of the increasingly conservative nature of education.[17]

Those who have worked as gender equity policy actors within the state have experienced the extent to which they have been positioned as outsiders within the apparatus of the state, enjoying a fragile presence within bureaucracies in a transitory moment wherein the state has 'bought time' on how next to regulate demands of feminism for deep structural reforms to institutional education. Early childhood educators have similarly been regarded as outsiders to the real business of education. Policymakers (those surviving the cuts) and early childhood educators need now to form strategic alliances across the education and the general community to find spaces in the new agendas of education to bring to the fore the foundational role of this sector, not only in education, but in the creation of a socially just society, where differences based in race, class, gender and dis/abilities are regarded as elements of the richness of community, and essential to the face with which Australia takes its place in a globalised culture. Early childhood educators need to work with policymakers at a generic level, and also need to activate the development of sector-specific gender equity policies within education systems and their own professional associations. Joining forces with sympathetic others in the education community to reject a cynical commodification of education, and promote an understanding of the emancipatory social reform issues, will be an essential strategy in keeping gender equity policies vital in early childhood education. As the support base within systems for implementation of gender equity policies is eroded by staff and budget cuts, early childhood educators will need to take up proactively, through alliances with sympathetic constituencies across all sectors of education, the policy spaces for gender equity in a social justice framework that interrogates critically all educational reform processes.

NOTES

1 These are analysed comprehensively in the new text by Taylor, S., Risvi, F., Lingard, B., and Henry, M. *Educational Policy and the Politics of Change.* Routledge. 1997.
2 Yeatman, A. *Bureaucrats, Technocrats, Femocrats: Essays on the Contemporary Australian State.* Allen and Unwin, Sydney. 1990.
3 Taylor, S., Risvi, F., Lingard, B., and Henry, M. *Educational Policy and the Politics of Change.* Routledge. 1997.
4 This expression was used by Eva Cox in *A Truly Civil Society.* ABC Books: Sydney, in the context of positing the argument that a nation's capital includes both social and economic resources.
5 Curriculum Corporation 1995.
6 Kamler, B., Maclean, R., Reid, J., and Simpson, A. *Shaping Up Nicely: The Formation of Schoolgirls and Schoolboys in the First Month of School.* Australian Government Publishing Service. 1994.
7 Walkerdine, V. *Schoolgirl Fictions.* Verso: London. 1990.
8 Department of Education Queensland. *Enough's Enough: Sexual harassment and violence – A resource kit for primary schools: Project Report.* 1994.
9 Alloway, N. Eight's Too Late. In *Unicorn* 21:25 4 November 1995.
10 *Foundation Stones: The Construction of Gender in Early Childhood.* A Gender Equity in Curriculum Reform project. Curriculum corporation: Melbourne. 1995.
11 *Frogs and Snails and Feminist Tales.* Allen and Unwin: Sydney. 1989. *Shards of Glass*: children reading and writing beyond gendered identities. Allen and Unwin: Sydney 1993.
12 *The Great Divide: The Construction of Gender in the Primary School.* Curriculum Development Centre: Canberra. 1989.
13 See *National Strategy for Equity in Schooling.* Ministerial Council for Employment Education Training and Youth Affairs 1994. This basis is the document that frames the ways in which states report on equity issues. There is no specific section on gender equity.
14 Marshall, C. (ed.) *Feminist Critical Policy Analysis: A Perspective from Primary and Secondary Schooling.* Falmer Press. 1997.
15 Kingdon, J.W. *Agendas, Alternatives and Public Policies.* New York, HarperCollins Publishers. 1994.
16 Alloway, N., Davies, B., Gilbert, P., Gilbert, R., and King, D. *Boys and Literacy: Meeting the Challenge.* A report to the Department of Employment Education Training and Youth Affairs. Published by James Cook University. 1995.
17 *Feminist Praxis as the Basis for Teacher Education.* In Marshall, C. op. cit.

Chapter 8

The politics of category membership in early childhood settings

Bronwyn Davies

The following chapter is taken from the book *Power/Knowledge/Desire: Changing School Organisation and Management Practices*, written by Bronwyn Davies (1996).[1] Throughout this project Bronwyn worked with the teachers who became researchers of their own practices and subsequently developed new practices in keeping with the *National Action Plan for the Education of Girls 1993–1997*. This chapter is about the teachers' struggle to come to see differently, and to undo taken-for-granted ways of seeing in educational settings. The chapter is written from their point of view.

Language is both extraordinarily powerful in its capacity to give us new ways to see the world and equally powerful in its capacity to hold in place the very things we are trying to interrupt (Davies, 1994). Despite our new-fledged desires, born of our access to post-structuralist discourse, we found ourselves knitting back up the unravelled world of the old discourses with the very patterns we thought we had just pulled undone. Over the eighteen months of this project, we talked and talked and talked, amazed at how many words it took to know with any certainty that we understood what each other meant. And yet so often, on return to school after a workshop, school reality would take over again, and we'd find we'd lost the way of seeing that felt so sure, so exciting the day before. It was particularly hard when other teachers or our principals cast doubt on what we thought we were coming to know, or when they demanded that we explain ourselves in situations where it was clear that nothing new was going to be able to be heard. But it was not just a struggle with others, it was also, sometimes, the way in which we thought about ourselves as teachers that crowded out the ways of thinking we were developing in the workshops.

One of the patterns we constantly struggled with was our own and others' tendency to engage in binary thought (Davies, 1989, 1993). If we saw something or someone as belonging in a subordinate category, it was easier to see them as powerless than it was to see them as powerful. It was a combination of binary thought and a tendency to essentialise people whom we located in binary categories that was especially difficult to erase as a habitual pattern of meaning making. It was hard, for example, to think of girls as oppressed and at the same time to see a girl acting in powerful and dominating ways and to recognise it as such. It was hard to see the children with disabilities, who were most often powerless in the face of their dominant, ascendant, able bodied class mates, as also and at the same time able to act powerfully. It was hard to see the way in which power shifted from one person to another and to recognise the sometimes fleeting nature of it.

In post-structuralist theory, the inevitability of having to belong to one or the other category of any binary pair, the inevitability of being powerful or powerless, depending on which category you belong to, is called into question. The binary pairs themselves, such as male/female, abled/disabled, white/black, powerful/powerless, are themselves put under erasure. That is, they are recognised as politically useful terms, even necessary terms, but they are also recognised as highly problematic. Categories are politically useful because you cannot call attention to a cultural pattern that consistently privileges one group over another if you cannot name the groups. Disabled people, for example, had to be named so that the problem of their invisibility and absence from mainstream culture could be recognised and acted on. Women have had to make more visible the categories of girl and woman for the analysis of their relative powerlessness *vis-à-vis* men to be recognised, analysed and interrupted. Aboriginal people have had to heighten the visibility of their category membership to persuade reluctant governments to take action about their ill treatment *vis-à-vis* whites. Homosexual people have had to do the same thing.

The catch is that the strong category membership claims made by each of these subordinate groups can have negative effects. One of them is the *essentialising* of the category that can go on – that is the slippage towards believing that the characteristics that are defined as belonging to people in a particular category are somehow naturally and inevitably characteristics of those people (Fuss, 1989). Worse, they are seen as the morally correct characteristics of that group of people – and often, by extension, of all groups. Early radical feminists, for example, had a lot of difficulty acting powerfully, or 'as a man might act', because that called their category membership in question and that was seen as immoral. The multiple differences *within categories* get blurred as the necessary political work of calling attention to the cultural patterns of disadvantage is done.

Much early liberal and radical feminism was, in some ways, more constricting than earlier patriarchal regimes. Those caught up in liberal feminist discourses had to outstrip the men at their own games and at the same time reveal their unquestioned membership of the category of female in their bodily presentation of themselves. Those caught up in radical feminist discourses were not restricted in those ways. They could dress as they wished, change their sexual preference, act politically quite differently from men. They experienced the exhilaration, the pleasure, the power of joining together to bring about institutional change, of sharing the woes of belonging to a downgraded category with others who had had similar experiences. But this had its price – there was a moral imperative to be like the other women and not to 'betray' your category membership.

The definition of woman slipped around as it shifted through these different discourses, but it did not loosen the hold of the idea that one is in some essential and fundamental sense *other* to man. It is in attempting to disrupt this essential otherness that putting the binary categories under erasure is addressing itself. Such work frees the category from the essentialising that is done and in some sense begins to erase both categories as meaningful.

The work of celebrating the category in order to undo old negative ascriptions (ascriptions you had believed to be true, just like any other member of the culture) is necessary political work. And it is political work that must continue, because binary thought is still the dominant mode of thought and the categories that are other to the ascendant categories are always at risk of being constituted as less normal, less admirable, less valued. Such a tendency is often subtle and unintentional and it takes persistent work to find the moments in which this happens and to challenge them. We need the categories even to notice the patterns, let alone disrupt them.

In this chapter, we will use some of the discussions we had in workshops to show the struggles we had with assumptions about various category memberships and the power of these to shape what we saw and the ways in which we interacted with the students.

There was an incident that absorbed our attention for some time, and we kept coming back to it, because for some time we couldn't get an agreed version of 'what happened'. Annie, Paquita and Bronwyn had spent some time together in the playground, where Annie and Paquita were studying playground violence and sex-based harassment. On the morning in question, Jessie came rushing over to us, chased by Jason, a boy with learning difficulties who had previously been in a school for children with disabilities. Jessie breathlessly asked Bronwyn if she would take her to the toilets. Bronwyn was in the midst of saying she didn't know where they were when Jason caught up and slammed her up against the gate. Jessie did not resist, or protest. She stood there quietly with Jason watching her. Jason began to wander off. Jessie slipped through the gate and walked slowly towards the toilets, looking back over her shoulder to see if he was watching her. Jason was apparently taking no notice. Jessie called out to him in a sing-song voice that she was going to the toilets. He took up the chase and she sped off to the toilets, easily winning the race.

When we discussed this event on several later occasions, Annie and Paquita were certain that it was an example of the kind of violence on the playground that they were concerned about. The story illustrated a *male* victimising a *female*. He had chased her and slammed her violently against the gate. While Bronwyn did not disagree that there had been violence, she believed that the story was one of female, able bodied power. Jessie had known how to use adult presence to gain a momentary advantage. In Bronwyn's observations of her, she had enticed Jason to chase her to the toilets, knowing she could outrun him. She deliberately engaged him in a competition that was exciting and that she could win. Yes, she had been slammed up against the gate, but she did not want to leave it at that.

It took a lot of talk around these two readings before we agreed that both of these readings were legitimate and both contributed to an understanding of 'what happened'. Both children probably knew the cultural pattern of males chasing and hurting females. They probably understood their game with each other at least in part through that storyline, he attempting to achieve himself as dominant and powerful, she attempting to escape that domination. (Interestingly, when the girls chased the boys, as they did in some of their play, the end point did not appear to be some form of violence of girl over boy.) At the same time, the establishment and maintenance of difference between 'them' and 'us', the abled and the disabled, was a binary pattern that Jessie could tap into in her achievement of demonstrated superior membership to Jason.

PAQUITA, ARIANNE AND THEO

The next incident we will look at happened when Paquita was out in the playground video-taping the children on the monkey bars. We show Paquita's transcription of the episode from the video-tape and then our discussion of the incident where Paquita makes problematic the action she took at the time. The original action involved two children, Arianne and Theo. Theo was one of the dominant boys who often took over and controlled the monkey bars in violent ways. Arianne is a physically skilful child. She is one of the few girls who uses the monkey bars in play time. Paquita's intervention was based on an unexamined assumption that Arianne, as a girl and as a child, was powerless, and that Paquita, as responsible adult teacher, should intervene to reprimand Theo for his unacceptable use of male power. It begins with Julie 'telling on' Theo:

Julie Arianne was using the monkey bar and Theo said, 'I'll look up your panties'

Paquita Could you ask Theo and Arianne to come here please ((Julie gets them.))
Paquita ((to Theo)) Did you say that you would look up Arianne's panties?
Theo (Nods 'yes')
Paquita ((to Julie and Arianne)) You have the right to use that equipment without Theo speaking to you like that. ((To Theo)) you've been harassing this person. Sit over there and do some thinking about your behaviour. You're off the playground. ((Theo sits down under a tree. Julie moves to another area of the playground. Arianne moves to a different area of the playground. Arianne does not go back to the equipment))

Paquita: I used this transcript in an early workshop to show how I was coming to see my teaching-as-usual as problematic. I wanted to explore the ways in which usual patterns of adult control cannot automatically end oppressive behaviour, and may even serve to heighten it. My naming of the behaviour as harassment may in fact have lent Theo more power, in some ways, rather than less:

Paquita I had quite a humbling experience with the transcription that's just above, with Julie and Arianne. I'd seen Arianne out on the playground and it only twigged to me the other night. . . . Julie . . . often comes up to me and she talks to me about a particular injustice that's happening, and she, you know, thinks I need to deal with it, and she calls me across and off I'd go. And she came up this day to say that Arianne was using the monkey bars and Theo, who's one of the group of boys who, you know that dominates that main piece of equipment, he said um, 'I'll look up your panties' and the teacher says 'Could you ask Theo and Arianne to come across please' and Julie goes and gets them and then the teacher said to Theo like 'Did you say that you'd look up Arianne's panties?' and, you know, I couldn't believe that Theo just nods his head ((laughter)) yes, because you know he doesn't usually do that, so that question was a bit of a walk in. Then the teacher says to Julie and Arianne 'You have the right to use the equipment without Theo speaking to you like that' you know, she's saying Arianne, telling her that the playground's quite all right when there's a teacher like this out there ((laughter)) to make sure this doesn't happen. And then she says to Theo, and over the three weeks I can't believe how particularly angry I was getting with Theo because I was seeing it, and I would move from the video to do an intervention ((laughter)) because I couldn't remain behind the video ((more laughter)) I said, you've been harassing this person, sit over there and do some thinking about your behaviour, you're off the playground, and Theo goes and sits down under the tree, and then Julie moves, this is the bit that just struck me the other night, Julie moves to another area of the playground and Arianne moves to a different area of the playground. Arianne doesn't go back to the equipment, and, what I was thinking was, here's a teacher doing structure, the teacher looking after the child on the playground duty. But Theo was off the equipment and the playground equipment was vacant ((laughter)).

It didn't do anything to help Arianne to have access to that equipment. . . . Julie and the teacher were involved in a discourse there that um, really wasn't being helpful to Arianne at all, because Arianne never comes up to the teacher to ask for assistance, she sorts her problems out in her way. So, if Julie had not come up to say you know, 'Theo's looking up Arianne's pants', Arianne might have still been over at the play equipment swinging her body wildly holding on to that piece of equipment with nowhere to go. Me getting into Julie being the good girl or helping sort out this stuff on the playground may have interrupted Arianne's powerful way that she quietly goes about, doing her business on the playground because, you know, I said 'pop off and sit under a tree' ((everyone talks at once))

Beth As though she couldn't do it herself, yeah that's right

Bronwyn Well, if, yes, going to the teacher for help is a fairly weak strategy. I mean that/

Paquita Yes, and that's Julie's strategy, not Arianne's ((everyone agrees))

Bronwyn You see, you're really admitting defeat if you're wanting to be a powerful girl on the playground to have to go and call on the teacher/

Beth And so of course it tends to be the girls who do

Bronwyn So, and so by you sort of coming in and supporting her she'd lost her sense of power on the equipment ((general agreement))

Patsy It was interesting wasn't it, that it was vacant, and she didn't go back? ((general agreement))

Paquita And, and you were talking about how we set up girls' days only, on the equipment, like that sort of structure and this just tapped into me personally being involved in the structure and how little effect that it had on Arianne's access

Bronwyn . . . that really needs to be looked at very carefully, the whole thing, and wondered about. Yes. Why she didn't go back, I mean, what's happening there? Is there no point any more? If she personally is not claiming that space and what is the implication, I mean what was made central in the talk was sexual harassment as the discourse, so, while she might have been able to ignore Theo as a pain and making a threat she could ignore, once that had become a big issue, that was then central to her identity, her panties and somebody looking up them and the boy being sent off the playground for it, and that becomes the sexual issue, and that's, it may be that is actually very debilitating thing in some sense, that you don't feel powerful any more because you are so conscious of your body as a sexual object that you wouldn't want to go and swing on there ((agreement))

Paquita When I used the word, I didn't use sexual harassment because when I was just about to say it, because that's what it was, I left out the 'sexual' because I thought that there was going to be an extra play on that you know/

Beth Yes, reinforce it, yeah/

Bronwyn But even so, it's sexual, we all know it's sexual ((general agreement))

Patsy And it had been focused on. I'm thinking that, perhaps what happened might've even upset the very delicate balance that there must be between Arianne and Theo and those other boys on that equipment . She's a tough girl and she can ignore it when they say they're going to look up her panties, to a degree, but once he's got into trouble over it, and he's been put under the tree, maybe she couldn't go back to the equipment then or that would have implicated her in the getting him into trouble

Bronwyn But there's no game any more is there? If the game is for her to claim the territory and there's nobody to claim it against, because the most powerful boy has been sent off, then what's the point? You see, if that's her game, is to fight over the territory, then the game's actually finished

Paquita There have been instances where we've caught her on video when she actually just dropped off when the boys are doing all their masculinity near the end, she's just dropped off and not bothered to engage with them

Beth Has she, have you seen her there by herself though, or with other girls? Has she been there, does she actually like doing that, the actual physical/

Paquita Yes, she loves it, she's really good at it

Beth Yes, so she doesn't mind being by herself ((general agreement))

Angel I'm just wondering if there's a, it sounds awful, but a sense in which he's been now reinforced that that's something (and you've taught him that that's something). It's punishable, therefore I've got something ((several yes's))

Bronwyn Well, he already knew he had it. I mean he couldn't have used those words if he didn't know he had it, but, but there is that sense in which boys in their antagonism to female teachers can have their own sense of power heightened by the female teacher saying that's not nice ((several yes's))

Paquita Whereas it was unspoken before, when she was hanging in there – and now it's been named ((some comments))

Bronwyn This is where, I think that it is absolutely fundamental that the principals establish school policy, in ways that all teachers and all students understand, that does not privilege and condone certain forms of masculinity, that says it just is not acceptable. It's the school, represented by the principal, that must make it very very clear that no matter how pleasurable and no matter how much power they might feel in that moment it isn't on in this school, end of story. So that's it, it can't fall into this trap that has happened here, or, it probably still can, but the likelihood of that is reduced, because it's not just you making a female personal judgement about what's 'nice' or 'not nice'

These two incidents highlighted for us the problematic and shifting nature of children's alliances with adults and the power of storying. It also seriously called in question the usual ways in which we might think, as adults, that we can change the way in which things are played out by our children in our culture. As children learn to speak, they learn, with that speaking, the cultural patterns through which dominance and subordination are achieved. The category *adult woman* is not necessarily a more powerful category than *male child*, particularly if what the male child learns from the adult is the power of any sexual words he might utter.

Much of the difficulty of getting a clear sense of what was happening here was to do with the way in which discourses bump into each other, confusing meanings and blurring category memberships. Adult–child binaries, male–female binaries and abled–disabled binaries take their meaning in different discourses, and yet clearly here they overlap and bump into each other as the players collectively and separately construct the meaning that is to be made in each telling of the situation.

Learning to speak, and, in the same process, learning to story the world so that others hear and take up that story as correct, is one of the ways in which we each become credible members of our culture. Those whose membership is in one of the subordinate categories, that is, a category read as other to the dominant (normal) category, sometimes have to work quite hard to position themselves as ones whose voice can be heard as meaningful in the same way that dominant category members are heard.

PAQUITA AND FAITH

Paquita: The following transcript and discussion around a series of incidents with one girl, Faith, reveal the way in which I began to see much of my teaching-as-usual as inadequate in dealing with children in the playground. Claims of violence and counter claims, the fractured, fragmented nature of interactions and conversations, the multiple demands on the teacher's attention, all make it very difficult to arrive at a clear idea of what is going on and what the teacher should be doing to prevent violence. I found myself falling into old assumptions, doubting that Faith, as a disabled girl, really knew what she was talking about. I found myself not hearing Faith or giving credibility to her words, because I had access to a 'better' form of words:

I am walking across the playground. Faith is a child with a disability that keeps her in a wheelchair. She has little physical control of hand, arm and head movements, has good language and communication skills, but slow speech and is difficult to understand. Faith is sitting by herself in the playground. I walk by her chair.

Faith ((calls to teacher)) Paquita! Paquita!
Paquita Hi, Faith
Faith Somebody was being mean to me
Paquita They were being mean to you?
Faith Yeah
Paquita Can you tell me what happened?
Faith Well she came along and she, go, like, this, to me
Paquita Stuck out her tongue?
Faith Yes.
Paquita Which person was it?
Faith Alice. And I can't find her now
Paquita Okay. Well, then, perhaps she's gone out on to the oval. How does that make you feel when she comes across and sticks out her tongue at you?
Faith It/ she makes me feel angry
Paquita I bet she does. Well, I'm going to go for a walk out on to the oval to see if I can find Alice ((Interruption))
Faith Yes
Paquita And what will you say to Alice when you see her?
Faith I will say that I'm very cross 'cause y/ I/ you stick out your tongue

Paquita	Mm. Angry, you said you felt angry
Faith	Mm
Paquita	And what do you want to tell her after you tell her that you are feeling angry?
Faith	'Never come near me again'
Paquita	Is it that you never want ((Interruption)) do you never want her to come near you or do you want her never to do that again to you?
Faith	I never want her to do that to me
Paquita	Okay. Well, let's go and see if we can find her. Are your brakes off? Do you take your brake off your wheelchair?
Faith	I can't reach
Paquita	I'll take it off then ((Interruption. They walk out on to the oval))
Faith	She was wearing black
Paquita	Black. Okay, there she is over there ((Alice sees them coming and stops playing and waits))
Paquita	Alice, can I talk to you, or can Faith talk to you? I was just passing by and I had to go right next to Faith and she called out to me. She said that there was a problem with something that you did to her on the playground
Alice	I didn't
Faith	I saw you
Alice	What?
Faith	I saw you stick your tongue out at me
Alice	I didn't
Faith	You did
Alice	I didn't
Faith	You did. That's the truth
Paquita	How did that make you feel, Faith?
Faith	That made me feel very angry
Alice	I didn't
Faith	You did. Alice, I saw you stick your tongue out
Paquita	((To Alice)) Do you know how difficult it is for Faith to look after herself when she has to wait for somebody to come by and wheel her in the chair? Very hard, and if that's something that you did, I think that's a very cruel thing to be doing
Alice	I didn't
Faith	Yes, you did. I saw you. That upset me
Paquita	((To Faith)) And what is it after you've said that you feel angry, what do you want Alice not to do?
Faith	I don't want you to come near me ever again!

Later, in the workshop, I went through this episode with the rest of the group in detail, explaining how it seemed to me when I transcribed it. My assumption of superior teacher knowledge seemed very foolish when looked at from outside. I caught myself in the act, I suppose, of hearing Faith somehow in the negative half of the able bodied/disabled binary and did not give her the credibility I should have. I was not clear whether I should believe her accusation. Alice's reported action remained, at the time, something that only *may* have happened. It was when I transcribed the tapes that I came to see Faith in quite a different way and to tell quite a different story:

Paquita	I'm just touched at how powerful I think Faith is. Faith's a little girl and she's in a wheelchair, and her physical disability stops her from even taking the brake on and off her wheelchair, so, she's really dependant on somebody moving her to the playground and parking her there for the hour and although she has language, it's really hard to understand her, so if you're wanting to have an interaction with Faith you need to have time and you need to listen very carefully. So, often, people will whizz past her because there's no time to do talking. But anyway, this is an interaction with Faith and with me and it's showing how powerful Faith is in resisting me kind of setting up this little discourse where I'm the teacher and this is the disabled person who needs my assistance, something like that. And Faith's sitting by herself on the playground and the teacher (me) walks near her chair and Faith calls out to me and I say 'Hi,' and she tells me that somebody is being mean to her and I don't understand it. And I say 'are they being mean to you'?
Bronwyn	Tell them how Faith's voice sounds so they've got more of an image
Paquita	You know, it's a sort of like a screech, it's hard for her to get the words out, it's like pain every word that she punches out into the world. I say, can you tell me what, what has happened. Well, she came along and ((reading the transcript)) 'she go like this to me, and she stuck out her tongue' so I do this stuff like um, help Faith by being a sort of a nice and good teacher, and Faith says 'yes' and I say 'which person is it'? And she says 'Alice I can't find her now perhaps she's gone out onto the oval' and then I move into this sort of um, sort of a humanist sort of counselling ((laughter)) mode and I say 'how does it make you feel when she comes across and sticks out her tongue?'
Nel	Textbook stuff ((laughter))
Paquita	And she says 'it makes me feel angry'. I bet it does. We're going to go for a walk out on the oval to see if I can find her. Um, and then I say, then there's an interruption and I say

'shall we, shall we go for a walk and, and you can find her?' so I'm doing that stuff about Faith needs to be participating and listened to, 'yes' she says, 'and what will you say to Alice when you see her' and Faith says ((using high pitched screechy voice)) 'I will say I am very cross because you stuck out your tongue' and the teacher says, um, 'angry, you felt angry'. So, I'm kind of re-wording Faith so it's more appropriate and Faith, thinks, um, 'well if this teacher's going to take me out onto the playground I better say um, rather than say, 'no I'm going to stick with my own words' ((laughter)). And the teacher says, 'and what do you want to tell her after you tell her that you are feeling angry' and Faith says 'I want to say ((using high voice)) never come near me again'. And the teacher says 'is that what you never want, do you never want her to come near you again or do you want her never to do that again to you' so I can, you know, she's breaking friendships, ties, that sort of stuff, and she, Faith compliantly says 'I never want her to do that to me again'. And the teacher says 'OK, Faith's got it right so let's go' ((laughter)) 'are your brakes off, do you take your brakes off you wheelchair' and she says 'I can't reach' 'I'll take them off' so they walk out and it goes on. And the bit that I think's interesting was when Alice denies 'I didn't,' and Faith says 'I saw you' and Alice says 'what', 'you stuck out your tongue at me', Alice 'I didn't' 'you did', 'I didn't' 'you did, that's the truth' and then I go 'how did that make you feel Faith', and Faith says, 'that made me feel angry'. She's remembered the stuff that got her out there because I said that and, and Alice says 'I didn't' and Faith says 'You did, you stuck out your tongue' and then the teacher says something revolting like 'do you know how difficult it is for Faith to look after herself when she has to wait for somebody to come by and wheel her in her wheelchair. Very hard, and if that's something that you did, I think that's a very cruel thing that you did' and Alice said 'I didn't' and Faith says 'Yes you did, I saw you. That upset me'. And the teacher says 'and what is it after you've said that you're feeling angry that you want to say to Alice' and in a loud voice she says to me ((using loud high scratchy voice)) 'I don't want you to come near me ever again'. I just loved that so much. You know like, here she is kind of being, positioned as the disabled person and highly obedient in order for somebody to move her, perhaps she has to play that bit, you know, engage in that discourse and still, right to the very end she holds onto telling that person off because she didn't want her to come near her again. So, that's kind of, that's what I wanted to explain, is how powerful I think Faith is

Bronwyn And then it, it goes on the next time Alice is rude to Faith, Faith actually had these ideas about how you could control, set up things in the classroom for behaviour management in the classroom, that people could get rewards for good behaviour in the playground and you should set it up so Alice gets a star whenever she behaves properly/

Paquita ((using the scratchy voice)) 'I think that she should get a smiley face if she does not stick her tongue out at me'

I never knew for sure whether Alice was innocent. I struggled with my own initial assumption that Alice knew what she was talking about and that Faith perhaps did not. In transcribing the tapes and revisiting the incident with Faith, I became more and more convinced that Faith had reason to be treated not only as a highly credible person, but as a powerful one as well, despite her highly visible membership of categories that are difficult to read as anything other than relatively powerless – girl, child, disabled. This disrupting of binary patterns happened here for me at a profound bodily level. I caught myself assuming without question my own superior knowledge and doubting a child with disability. The disruption of those binaries was a highly charged, even exciting experience.

JOANNE, PETA AND CLAIRE

So that is a struggle in one direction, to recognise power in a disabled girl child when it is so easy to see her through the multiple binaries in which she is always a member of the subordinate/powerless term.

Another struggle was to know how to interact with girls who were disruptive of their category membership. The celebration of this that we hoped we might automatically engage in was something we found ourselves, on occasion, struggling over. Peta and Claire are girls who are seen as powerful by everyone, even adults and boys. Theirs is a strength that comes not from celebration of their femaleness, but from an outright rejection of it. In one incident in a lesson on sexual education, Peta's rejection of femaleness/femininity is seen to lead the other girls to use model babies for footballs rather than to wonder at the power of women's bodies. The boys in this lesson on foetuses were exemplary, marvelling at the ways in which babies form in women's bodies. The girls did not respond in this way. Again, in a workshop, we talked around these issues:

Jess I was thinking of Peta again, because she's . . . she's intimidating to me, ((laughter and comments)) yeah, and she's just a very, very ((everyone talking)) powerful girl within the group . . .

Joanne	Like she's very physical. Violent. . . . When I talked to the boys they all said that they wouldn't sexually harass Peta ((laughter and comments)) and they bring that up so I said 'Yup, we wouldn't sexually harass Peta', one of them says 'it's not only girls who fear boys, some boys fear girls like Peta' ((laughter and comments))
Bronwyn	So was Peta thc ring leader in the foetus episode?
Joanne	Er, yeah, she was, her and Claire, and Merissa's the other one. She looks exactly like a boy, she's really short and stumpy and wears football jumpers and football shorts and chews gum and drinks whole bottles of coke for breakfast ((everyone laughs)), she's short and so (punch happy). ((several comments)) Yeah, like she sticks her tongue up her nostrils ((laughter))
Nel	That's a neat trick ((everyone continues to comment))
Joanne	She's that type of girl, she does this wonderful pregnancy trick, she lies on her back and she pulls her T shirt over her stomach and she says 'Look, I'm pregnant' and she can force all her stomach muscles up and she can look about eight months pregnant ((laughter and comments)) . . .
Bronwyn	So, tell the story of the/
Joanne	Um, foetuses. I had these really beautiful models. There were nine of them, and there's twins as well, of uteruses with foetuses in different stages in them. The seven month old one, and the twins, you can take out. When I showed the boys, who had been wonderful in sex ed, they just sort of swarmed to it and touched it gently and wanted to know what was what and questioned that and talked about all their stories of babies they knew and showed so much interest and wonder that it was so amazing ((general agreement)). And that was just great to be able to tap into that and really appreciate that women's bodies are so wonderful, amazing. And the girls stood back, didn't want to look at it, didn't want to touch it, and then they got the babies and threw them around like footballs ((laughter and comments))
Bronwyn	Something very interesting going on there ((general agreement and commenting))

Peta can be seen to be as much caught up in the male/female binary as any little girl playing dollies in the home corner. In defining femaleness as other to the powerful ways of being she apparently desires, she is caught up in processes that perhaps necessarily entail the negation of her female body as she struggles to find her own forms of (not-female) power. If she had had access to ways of understanding identity other than in terms of the male/female binary, she could perhaps see her strength and power as one of many possible ways of being that were available to her, and not necessarily incompatible with the possibility of the physical creation of others' lives.

She probably does not have access to the idea(l) of being able to move beyond the binary. Instead, she finds herself caught in being either female/weak, or anti-female/strong. Reproduction is dangerously close to sexuality (it was, after all, a sex education lesson) and it is women's/girls' sexuality that is used more than anything else, in school contexts, to hold them in their subordinate position (Davies, 1993). In the present social patterns Peta sees around her, it is readily observable that the displacement of women in any hierarchies of power occurs when they are sexualised, or become pregnant and 'mothers' of small children. The object bodies with their babies can be seen by the boys with wonder, and the comfort of distance. For the girls, such distance would be hard to achieve if they are resistive to the idea of their subordinate category membership. If they are already subjected to the sexualising of their bodies in ways that control them and objectify them, and if these objects in the classroom represent the inevitable outcome of that sexualising, it is not too difficult to sympathise with Peta, turning the babies into footballs so that she could retain, for now, a naming of her body as powerful and under her control.

CONCLUSION

Through video-taping the playground, we were able to begin closely examining what we saw happening there in a way we were not able to do when it was simply our teachers' eyes we looked with. Looking as researchers enabled us to catch details in the children's activities that we did not usually see, but it also enabled us to look in detail at our own conversations and actions from outside of ourselves. Transcribing and presenting the material for discussion in workshops extended this capacity to see what had previously been invisible. Ourselves as teachers-in-authority, as ones who know, and in particular as ones who know right from wrong, looked quite strange to us when we turned our gaze on ourselves. This strangeness enabled us to see a much more complex social world being played out amongst the children than we had seen before. And it was in the light of this entry into the subtle, complex and contradictory meaning making going on in the playground that we were able to design a successful school level strategy for interrupting the violence that had been the central and distressing feature of our playground.

A central feature of our project was its collaborative nature. We worked with each other on the data we collected. We worked collaboratively to make sense of it and we moved together towards the insights we were developing. We planned the second stage of bringing about change in workshops, although we also had Bronwyn working with us on our school sites, helping us to think through what might be done in light of the particular structural and social features of our individual school.

It is important not to make the success of this project sound as though it was simply achieved as a result of teachers becoming researchers. Social change can be understood as a pattern of intertextual shifts. The texts that interleave and permeate each other are produced at levels of structure, discourse and desire. None of these operates on its own. Structure operates at the level of departmental policies, national agendas, specific institutional structures, classroom structures and social structures. Multiple discourses and patterns of desire are relevant within each of these levels. Technical or corporate managerial strategies primarily address the level of structure. When they insert a new discourse into the policies and structures, such as that of gender equity, there tends to be an assumption that its meaning is self-evident. But, as we found in this study, the discourses of gender equity were often very poorly understood. Much of the frustration experienced by us as teachers attempting to bring about change was that our strategies would get bogged down in disputes about what things meant. Intersecting with this problem of discourse was the lack of desire on the part of many of our colleagues to bring about or even facilitate change. There was a superficial correctness that some might come at in public, but there was a nod and a wink the minute they were not being monitored. In addition, we were often caught up in contradictory discourses, the schooling-as-usual discourses being very powerful in precluding other ways of thinking.

The impact of the discursive construction of teachers as non-scholars, as busy, practical, vulnerable, non-agentic people, is that these features are almost totally incompatible with us becoming researchers. Teachers-as-researchers are people who can examine their own gendered practices, analyse them, critically consider them in the light of the available literature and think through what changes would be necessary to bring about changes compatible with current values. Instead, apart from this project, we have systems attempting to assert those values in the shape of policy documents, and inserting them into the system largely through the structures of corporate managerialism. We have money spent on short in-service courses and on practical materials that might enable new practices to be put in place. We have teachers asking for practical strategies and then finding very often that they can't implement them because they don't know how to think through, for example, the effects of their questioning-as-usual, and so the new materials are only a superficial and soon abandoned add-on.

The discourses and structures of corporate managerialism shaping principals' practices are very often not clear to us as teachers, whose practice is shaped by a different set of ideals. Corporate managerialism is in direct conflict with the discourses with which we set out to become researchers of our own practices, and authors of the analyses of those practices. It may also directly clash with discourses about giving students a voice, since the process of marketing can allow only good news to be heard.

At the same time, the commitment to principles of social justice in state and national educational bodies means that spaces where projects such as this can take place have been created. In this project, we were given time out to attend workshops, to form a group with like-minded others, to become researchers of our own practices, to understand the constitutive force of discourses and to begin to plan changes. In some cases we were able to carry them through. The structures of the schools and the discourses through which schools are constituted, however, rarely made it possible for us to achieve even simple steps like the establishment of a gender equity committee with a real sense of power and purpose or the establishment of workable practices for dealing with sexual harassment. Teachers need space (physical, emotional, discursive) to become scholars. They need guided practice at becoming researchers of their own and schools' practices. They need an authority system in which they are able to develop a sense of agency and a set of relevant competencies to carry through the actions that become evident to them as needed in light of new policies. They need informed support networks with whom they can establish access to and competent use of new discourses, in which they can talk through issues affecting their own and others' practices and with whom they can plan changes. They need principals and other people in authority who will come in with *informed support* of whatever kind is necessary and who will not block or undermine their action.

Principals and their staff can best use policy when it is able to be implemented in ways that coincide with an already achieved understanding of what, for example, cultural difference is, rather than when it is something they have thought about only in relation to a national or departmental imperative. If they have not already thought it through, in-service days and short courses are totally inadequate to deal with the depth of change required in coming to develop a new personal philosophy/discourse and an understanding of how that might be put into practice.

What this project suggests is that we must find ways to enable students, teachers and principals simultaneously to disrupt old certainties, to discover the political and personal problems they entail and to forge new patterns of meaning making that allow them to take themselves up in other than binary terms. It will be necessary to work at the structural level, examining the ways in which the contexts of schooling, the popular culture and the current school knowledges establish and maintain binary thought. It will be necessary to examine the discourses through which knowledges are constructed by teachers and students and through which they constitute themselves and each other. And it will also be necessary to find ways to enable principals, students and teachers to examine the patterns of desire that lead them to take up one discourse rather than another (Davies, 1995, 1997).

NOTE

1 Davies, B., with Allen, S., Batten, R., Browne, P., Bessell, S., Cameron, R., Dawning, F., Hannay, R., Param, L., Poultney, L. and Walsh, B. (1996) *Power/Knowledge/Desire: Changing School Organisation and Management Practices.* Canberra, Department of Employment, Education and Youth Affairs, 1–259. This project was funded through the Commonwealth Quality Schooling Programme and the Curriculum Development Projects Programme.

REFERENCES

Davies, B. (1989) *Frogs and Snails and Feminist Tales. Preschool Children and Gender.* Sydney, Allen and Unwin.

Davies, B. (1993) *Shards of Glass. Children Reading and Writing Beyond Gendered Identities.* Sydney, Allen and Unwin and New Jersey, Hampton Press.

Davies, B. (1994) *Post-structuralist Theory and Classroom Practice.* Geelong, Deakin University Press.

Davies, B. (1995) What about the boys? The parable of the bear and the rabbit. *Interpretations* 28(2) 1–17.

Davies, B. with Allen, S., Batten, R., Browne, P., Bessell, S., Cameron, R., Dawning, F., Hannay, R., Param, L., Poultney, L. and Walsh, B. (1996) *Power/Knowledge/Desire: Changing School Organisation and Management Practices.* Canberra, Department of Employment, Education and Youth Affairs, 1–259.

Davies, B. (1997 forthcoming) Critical Literacy in practice: language lessons for and about boys. *Interpretations.*

Fuss, D. (1989) *Essentially Speaking. Feminism, Nature and Difference.* New York, Routledge.

Chapter 9

Improving our gender equity 'tools'

A case for discourse analysis

Glenda Mac Naughton

WORKING FOR GENDER EQUITY IN EARLY CHILDHOOD: THE STORY SO FAR

It has been over twenty years since the first guides to gender equity for early childhood staff were published (e.g. Cohen and Martin, 1976; Guttenberg and Bray, 1976; Davis, 1979). In this time, early childhood staff have been advised to achieve greater gender equity in their work with children by making children's learning materials, language and behaviours free of traditional sex-role stereotypes and by providing children with equal opportunities to access all learning materials (Birmingham Women's Liberation, 1975; Wangman and Wagner, 1977; Davis, 1979; Aspinwall, 1984; Perritt, 1988; Equal Opportunities Commission, 1992).

More specifically staff have been consistently advised to:

- encourage girls to play with constructional materials to improve their future scientific and mathematical competence (Davis, 1979; Women's Action Alliance, 1980; Mac Naughton, Mortimer and Parish, 1986; Equal Opportunities Commission, 1992);
- encourage girls to be involved in 'non-traditional' role play to increase their interest in a broader range of occupational choices (Cohen and Martin, 1976; Wangman and Wagner, 1977; Women's Action Alliance, 1980; Equal Opportunities Commission, 1986; Mac Naughton, Mortimer and Parish, 1986; Equal Opportunities Commission, 1992).

These goals derive from and illustrate the prevalence in the early childhood literature of liberal feminist approaches to gender equity. Broadly speaking liberal feminists believe that:

- all women should have the same rights and opportunities as those enjoyed by men;
- many women do not have equal opportunities to contribute to our world in many spheres of life including employment, education and the family;

- such inequalities exist because of sexism;
- sexism creates and reinforces the belief that women are inferior to men and, therefore, should not have the same rights as men and should not share the same status as men;
- to create greater gender equity sexism needs to be challenged.

Liberal feminists believe that these goals will be achieved by girls and women learning to do, say, feel and believe the same things as boys and men. For example, sexism will be challenged and gender equity will be created by women and girls being able to:

- dress the same as men and boys (e.g. wear trousers and have short hair);
- socialise like men (e.g. going out alone, drinking beer and being the one to ask the man for a date) and boys (e.g. being the leader in play, being involved in superhero play and throwing balls like boys do);
- do the same jobs as men, in the ways that men do (e.g. being as tough a boss as a man, carrying as heavy weights as a man, running as fast as a man) and doing the same things as boys do (e.g. being the doctor in hospital play and being the shopkeeper in shop play).

Hence, when early childhood staff are advised to create gender equity by encouraging girls to participate in traditionally male activities and by encouraging role reversal between boys and girls, such advice rests on a liberal feminist approach to changing sexist social relationships in our society.

This chapter looks at the work of one early childhood worker (Fay) who heeded such liberal feminist advice. Fay's gender equity work in block play and homecorner will be used to explore the theoretical and strategic implications of using liberal feminist approaches to gender equity in early childhood settings. Her story illustrates the practical implications of using a liberal feminist approach to gender equity and thus serves as a useful lens through which to reflect on what is gained and what is lost through basing gender equity work in early childhood on liberal feminism.

INTRODUCING FAY

Fay joined a research group of twelve early childhood educators who decided to explore the practical dilemmas and issues involved in challenging traditional sex-role stereotypes in their centres. They met monthly to talk about the gender issues surfacing in their work and to decide what to do about them. For several months they monitored children's play choices and interests. Their findings echoed much other early childhood research (see, Dunn and Morgan, 1987; Dermon-Sparks *et al.*, 1989; Alloway, 1995; Epstein, 1995). The research group found that there were traditionally gendered play patterns between the children in each of their centres. For instance, boys dominated in the construction material areas, such as play with wooden indoor blocks and Lego, and girls dominated in the homecorner and in the less physically active play areas. Not surprisingly, given the research project's aims, the educators tried to alter these patterns.

On joining the research group, Fay was uncertain about what 'gender equity' could and did mean but, broadly speaking, thought it meant girls and boys doing and being the same. She believed that it was important to treat boys and girls in the same way, with no special treatment for either gender. As she explained:

> [Equity means] . . . something along the lines of making girls equal to boys, or something, maybe, because I have these really strong feelings about equal pay, equal work, equal whatever, and if you want equal whatever, you do equal whatever. So I thought it was along those lines to make girls equal to boys, and I don't believe it. I believe everyone is equal anyway.

Fay's understanding of equity was strongly intertwined with her understandings of how to be a 'good' early childhood teacher. Fay's understandings were personal to her but expressed three ideas of 'good' teaching in mainstream early childhood literature historically and currently (see, for example, Morrison, 1995). Firstly, she understood her role as an observer and facilitator of 'natural' development. Her role was to encourage children's development by providing an appropriately balanced environment for each child to reach their full developmental potential. Secondly, she believed that her centre should be organised to enable children to have free choice. These two understandings meant that Fay needed to focus on correctly structuring the physical learning environment so that children could choose the materials that would facilitate their full development. For example, the teacher's role in block play was to present the 'right' materials in the 'right' way. Finally, Fay believed that children needed a developmentally balanced curriculum to develop to their full potential. They needed access to materials that facilitated all aspects of their development. Block play and homecorner each contributed in their own ways to such balance in the curriculum.

FAY'S ACTIONS FOR GENDER EQUITY

The connection between Fay's understandings of gender equity and of her role in children's learning influenced her first actions in the research group. She decided to observe boys' and girls' play patterns. She wanted to know 'where the children were at' before acting. This was consistent with and derived from her belief that her role as a teacher was to observe and monitor children's 'natural' development.

Fay uncovered differences in the boys' and girls' use of blocks that were almost identical with those found by others in the research group: a particular group of boys dominated the area and not one girl entered. The differences were problematic, given Fay's beliefs about developmental curriculum and gender equality. Not all children were playing with blocks, and therefore not all children were gaining the developmental benefits of these materials. More specifically, girls were missing out on a key developmental opportunity. Given Fay's emphasis on the need for the 'right' materials in children's learning, it was not surprising that she raised the relevance of the physical properties of blocks for gender equity and she wondered if the current design of indoor blocks was *inherently* suited to boys.

By the end of the third research group meeting, Fay's heightened awareness of gendering issues in block play via her own observations had coalesced with the research group discussion of the possibilities for gender equity in the physical re-presentation of block play. During a discussion triggered by another group member (Edna) about normal approaches to block play, Fay said that she had decided to totally re-organise her presentation of block play.

During the following eight months Fay focused on physically re-presenting block play to disrupt the gender stereotyped play she had observed. First of all, Fay removed the physical barriers between block play and homecorner, creating a large open space in which materials normally offered in the separate areas of block play and homecorner were combined. Three months later, Fay reported that, despite her removal of the physical barriers, such as shelves, between homecorner and block play areas, the children took three months to mix equipment between them. During this time, she named the combined space 'the dramatic play area', hoping that this would suggest a less gender-tagged play space to the children, thereby, reducing gender-divided play within it. Fay persevered with this change for an additional two months.

When this change did not prove successful, Fay experimented further with re-presentation. She re-structured her centre into four areas: 'creative play area', 'imagination area', 'discovery area' and 'quiet area'. The 'imagination area' replaced homecorner and block play and consisted of a changing combination of block play and homecorner materials.

During these eight months, Fay emphasised her desire to create equal access to block play for boys and girls. She believed that these strategies would create a gender-neutral area that both boys and girls would see as relevant to them. Re-naming the play space and integrating materials traditionally used by boys (blocks) and by girls (dolls) into a single space were her main strategies. This, she believed, would be sufficient to encourage them into the area. She was supported in this belief by her understandings of 'good' early childhood teaching and of gender equity. Her beliefs about good teaching indicated that children learn best with minimal adult intervention and her beliefs about gender equity indicated that providing equal access would create gender equity.

THE OUTCOMES OF FAY'S ACTIONS

Fay's work led to contradictory changes in play patterns between boys and girls. After four months of a combined block/homecorner area, Fay was frustrated at girls' and boys' reluctance to play together in the combined area. The children learnt the new names quickly. However, the intention of renaming the areas was to prevent children gender-tagging the spaces, but this didn't happen.

Several children re-created the areas in traditionally gendered ways. For example, video-taped segments of play taken in Fay's centre indicated that the 'imagination area' was defined by a group of girls as their space and as a space separate from boys. Girls had constituted the 'imagination area' using their normal homecorner storylines. Attempts by different boys to enter this space were rebutted in a variety of ways. For example, one girl asserted, 'This is still the "imagination area"', another asserted, 'No boys in the "imagination area"'. In response, one boy threw a cup from 'the discovery area' into 'the imagination area'! A group of boys had clearly identified the discovery area as boys' space. Fay's written observations give a flavour of some of this play:

> Block play/homecorner (physical barriers removed).
> 9.55am.
> Boys (4) have used large blocks and have cars. Very noisy and boisterous play. Throwing cars from one end to the other. B.C. voice very loud and organising the play. B.C. told the girls he was having all the blocks. Girls (4) confining themselves at this time to bedspread area. K.T. began to stand up for her rights over blocks but B.C. just dominated and continued to take the block unit I told him to move.

Clearly, Fay's initial aims had not been fully realised. Despite experimenting with 'gender-neutral' physical structures, she couldn't significantly shift the gender divisions between boys' and girls' use of space. Boys were still physically expansive and noisy; girls were still tentative and restrictively using space. Interactions between girls and boys were still problematic.

After eight months of experimentation, Fay reflected: ' I'm thinking oh, well, *back to the drawing board* [her emphasis]. She had discovered that her physical changes in the presentation of materials were not sufficient in themselves to change gender relations.

FAY'S THEORIES OF CHANGE: WHY DID THEY FAIL HER?

The strategies Fay used to change gender relations in her centre echoed much of the liberal feminist gender equity advice early childhood staff have been given during the last twenty years. For seven months, Fay had tried to encourage girls to use construction materials and to expand girls' non-traditional play with these materials. In this work, she faced an uphill battle trying to create more equitable access and participation in blocks and homecorner. Why was this? There are several possible interpretations.

Failure could be attributed to Fay's inadequacies as a teacher. Yet, Fay was an extremely experienced, mature and competent teacher in all other areas of her work. Failure could also be attributed to the children themselves. Maybe the children's reluctance to play in less gender-differentiated ways in more gender-neutral spaces derives from innate gender differences between boys and girls. Perhaps children are pre-programmed to prefer different play spaces and play materials and to play in same-sex groups. Yet, we know from research (Epstein, 1995; Mawson, 1995) that this is not the case. Boys and girls can, and do, play with each other. Boys and girls can, and do, play in less gender-differentiated ways. Another possibility behind Fay's failure to shift gender relations in her centre could be that her strategies for creating change were mistaken. It is this possibility that we will explore in some detail, with the value of hindsight.

Fay's strategies for shifting gender relations in her centre were influenced by: her theory of how children learn and, thus, unlearn or relearn gender roles; her theory of how to create a world free from gender inequality; and her theory of how best to promote young children's learning. We shall look at each of these theories in turn to explore how they shaped Fay's work and why they produced mistaken strategies for changing gender relations in her centre. As each of Fay's 'theories' of children's learning have strong resonances with liberal feminist theories of gender, this discussion will provide a focal point for evaluating such approaches to gender equity in early childhood settings.

Fay believed that children learn their gender roles from the gendered messages around them. These messages were evident in how the early childhood centre was structured into clear 'gender-tagged' domains such as block play and homecorner. In each of these domains, the equipment provided children with clear gender-stereotyped messages about who should play in each domain and what storylines should inform the play in each domain. Fay believed that children were learning how to think and act in homecorner and block play by absorbing the gender-messages embedded in the naming, organisation and presentation of the materials in each domain. Hence, to create less gender-differentiated (and thus more equal) access and participation in areas such as block play and homecorner, Fay needed to change the gender messages embedded within them. This could be accomplished by re-naming, re-organising and re-presenting materials. Through such changes, girls and boys could absorb new gender messages about who should play in each area and how and, in doing so, could become less 'gender-tagged' and more like each other.

Fay was not alone in understanding how children learn gender in this way. Her ideas sit within an approach to learning gender shared by liberal feminists that relies on what Davies (1988, p. 10) called 'osmosis' socialisation accounts of children's identity formation. Such accounts assume that gender differences in our society are created and maintained through a process similar to osmosis. For instance, sexist gender differences in our society are created and maintained because children and adults automatically absorb sexist messages from other children, from adults and from the media (or the block area and homecorner area).

Osmosis socialisation theory also assumes that children and adults absorb such messages uncritically (Mac Naughton, 1995). Hence, children who watch sexist television programmes or listen to sexist stories will automatically and uncritically absorb sexism. Likewise, children who play in gender-tagged blocks and homecorner areas will automatically and uncritically absorb the gender messages from these areas. If these messages reinforce traditional gender-role stereotypes, then children will learn to act in sexist ways. By implication, the reverse is also true. If these messages reinforce non-sexist gender roles, as Fay believed her 'imagination area' did, then children will learn to act in non-sexist ways.

However, Davies (1988) believes that strategies to create greater gender equity based on osmosis socialisation accounts are grounded in a flawed theory of how children learn gender. Such theory fails to acknowledge human agency, human resistance, and an individual's ability to re-make dominant practices, meanings and understandings (e.g. Connell, 1987; Weiler, 1988).

Human agency refers to the ability of people to take an active role in their own lives, to be 'agents' for how they live their lives. Osmosis socialisation theory assumes that children are not active in their own gender socialisation (Connell, 1987; Davies, 1988) but that they merely absorb information about gender uncritically. For instance, in osmosis socialisation theory, children cannot decide how to 'do' their own gender and they cannot take critically informed decisions about how to be masculine and how to be feminine. They merely do whatever they are told by the messages around them.

Such theory leads to strategies for change that treat individuals as 'passive recipients of social structure' (Davies, 1989b, p. 239) and of the social messages we give them. However, Davies (1989a) and Walkerdine (1990) found that not all girls passively or consistently accept the traditional female roles in the world about them. As Davies explained:

> Any adult who has attempted to 'socialise' a child knows that this process is fraught with difficulties and that children do not straightforwardly accept what adults tell them or the way adults do things.
> (Davies, 1988, pp. 10–11)

Thus, the theories of gender development that underpin liberal feminist theory cannot explain how and why girls and women want to continue, or want to challenge, traditional gendering. For instance, liberal feminist theory cannot explain why some girls want to continue to play in homecorner rather than with blocks when they have equal access to block play; or why some girls happily reject dresses and always want to be doctors, not nurses, in the hospital play.

In addition, as we know, children are surrounded by different messages about gender. Some messages from parents, early childhood staff and the media will be non-sexist, some will be very sexist. What happens when children are surrounded by such differences? Which messages do they absorb? Do they automatically and uncritically absorb the non-sexist or the sexist messages? How do they decide which messages to ignore and which to take notice of? Osmosis socialisation theory's view of gender learning cannot answer these questions as it deals only with the impact of the environment on the passive child.

This theoretical failure to understand the reasons why girls and women make the choices that they do has been allied with the failure of many early childhood staff to create a desire for greater gender equity amongst the children in their centres. Critics of liberal feminist approaches to gender equity (e.g. Davies, 1988; Alloway, 1995; Epstein, 1995) argue that strategies for creating gender equity based on the assumption that children passively learn gender via absorption are doomed to failure because children can resist our efforts to socialise and/or re-socialise them.

Fay's experiences included several such moments of resistance from the children in her group. She tried to alter children's gender socialisation through altering the messages she provided to the children and waiting for them to absorb these new messages. Children resisted these in many ways and there was little evidence of any long term change in how the children in her group 'did' their gender.

As with Fay's theories of how children learn gender, her theories of a world free from gender inequalities had all the hallmarks of liberal feminism. Like liberal feminists, she believed that gender inequalities exist because women do not have equal opportunities to contribute to our world. Hence, for Fay, greater gender equity is created by ensuring equal opportunities and rights for women and girls. These liberal feminist ideas reverberated throughout Fay's strategies for creating gender equity in her centre in three ways. Firstly, they influenced how she interacted with the children. Secondly, they influenced what she said to the children. Thirdly, they influenced the materials she used with the children.

The belief that gender equity for women means being able to do the same as men do and having the same opportunities as men, led Fay to focus on equity of access issues to block play. She encouraged the girls to do what the boys were doing (playing with blocks) because she believed that girls are essentially the same as boys, so they can do anything boys can do if they are given the opportunity. She believed that if girls were given equal access to materials and play space in her centre, then inequalities in the use of blocks would disappear.

Fay's emphasis on equal opportunity and her views of how children learn gender sat comfortably with her theories on 'good' teaching in early childhood. These theories derived from developmental approaches to early childhood teaching that prescribe involvement in all curriculum sites as necessary for balanced and, therefore, full development. From such a perspective, non-involvement in block play was problematic.

Fay's view on the teacher's role in children's learning limited her options for changing girls' behaviour and, therefore, for creating equal developmental opportunities for them. In her developmental theory, presentation and structuring of materials were the least developmentally restrictive ways to alter children's choices. If there were problems in children's choice and use of materials, then changing their selection and presentation was the most logical way forward for someone committed to facilitating the child's 'natural' development.

In summary: although Fay would not name her gender equity work 'feminist', her goals resembled those of liberal feminists and her beliefs about how she could achieve these goals resembled those of liberal feminists and developmentalists about how to influence children's gender learning. These goals and these beliefs about children's learning formed Fay's strategies for how to work for gender equity in her centre and how to judge when it had been achieved.

FAY'S THEORIES OF CHANGE: WHY DID SHE PERSIST DESPITE 'FAILURE'?

It is clear that Fay's chosen change strategies and the theories of learning that shaped them were flawed: the changes in children's gendering she anticipated failed to materialise. Despite this, Fay persevered in trying to create her planned changes in children's gendered behaviour for many months. To explain why she persisted so resolutely in the face of 'failure', we can draw on a powerful tool for critiquing approaches to gender equity work in early childhood settings known as feminist post-structuralist discourse analysis.

Put simply, discourse analysis is the process of 'taking apart' and critically reflecting on our social beliefs and practices, our emotional investments in them and the contribution of social institutions to beliefs, practices and emotions. Through such 'taking apart' we learn how social relations work, whose interests they work for and how we might do them differently in order to benefit groups who are discriminated against in our society. Feminist discourse analysis aims to 'take apart' social relations in order to eliminate sexism and the forms of the discrimination that maintain it.

When applied to gender equity strategies in early childhood settings, feminist discourse analysis involves 'taking apart' and critically reflecting on our early childhood beliefs and practices, our emotional investments in these and the contribution of social institutions to our beliefs, practices and emotions. Through such 'taking apart' we learn how early childhood programmes work, in whose interests they work and how we might do our work in them differently in order to benefit girls and boys experiencing gender inequalities within them.

To 'take apart' early childhood programmes, we can use three concepts that have specific meanings within the particular feminist approach to discourse analysis used in the remainder of the chapter: discourse, power and subjectivity. The particular approach taken here is known as feminist post-structuralism.

Discourse

In everyday language, the term discourse is often used to refer to talk between people. To illustrate, the statement 'Jo is discoursing with Lee' would in everyday language simply mean 'Jo is talking with Lee'. However, in the feminist theory, discourse has a more specialist meaning. Here discourse refers to the historically and culturally specific categories through which we give meaning to our lives, practice our lives, invest emotionally in our lives and constitute our social structures. So, discourse in feminist post-structuralist theory has three inter-related dimensions to it.

1 Discourse refers to the categories we and others use to understand social life. For example, gender provides many categories through which we give meaning to our lives. Specifically, we use categories such as masculinity and femininity to understand ourselves and others. There are a host of categories within our language that define and delineate people on the basis of gender, such as wife, husband, mother, father, sister, brother, waitress, waiter, etc. These categories categorise people on the basis of their gender.

2 Discourse refers to the social practices that arise from these categories. Categorising people produces expectations about how we should act towards others and how we should 'be ourselves'. For example, the category of gender gives rise to a number of social practices, such as dressing, acting, thinking, feeling, that will be gender-specific. Women and men are expected to dress, act, think and feel differently. For instance, in much of the western industrialised world, if dresses are to be worn it should be by the woman, not the man. So, we learn to dress, act, think and feel in differing ways, depending on which gender category we belong to.

3 Discourse refers to the emotional investments we make in our social practices. These are referred to as our 'patterns of desire'. As we learn which social practices 'go with' which social categories in our society, we also learn that there is pleasure in getting the match between practice and category 'right' and pain in getting it 'wrong'. Consequently, we invest emotionally in getting practices right. For example, when we categorise ourselves as traditionally masculine or non-traditionally feminine we gain pleasure from being involved in social practices and relationships that affirm our categorisation. We invest in getting our view of being masculine or feminine 'right' (Davies, 1989a).

Hence, within post-structuralism, discourse has been recast to include the emotional and social practices through which meaning is constituted in our lives. To illustrate: if poststructuralists refer to Fay's gender equity discourses, they are referring to more than how she talks about gender equity. They are referring to the complex interactions between:

- the categories she uses to categorise people on the basis of gender;
- the social practices in and through which she has learnt the meaning of the words. These practices include how other teachers react to her when she talks about gender equity, the training she has had, the books she has read and the television programmes she has watched;
- the emotional investments she has made in her meanings for gender equity. These investments include how Fay's definitions of gender equity give her pleasure and fit with her current patterns of desire as a woman, as an early childhood teacher and as a member of a gender equity research group;

Post-structuralism's recast notion of 'discourse' attempts to encapsulate these complex interconnections between language, meaning, the individual and the social. It is these complex interconnections that are referred to when post-structuralists refer to Fay's 'gender equity discourses' or 'teaching discourses'.

Discourse and power

Post-structuralists (e.g. Weedon, 1987) believe that discourses enable particular groups of people to exercise power in ways that benefit them. They are able to do this because discourses constitute particular ways of being as normal, right and, therefore, desirable (Davies, 1993). For instance, the particular meanings given to social categories such as 'girl' or 'boy' have an implicit moral sense within them of what is normal and/or right. In our society, categories such as 'wimp' and 'sissy' are part of how males are categorised. Whilst they are part of the discourse of being male, they are rarely seen as desirable, normal or right ways for boys to be 'boys'. This sense of what is right and/or normal is socially constituted and produced in discourse.

For a post-structuralist, moral systems are more than just an individual's expression, or just some accidental and arbitrary occurrence. They exist because 'particular ways of speaking have been institutionalised, have taken on a life of their own, have, in fact, become constitutive of people and their actions' (Davies and Harre, 1991/2, p. 3). This happens when discourses are articulated and circulated via the major institutions within our society.

Thus, whilst there is some choice about who we become, our desires are shaped by the way in which powerful discourses circulate in, and via, social structures and institutions. This makes more possible some ways of being, and not others (Davies, 1989a). From a post-structuralist perspective, therefore, all ways of being have social and political implications. As Weedon explains:

> How we live our lives as conscious thinking subjects, and how we give meaning to the material social relations under which we live and with which we structure our everyday lives, depends on the range and social power of existing discourses, our access to them and the political strength of the interests which they represent.
>
> (Weedon, 1987, p. 26)

Consequently, contradictory discourses about what is normal, right and best circulate and compete with each other in a society at a given point. Some discourses dominate, resulting in certain moral systems becoming dominant at specific moments. This is not because some discourses are 'more truthful' or 'right' but because they have more political strength than others, derived from their institutional location. This is so for all discourses, including gender equity discourses and early childhood teaching discourses. Not all gender equity discourses have equal social power, because particular options about how to understand and practise masculinity and femininity are constantly reaffirmed institutionally. Each person's gender discourses will be influenced by the institutional and material power of those discourses. Not all early childhood teaching discourses have equal social power, because particular options about how to understand and practise being an early childhood teacher are constantly reaffirmed institutionally. Each early childhood worker's teaching discourses will be influenced by the institutional and material power of those discourses.

So, for a post-structuralist, some understanding of gender equity and of early childhood teaching that circulates in our society will be powerful, and some will not. Those that lack an institutional base will be marginalised or silenced by being positioned through discourse as abnormal, wrong or undesirable.

Subjectivity

'Subjectivity' describes who we are and how we understand ourselves, consciously and unconsciously. These understandings are formed as we participate in, articulate and circulate discourse. As discourses form subjectivity, they constitute the very foundations upon which early childhood staff choices are made about what to do, what not to do, how to do it and who to do it with. So, to understand decisions that early childhood staff take consciously and unconsciously about what to do with children, how to do it and how to evaluate what they have done, we must identify and analyse the discourses constituting their teaching. Consequently, discourse analysis is a central feminist post-structuralist tool for evaluating gender equity teaching decisions in early childhood settings. For instance, it can help us evaluate Fay's gender equity decisions and why she persisted with the choices she did.

Discourse analysis: the process

Discourse analysis involves identifying relationships between individuals, social structures and institutions. Within feminist post-structuralist discourse analysis, this involves six inter-related processes:

- Identifying how we categorise people, including ourselves. These categories will be formed and expressed via our language.
- Identifying the social practices through which meanings are given to the categories we learn.
- Identifying the patterns of emotional meanings and investment we have in particular categories.
- Naming the discourses that are formed by our categories, practices and emotional investments.
- Identifying the institutional basis of discourses.
- Evaluating the social power relations and effects of different discourses.

These six processes combine to produce an analysis of who benefits and how from the articulation and practice of particular discourses. Applied to early childhood teaching, discourse analysis produces an understanding of who benefits and how from articulation and practice of particular early childhood teaching discourses, including those related to gender equity. Staff can use this understanding to reflect critically on teaching practices for gender equity and to recast these practices in the light of what they learn. The intention in using discourse analysis in this way is to improve gender equity programmes through finding more powerful ways of assessing their implications.

Discourse analysis of Fay's work

We shall now use discourse analysis to explore Fay's teaching decisions in block play and homecorner, culminating in a discussion of who benefited and how from Fay's articulation and practice of her gender equity and early childhood teaching discourses.

Identifying the frameworks through which we categorise people and ourselves in language constitutes the initial phase within discourse analysis. These categories are formed and expressed via our language. A feminist post-structuralist analysis of gender equity strategies in early childhood settings therefore involves identifying and analysing the frameworks through which early childhood staff categorise themselves and others as teachers and learners.

Fay categorised herself as an early childhood teacher who believed in a 'middle of the road' approach to gender equity and who was 'not-feminist'. She also categorised herself as a 'good' early childhood teacher. Fay categorised the children according to how traditionally gendered they were or not. She talked of 'girly-girls', 'boyish-boys' and 'children who crossed the gender boundaries'. Her aim in her gender equity programme was to ensure that children could 'cross the gender boundaries'. By this, Fay meant that girls would do what boys normally did, such as climb trees and play with blocks, while boys would do what girls normally did, such as play in homecorner and make very decorative collages. For one gender to do what the other did was to make the genders the same and, therefore, equal. Her categorisation of children struggled to find a way of talking about children that moved her beyond what she understood to be a normal girl and a normal boy. They *were* different and yet she *wanted* them to be the same.

With a clear sense of the categories that Fay used to make sense of herself and the children, the next stage in discourse analysis involves identifying the social practices through which meanings are given to these categories. As discussed above, a characteristic of discourse is that it is in and via social practices that we give meaning to the categories we learn to use to order our social world. Analysing working for gender equity, therefore, involves identifying the social practices through which early childhood staff come to understand what is meant by the social categories that build their discourse.

Fay's definition of being a 'good' early childhood teacher was formed through past and current social practices. These included having studied early childhood teaching at a specialist early childhood training college, using what she had learnt in her work with children on a daily basis, meeting with colleagues who followed similar practices to her own and updating her knowledge of early childhood teaching through attending professional development courses. These social practices gave meaning to the category of early childhood teacher and formed her understandings of a 'good' early childhood teacher.

Fay's definition of being a teacher working for gender equity was formed through her involvement in the gender equity research group and through watching television and reading newspapers. Through the media, she formed an understanding of what a 'middle of the road' non-feminist gender equity teacher does. They don't go 'too far' or interfere 'too much'.

Since discourse constitutes emotions and subjectivity, the next aspect of discourse analysis involves identifying patterns of desire associated with particular ways of categorising ourselves and others. These provide the power behind what is learnt via discourse.

Fay had a variety of social categories through which she could understand herself as an early childhood educator in our society. For example, as a feminist or non-feminist teacher and as a developmentally appropriate or not developmentally appropriate teacher. There was a choice for Fay about how to position herself as an educator working for gender equity. She could be a 'not developmentally appropriate, feminist teacher' or a 'developmentally appropriate feminist teacher', or any other combination. Each choice would have had emotional consequences because of her own history of emotional investment in particular ways of being a teacher.

Fay already had well-developed patterns of desire, which had been built up during twenty years of teaching, that constituted her as a teacher committed to developmental approaches to teaching. Fay had been respected and rewarded for her approach to teaching in several ways. She had gained and kept employment, she had been used as a teacher trainer by early childhood training colleges, she had advice sought from her from parents on the education of their children and she had advice sought from her by colleagues. There had been little in her professional life that had challenged this particular way of being a teacher. In Fay's life, it was the normal, right and best way to be a teacher. It was what she had been taught during pre-service training and what all of her colleagues, to her knowledge, understood as 'best'.

This meant that all of her existing patterns of desire supported her decisions to continue to be a teacher who had minimal involvement in children's learning and who relied strongly on the material environment to change children's learning, including their gender learning. She had learnt to enjoy the sense of rightness that teaching this way gave her, and it was how others in her profession expected her to be. It was also what she believed to be right. Hence her patterns of desire were formed in, and through, her sense of rightness about teaching. In other words, they were formed through the moral systems of her teaching discourses. Understanding the emotional force behind the morality (rightness) of Fay's teaching discourses helps to explain why she persevered so persistently in the face of 'failure'. She not only knew that her goals and strategies were right, she had also heavily invested emotionally in them being right. She both *knew* and *felt* she was right.

Identifying the emotional investments associated with the moral systems forming our discourses of teaching is an important dimension of discourse analysis. In Fay's instance, it helps us understand perseverance in the face of 'failure'. More generally, it helps us understand why early childhood staff often find it difficult to change their ways of teaching and shift from the theories of teaching and learning gained in pre-service training.

Discourse analysis also involves analysing the extent to which the particular discourses being analysed have institutional authority and the political implications of this. It is by locating discourses socially and institutionally in this way that we can learn:

> what power/knowledge relations constitute this field, how power is exercised, whose interests are silenced, marginalised or excluded and how it is open to change.
>
> (Weedon, 1987, p. 169)

The institutional basis to Fay's developmental discourses was apparent when she referred back to how her training had constructed her teaching knowledge. Much of what she had learnt about feminism was from the print and broadcast media. So, what Fay understood about teaching for gender equity had institutional authority. The academy established and gave moral authority to her discourses about children's learning, and the media established and gave moral authority to her discourses about gender equity. This institutional articulation and circulation of Fay's discourses added to the moral force they had within her daily life. Not only did Fay know and feel that she was right: her discourses were institutionally sanctioned by the academy and by the media. Given the moral and institutional force underpinning Fay's discourses, it is not surprising that she persevered for so long with her approach to gender equity before going 'back to the drawing board'.

The final phase of discourse analysis involves evaluating the social and political implications of the discourse. Feminist post-structuralist discourse analysis emphasises the gendered power effects of the discourse. The aim is to evaluate the extent to which sexist power relationships have been disrupted or reinforced and the extent to which more or less equitable gender relationships are supported via the discourse.

To explore the gendered power-effects of Fay's developmental and gender equity teaching discourses it is necessary to think about the extent to which sexist power relationships between the children in her centre were challenged or reinforced and if more equitable gender relationships were established. With the benefit of hindsight, it is possible to see that Fay's developmental and gender equity teaching discourses reinforced sexist relationships between the children and did not create any greater gender equality between the children. To expand: children's traditional ways of doing gender did not alter. The traditionally gendered boys who had dominated block play were able to continue doing gender in the ways that they had at the beginning of Fay's 'experiment'. They could do this in the 'discovery area' and in the combined blocks and homecorner area. They did not need to change how, with whom or with what they played. All that needed to change was *where* they were boys, not *how* they were boys.

The same was true for the traditionally gendered girls who enjoyed playing with each other and playing in homecorner. All that needed to change was *where* they were girls, not *how* they were girls. This meant that when the traditionally gendered boys took over the 'discovery area', the girls responded to the boys as they always had: they moved away and avoided any confrontation with them. The girls had gained no greater access to play space and the boys had maintained a specific area of play space as theirs. For non-traditionally gendered boys and girls, little had altered. The opportunities to have non-traditional ways of being supported or taken up by other children had not altered.

The chances of sexist relationships and ways of being disrupted through Fay's gender equity strategies were minimal. Her strategies 'led' Fay to hope for and watch for the 'natural' emergence of children's essential sameness (androgyny). While she did this, her attention was diverted from the continuing hierarchical organisation of gender relations between boys and girls in her centre. She missed the fact that boys had established the 'discovery area' as theirs through force and had kept the girls out via intimidatory tactics such as throwing tea-cups (girls' things) out of it. Until this could be seen, little could be done about it.

From this evaluation of the gendered power effects of Fay's teaching discourses, it is possible to argue that Fay failed in her gender equity work because of the discourses through which she understood, practised and felt this work. To undertake her gender equity work differently, Fay would need access to alternative feminist discourses of teaching.

ACCESSING ALTERNATIVE GENDER EQUITY DISCOURSES

There are several ways of understanding what the goals for gender equity programmes could and should be and of understanding how children learn gender. Each will be aligned with some form of feminist theory. 'Feminist theory' covers many approaches to understanding women's roles, experiences, positions and possibilities, as 'feminisms' differ in how they explain women's oppression. This chapter has explored the theoretical basis and practical outcomes of liberal feminist approaches to gender equity in early childhood. This is because it has been the dominant feminist influence in early childhood gender equity programmes; the contribution to these programmes of other feminisms, such as socialist feminism and radical feminism, have been minimal.

For early childhood staff wanting to move away from developmental and liberal feminist approaches to this work, feminist post-structuralism offers one way forward. In recent years, there has been considerable interest in the theoretical and strategic potential of using feminist post-structuralism to inform gender equity work in early childhood (see, for example, Davies, 1989; Mawson, 1993; Mac Naughton, 1994; Alloway, 1995; Danby 1996).

Broadly speaking, feminist post-structuralists share with liberal feminists the view that women experience considerable sexism and that it needs to be challenged. However, unlike liberal feminists, they believe that gender inequalities exist because we live in a society that has dominant ideas about the correct way to be male and female. This produces a gender order where some ideas are seen to be better and more right than others. It is the gender order that creates inequalities. If there were no one correct way to be male or female then inequalities could not exist.

The current gender order is a patriarchal gender order. This means that masculinity is prized above femininity and particular forms of masculinity (dominant) and femininity (submissive) are prized above all other forms of masculinity and femininity. It is the attempt to categorise us into male and female within the current patriarchal gender order that is the problem.

For feminist post-structuralists, sexist gender relations will disappear when we no longer need to oppose male and female ways of being and when we can all choose to be masculine and feminine in different ways at different times. Liberation will occur through challenging the dominant way of understanding who we are and creating alternative and oppositional understandings of what it means to be male and female. This will change power relations between the sexes. We should, therefore, celebrate difference and challenge the traditional gender order if we want to change women's place in the world and empower women and children.

To construct such challenges, we need to understand how children learn their gender. Feminist post-structuralists such as Davies (1989a, 1993) believe that children learn their gender by positioning themselves inside the discourses of masculinity and femininity available to them in our society. Through these discourses, children learn that there are proper ways of being male and female from an early age. By 4 years of age, children are correctly located within the dominant way of being male (hegemonic masculinity) and female (emphasised femininity) (Davies, 1989a). Adults are important in reinforcing or challenging the gender order because children constantly see themselves through adult eyes. Children constantly check how adults react to their ways of being and look for signs from adults that they are correctly gendered. If those signs are not forthcoming, children puzzle over what they can do to be correctly gendered.

Children need to work particularly hard on themselves to be correct if their desires are other than the dominant male or female desires. They have to work on their own pattern of desires. Adults can help them in this process:

> even when (children) resist a particular . . . position . . . (they) cannot escape the implications of femininity. Everything we do signifies compliance or resistance to dominant norms of what it is to be a woman.
>
> (Weedon, 1987, pp. 86–87)

Post-structuralism emphasises the need to rethink how we help children to construct alternative notions of what it means to be male and female. Post-structuralists such as Davies (1989a) and Walkerdine (1990) believe that learning gender is an ongoing, active struggle by children to make sense of the messages around them, and early childhood staff need to engage actively in this struggle with them. Staff cannot passively wait for children to absorb non-sexist messages from the world about them, but should actively engage in dialogue with children that challenges what the children will have already learnt about the correct way to be male and female.

So, if Fay had positioned herself within feminist post-structuralist discourses, she would have become more actively engaged in children's learning than she was. She would have needed to:

- find ways to work with children to make the current male and female dualism irrelevant. This would have involved checking if and how she was helping children position themselves correctly in the existing gender order and checking what options she was making available to the children to position themselves differently from the dominant way of being male and female.

- talk about the differences between girls and the differences between boys as well as the things that girls and boys share, rather than only differences between girls and boys.
- extend children's understanding of how to be male and female but ensure that she did not do so in ways that reinforce the existing gender order (male dominant, female submissive).
- encourage children to understand how their actions and reactions affect other children's power to do what they want to do and be who they want to be.
- empower children to explore different ways of being masculine and feminine.

Through such active involvement in re-constructing children's gendering, Fay may have successfully challenged sexism between the children and created greater gender equity in her centre. In evaluating the extent to which this was so, discourse analysis would have been a useful tool to add to her teaching repertoire. It would have enabled her to judge the success or otherwise of such strategies.

Since the late 1980s, there has been considerable debate about the extent to which liberal feminist strategies can and do lead to any long-term change in gender relations between men and women. Weiler (1988) convincingly argued that liberal feminist educational strategies are theoretically and thus strategically flawed. One of the major reasons why they are theoretically flawed is because the theories of why there are gender differences between males and females and of how these differences are created and maintained are simplistic. We have explored the reasoning behind these assertions in this chapter.

These criticisms relate directly to strategies that still predominate in much of the early childhood literature on gender equity. It is, therefore, timely to reflect on the extent to which the mainstream approaches to gender equity in early childhood may also be strategically and theoretically flawed. Fay's work provides a beginning for such reflection. It highlights how key elements of the advice still being given to early childhood staff in key policy documents (e.g. OPCC, 1991; EOC, 1992; DHS, 1996) and in much current mainstream professional literature (e.g. Spodek and Saracho, 1994; Morrison, 1995) is theoretically and, therefore, strategically flawed.

DOING DISCOURSE ANALYSIS

Early childhood staff have to make many choices about how to do their gender equity work: what their goals will be; what theories of learning gender will inform their work; and what strategies they will adopt in their centres. Discourse analysis can provide early childhood staff with a powerful tool for evaluating how they approach gender equity currently and how they might do it in the future.

In summary, discourse analysis, as conceptualised in this chapter, involves:

- Identifying how we categorise people, including ourselves.
- Identifying the social practices through which we give meanings to the categories we learn.
- Identifying the patterns of emotional meanings and investment we have in particular categories.
- Naming the discourses that construct and are constructed in our teaching.
- Identifying the institutional basis for different discourses that construct and are constructed in our teaching.
- Identifying the social power relations and effects of the different discourses that construct and are constructed in our teaching.

Discourse analysis can help early childhood staff wishing to reflect on and recast their work for gender equity with young children through providing an alternative foci for child observation, for teaching action and for professional self-evaluation. The following questions and processes provide a starting point for early childhood staff wishing to use discourse analysis to rethink these aspects of their professional practice.

Child observations

Early childhood staff traditionally observe children's developmental progress across a variety of developmental domains such as cognitive development, emotional development, etc. Questions such as 'What developmental skills are the children using in completing this task?', 'What are the children's developmental strengths and weaknesses in a particular developmental domain?' and 'How is the children's learning being influenced by their developmental abilities?' guide this observation. These questions can mask how fundamental gender is in children's development and learning (Mac Naughton, 1995). To overcome this difficulty within developmental observations, staff need to focus specifically on how gender is constructing learning and development within and between children. Staff can use discourse analysis to generate questions similar to those that follow to guide such a shift in observational focus.

- To what extent do specific children use gender as a category in their daily interactions with themselves and others? What gender categories do they use?
- How do specific children practise gender? What daily practices give

meaning to their understanding of themselves and others as gendered beings?

- What emotional investment do specific children have in particular ways of being masculine and feminine? What would be the emotional benefits and costs for them of doing masculinity and femininity differently? To what alternative understandings do they have access?
- How would I name specific children's discourses of gender?
- What institutional support do specific children have for their discourses of gender?
- Whom do specific children's discourses of gender benefit? How do they benefit girls and women? How do they benefit boys and men? Which girls and women do they benefit? Which boys and men do they benefit? How do they benefit specific children? In whose interests are the children's discourses of gender?
- Who would benefit if specific children's discourses of gender constructed and were constructed by alternative discourses? What might these alternatives be? How would they benefit girls and women? How would they benefit boys and men? Which girls and women would they benefit? Which boys and men would they benefit? How would they benefit specific children?

Teaching actions

Staff need to be actively involved in children's daily gendering practices to create greater gender equity in early childhood settings. As Fay's story has illustrated, hoping that children will absorb non-sexist messages around them is insufficient to challenge gender inequalities between children. Staff wishing to take a more active teaching role for gender equity can use discourse analysis to generate questions similar to those that follow. Answering these questions can help staff plan and evaluate their gender equity teaching actions.

- To what extent do I use gender as a category in my daily interactions with the children? What gender categories do I use?
- How do my interactions influence how children practice gender? What aspects of my daily curriculum practices give meaning to children's understanding of themselves and others as gendered beings?
- What emotional investment do I have in the particular ways of teaching that masculine and feminine of specific children? What would be the emotional benefits and costs to me of teaching differently? What alternative understandings do I have of how to teach for gender equity?
- How would I name my current approach to teaching gender?

- How do and could my curriculum decisions and teaching actions provide institutional support to specific children for their discourses of gender?
- Who benefits from my curriculum decisions and teaching actions for greater gender equity? How do they benefit girls and women? How do they benefit boys and men? Which girls and women do they benefit? Which boys and men do they benefit? How do they benefit specific children? In whose interests are my actions for gender equity?
- Who would benefit if specific children's discourses of gender were challenged by me in my teaching actions? What might I do to create these challenges? How might my actions benefit girls and women? How might my actions benefit boys and men? Which girls and women might they benefit? Which boys and men might they benefit? How might they benefit specific children?

Professional self-evaluation

Discourse analysis also offers a tool for individuals and groups of early childhood staff wishing to conduct indepth reflection on their broader role as a professional in the gendering of young children. Questions that arise from discourse analysis and that could be used to guide such reflection include the following:

- How do I categorise myself as an early childhood educator? What are the main theories/ideas that define my teaching? Am I a feminist educator or am I a traditional early childhood educator? What sort of feminist or traditional educator am I?
- How do I practise being an early childhood educator? What daily practices give meaning to my understanding of myself as an early childhood educator and to my theories of teaching and learning?
- What emotional investment have I in my current theories of teaching and learning? What would be the emotional benefits and costs of teaching differently? What would be the emotional benefits and costs of understanding children's learning differently? To what alternative understandings do I have access?
- How would I name my discourses of teaching and learning?
- What institutional support do I have for my discourses of teaching and learning?
- Whom do my discourses of teaching and learning benefit? How do they benefit girls and women? How do they benefit boys and men? Which girls and women do they benefit? Which boys and men do they benefit? How do they benefit me? In whose interests are my discourses of teaching and learning?
- Who would benefit if my teaching constructed and was constructed by

alternative discourses? What might these alternatives be? How would they benefit girls and women? How would they benefit boys and men? Which girls and women would they benefit? Which boys and men would they benefit? How would they benefit me?

WHY THEORY MATTERS: SOME FINAL THOUGHTS

There is considerable research in this book that provides alternative theories through which to understand children's gender learning. Suggestions for further exploration of feminist post-structuralist goals and approaches to children's gender learning are identified in the further reading section below. As we in early childhood teaching struggle to improve our theories and strategies of teaching for gender equity, it is worthwhile reflecting on Foucault's warning that everything is dangerous. We must never assume that we have finally found the right way forward. We must constantly search for stronger and more effective ways to theorise and hence develop strategies for a more positive and just world for all. Discourse analysis can help in this search.

FURTHER READING

Alloway, N. (1995). *Foundation Stones: The Construction of Gender in Early Childhood.* Carlton: Curriculum Corporation.
Davies, B. (1989). *Frogs and Snails and Feminist Tales*. Sydney: Allen and Unwin.
Davies, B. (1990a). Agency as a form of discursive practice. *British Journal of Sociology of Education, 11*(3), 341–361.
Davies, B. (1990b). Lived and imaginary narratives and their place in taking oneself up as a gendered being. *Australian Psychologist, 25*(3), 318–332.
Davies, B. (1993). *Shards of Glass*. Sydney: Allen and Unwin.
Epstein, D. (1995). 'Girls don't do bricks'. In J. and I. Siraj-Blatchford (eds), *Educating the Whole Child: Cross-curricula Skills, Themes and Dimensions* (pp. 56–69). Milton Keynes: Open University Press.
Mac Naughton, G. (1994). It's more than counting heads in block play: rethinking approaches to gender equity in the early childhood curriculum. Paper presented to the *20th Triennial conference Australian Early Childhood Association*. Perth, WA.
Mac Naughton, G. (1995). A post-structuralist analysis of learning in early childhood settings. In M. Fleer (ed.) *DAPcentrism: Challenging Developmentally Appropriate Practice* (pp. 35–54). Watson, ACT: Australian Early Childhood Association.
Walkerdine, V. (1990). *Schoolgirl Fictions*. London: Verso Books.

REFERENCES

Alloway, N. (1995). *Foundation Stones: The Construction of Gender in Early Childhood.* Carlton: Curriculum Corporation.
Aspinwall, K. (1984). *What Are Little Girls Made Of? What Are Little Boys Made Of?* London: National Nursery Nurses Educational Board.

Birmingham Women's Liberation (1975). *Out of the Pumpkin Shell.* Birmingham: Birmingham Women's Liberation.
Children's Services Office (1991). *Planning for Learning: A Framework for Planning Curriculum in Children's Services.* South Australia: Education Department of South Australia.
Cohen, M. and Martin, L. (1976). *Growing Free: Ways to Help Children Overcome Sex-Role Stereotypes.* Washington, DC: ACEI.
Connell, R. (1987). *Gender and Power.* Sydney: Allen and Unwin.
Danby, S. (1996). Rites of passage: masculinity in the block area. Paper presented to Reconceptualizing Early Childhood Education: Research, Theory and Practice, Sixth Annual Interdisciplinary Conference, Madison, Wisconsin, October 10–12.
Davies, B. (1988). *Gender Equity and Early Childhood.* Canberra: Commonwealth Schools Commission.
Davies, B. (1989a). *Frogs and Snails and Feminist Tales.* Sydney: Allen and Unwin.
Davies, B. (1989b). The discursive production of the male/female dualism in school settings. *Oxford Review of Education, 5*(3), 229–241.
Davies, B. (1990a). Agency as a form of discursive practice. *British Journal of Sociology of Education, 11*(3), 341–361.
Davies, B. (1990b). Lived and imaginary narratives and their place in taking oneself up as a gendered being. *Australian Psychologist, 25*(3), 318–332.
Davies, B. (1993). *Shards of Glass.* Sydney: Allen and Unwin.
Davies, B. and Harre, R. (1991/2). Contradiction in lived and told narratives. *Research on Language and Social Interaction, 25,* 1–36.
Davis, W. (1979). *Towards a Non-sexist Classroom.* South Australia: Education Department, Women's Advisory Unit.
Department of Education (1987). *Guidelines for Preschool Curriculum Development.* NSW: Department of Education.
Department of Human Services (1996). *Babies, Toddlers and Two Year Olds: A Curriculum Resource for Developing Child Centred Programmes for Children Under Three.* Melbourne: Government of Victoria.
Dermon-Sparks, L. and the A.B.C Task Force (1989). *Anti-bias Curriculum: Tools for Empowering Young Children.* Washington, DC: National Association for the Education of Young Children.
Dunn, S. and Morgan, V. (1987). Nursery and infant school play patterns: sex-related differences. *British Educational Research Journal, 13*(3), 271–281.
Epstein, D. (1995). 'Girls don't do bricks'. In J. and I. Siraj-Blatchford (eds), *Educating the Whole Child: Cross-curricula Skills, Themes and Dimensions* (pp. 56–69). Milton Keynes: Open University Press.
Equal Opportunities Commission (1986). *An Equal Start?* Manchester: Equal Opportunities Commission.
Equal Opportunities Commission (1992). *An Equal Start: Guidelines on Equal Treatment for the Under Eights.* Manchester: Equal Opportunities Commission.
Fleet, A. and Clyde, M. (1993). *What's in a Day: Working in Early Childhood.* Sydney: Social Science Press.
Guttenberg, M. and Bray, H. (1976). *Undoing Sex Stereotypes.* New York: McGraw-Hill.
Mac Naughton, G. (1994). It's more than counting heads in block play: rethinking approaches to gender equity in the early childhood curriculum. Paper presented to the 20th Triennial conference, Australian Early Childhood Association. Perth, WA.
Mac Naughton, G. (1995). A post-structuralist analysis of learning in early childhood settings. In M. Fleer (ed.) *DAPcentrism: Challenging Developmentally*

Appropriate Practice (pp. 35–54). Watson, ACT: Australian Early Childhood Association.

Mac Naughton, G., Mortimer, J. and Parish, K. (1986). *Working Together: Guidelines for Good Practice*. London: Greater London Council.

Mawson, B. (1995). The Construction of Gender in the Kindergarten. Minor Masters thesis, University of Tasmania.

Morrison, G. (1995). *Early Childhood Education Today* (6th ed.). New Jersey: Merrill.

Office of Preschool and Child Care (1991). *Early Childhood Curriculum Guidelines for Children 3–5 years of age*. Melbourne: Office of Preschool and Child Care.

Perritt, R. (1988). *Girls and Boys: An Australian Early Childhood Association Resource Booklet*. Watson, ACT: Australian Early Childhood Association.

Spodek, B. and Saracho, O. (1994). *Right from the Start: Teaching Children Ages Three to Eight*. Boston: Allyn and Bacon.

Walkerdine, V. (1990). *Schoolgirl Fictions*. London: Verso Books.

Wangman, N. and Wagner, S. (1977). *Choices: Learning about Sex Roles*. Minneapolis: Jenny Publishing Co.

Weedon, C. (1987). *Feminist Practice and Poststructualist Theory*. Oxford: Basil Blackwell.

Weiler, K. (1988). *Women Teaching for Change: Gender, Class and Power*. Massachusetts: Bergin and Garvey Publishers, Inc.

Women's Action Alliance (1980). *Maximising Young Children's Potential: A Non-sexist Manual for Early Childhood Trainers*. Newtown, Mass: WEEA Publishing Centre.

Chapter 10

The serious and playful work of gender

Talk and social order in a preschool classroom

Susan Danby

This chapter reports some observations made of the social interactions of girls and boys, aged 3 to 5 years, in play situations in a preschool[1] classroom of a childcare centre. It provides an alternate framework for early childhood educators to become aware of how preschool children construct their gendered social organisations. As girls and boys organise and build their social worlds of play through their talk-in-interaction, they are building their social orders. In this chapter, an analysis of one episode of children's play has, as its focus, the methods that some girls and boys use in their talk and activity to make sense of their everyday interactions. The analysis of play shows the children's real life work of constructing and maintaining gendered social orders in their lived everyday worlds. A close reading of the transcript of an episode illustrates how two girls turn the boys' masculine practices of ritualised threats into a performance. By so doing, they show that while they know the masculine discourse, and can perform it themselves, they do not actually 'own' it in the way that the boys do. In this way, gender is established not as a social identity but as a dynamic practice that is ongoing, built by relational encounters and shaped by the collective performances of the participants.

DEFINING PLAY AS THE WORK OF CHILDHOOD

Early childhood pedagogy posits a particular view of play that is described as difficult to define but easy to recognise through the numerous characteristics attributed to it. For example, Garvey (1990, p. 4) defines play as having five major characteristics:

1. play is enjoyable and positively valued by the player;
2. play has intrinsic motivations with no extrinsic goals;
3. play is spontaneous and voluntary;
4. play involves active engagement; and
5. play has systematic relations to what is not play.

Garvey (1990, p. 5) points out that this relationship of play to what is not play is what motivates research to specify the links 'with creativity, problem-solving, language learning, the development of social roles, and a number of other cognitive and social phenomena.'

Garvey's (1990) definition of play is widely accepted within traditional early childhood pedagogy (Piscitelli, 1992). An acceptance of this definition constructs a version of childhood that proposes that play is an enjoyable time in a young child's life, but also crucial for developing socialisation, cognitive and other abilities. This notion of play, which has been appropriated by early childhood educators, becomes the vehicle for 'learning' discourses, described within mainstream early childhood literature as 'developmentally appropriate practice' (Bredekamp, 1987). Within this perspective, imagination and creativity derive from play opportunities (Mann, 1996). Indeed, play is conceived as central to early childhood curriculum (Feeney, Christensen and Moravcik, 1991; Scales, Almy, Nicolopoulou and Ervin-Tripp, 1991; Spodek and Saracho, 1994).

This insistence on play contrasts with a pedagogic method known as an 'academic approach.' This approach limits the provision of resources and choice of activities (National Childcare Accreditation Council, 1993), as children are expected to engage in discrete learning tasks such as memorising facts or acquiring skills out of context (see, for example, Kessler, 1992; Wien, 1995). These types of activities are deemed inappropriate by mainstream early childhood pedagogy (Bredekamp, 1987; Koralek, Colker and Dodge, 1993). Against this background, play has always been regarded by early childhood educators as the preferred form of activity.

THE WORK OF CONSTRUCTING SOCIAL ORDERS

Each theory of childhood 'constitutes' or 'constructs' the child in particular ways (Baker, 1998; Jenks, 1982/92). Within contemporary Western culture, childhood is seen as a natural category of life belonging to a particular group known as 'children.' Within this naturalised category of childhood, particular activities are ascribed as belonging to this category (Atkinson, 1980; Jenks, 1982/92). Play is one such activity. So is believing in Santa Claus. If children play, believe in Santa Claus and do other 'natural' activities of childhood, they are said by parents, teachers and other adults to be participating in their appropriate stage-of-life categories (Atkinson, 1980). If, however, an adult participates in the same way, the adult is said to be acting like a child or 'childish.' Within this view of childhood, childhood is a sequence of developmental stages. Further, children are seen as incomplete versions of adults, but working towards future fulfilment (Atkinson, 1980). This conception of 'childhood' emphasises '*not ... what children are*, but ... *what they are not*' (Oakley, 1994, p. 23).

This chapter presents an alternative view and argues that play constitutes the real here-and-now social worlds for children. The focus is on analysing not how children play in preparation for future development, but how they work to organise and make sense of their day-to-day, moment-to-moment everyday social worlds. In their play, children encounter the everyday work of building social orders. This approach views children as competent players in their social worlds, in contrast with the traditional view that sees children as semi-formed or incomplete adults; or as Speier (1976) puts it, 'precompetent.' Denzin (1982/92, p. 192) clearly describes the work of young children:

> When they are left on their own, young children do not play, they work at constructing social orders. 'Play' is a fiction from the adult world. Children's work involves such serious matters as developing languages for communications; defining and processing deviance; and construction rules of entry and exit into emergent social groups. Children see these as serious concerns and often make a clear distinction between their play and their work. This fact is best grasped by entering those situations where children are naturally thrown together and forced to take account of one another.

By acknowledging the social orders of children, social orders of adults can also be identified. Speier (1976, p. 99) argues that the social orders of adults and children can be likened to the relations of colonisation. As with colonisation, there are two cultures (adults and children) in contact with each other, with one culture having the administrative management of the other. A colonial administrator seeks to bring the native culture within the rationality of the 'higher' order, while recognising difference from that order. The teacher's involvement can be likened to that of a 'colonial administrator,' whose duty is successfully to manage 'the native culture.' The children, the other culture, do their own membership work using play practices to build and maintain their social order. Children operate to produce their own social worlds within the social spaces created by adults (Gracey, 1972; Kessler, 1992). Such play outside the vision of the teacher has also been outside the vision of conventional developmental approaches to early childhood pedagogy.

CONSTRUCTING GENDERED SOCIAL ORDERS: RITUALS AND THE DISCOURSE OF HEGEMONIC MASCULINITY

Davies (1989) proposes that the work of childhood is the work that every child does to establish gendered practices and identities. She writes,

> Each child must get its gender right, not only for itself to be seen as normal and acceptable within the terms of the culture, but it must get it right for others who will be interpreting themselves in relations to it as

> other. To the extent that it is a competent member of society, it can be seen to be competently constructing the gendered world, achieving the practices, the ways of knowing and of being that make sense within the narrative/interactive structures of the society it lives in.
>
> (Davies, 1989, p. 20)

Thus the work of the members of the classroom, as members of culture, is to construct and shape gendered practices. This perspective does not fit within the conventional early childhood paradigm that views play as fun and as having no external goals. Instead, this is real-life work, with real-life consequences if children do not 'get it right.'

Traditional early childhood pedagogy posits play either as an ungendered phenomenon or as a manifestation of biological sex differences (Cook-Gumperz, 1992; Davies, 1989). This perspective sees the gendered ways in which children construct their worlds as a natural consequence of biological determination. Just as the categories of 'child' and 'adult' have come to be seen as the 'natural' categories of a lifetime (Atkinson, 1980), acting as male or female has also come to be seen as 'natural' (Davies, 1989). Yet children's learning cannot be fully discussed without understanding that gender (the social – not biological – construction of being masculine or feminine) is an essential organising element of all children's learning (Davies, 1989; Mac Naughton, 1995). As Oakley (1994, p. 22) points out, 'attention to gender has an important role to play in the "denaturalizing" of the phenomenon of childhood.'

In play situations, the very serious work of constructing social order (Denzin, 1982/92; Goodwin, 1985, 1990) is finely attuned to a recognition that there is more than one social order to manage: gender is one type of social order; age is another. As the children play, girls and boys work on each other to build and shape their gendered social orders. As recent studies illustrate, even before school-age, girls and boys already show understandings of gendered social orders. For example, girls and boys use the structural features of talk and action differently, with boys' interactions appearing to be more highly aggravated, with more physical action and contact, than that of girls (Sachs, 1987; Sheldon, 1990, 1992, 1996).

This chapter views play as children's serious real-life work of constructing and shaping gender. The episode of play discussed later shows that gender is not an established social identity but a dynamic practice built and shaped by ongoing interactions. These encounters are bound by the collective performances of the participants.

In previous analyses of episodes involving boys' and girls' groups, I showed how gendered social orders are brought into being by the children's strategic and pragmatic use of talk and action (Danby, 1995, 1996; Danby and Baker, 1998). Analysis of talk and action shows a group of boys constructing and shaping their local hegemonic version of masculinity in the block area (Danby, 1995). Hegemonic masculinity (Connell, 1995, 1996) is what I have called the ritualised practices of the older boys in block area. A highly scripted ritual of terror is used by the older boys to initiate the younger boys into their powerful social order of the block area. Close analysis of the boys' episodes described a detailed procedure, a ritual faithfully followed. The ritualised practice (as identified and practised in this particular preschool room) has nine phases which are identified in Table 10.1. Alongside each phase is a brief description of the interactions that occurred during that phase in one particular episode that started with Connell and John using large blocks to make a road. Colin and David were nearby. In this instance, John acted as David's apprentice to display their hegemonic masculinity.

The local ritual acts as a rite of passage to signal the transition from newcomer to participating masculine member of the block area. Both Garvey (1990), in her work on spontaneous play, and Thorne (1993), in her work on gender play, saw rituals as defined by a repetitious predictable performance. Garvey (1990, p. 111) defines 'ritual' as a feature of

Table 10.1 The local ritual of hegemonic masculinity: nine phases

Phase 1	'Go away': protection of interactive space	John protects his play space from Connell by telling him to 'go.'
Phase 2	Calling on reinforcements or 'the cavalry' arrives	David, who is nearby, aligns himself with John.
Phase 3	Resistance: verbal or physical	Connell resists David's and John's attempts to exclude him.
Phase 4	Call on discourse of strength/size	David and John display through their talk and action that they are big and strong.
Phase 5	'Bash you': threats of violence	David issues violent physical threats to Connell.
Phase 6	Enter the apprentices	John follows David's lead as they jointly issue direct threats of violence and call on figures of authority (e.g. police).
Phase 7	The climax: repetition of sound and close physical proximity	David uses a combination of loud vocal noises and physical action.
Phase 8	The cry for help	Connell cries.
Phase 9	The arrival of the teacher	The teacher enters and asks David about the problem.

> spontaneous play ... based on any resource: motion, object play, language, social conventions.... A ritual, then, is defined not by its content or by the resource it builds on, but by its distinctive form: controlled repetition. The nature of the control is generally rhythmic, and the behaviour takes on a predictable regularity of tempo.

This special form of play requires participants to understand how to continue this particular type of interaction which needs no new views or subject matter to be introduced (Garvey, 1990).

What is highlighted here is how two girls take up and use aspects of the boys' ritualised discourse of hegemonic masculinity as part of their own game. While they use only some elements of some phases, they show that they can appropriate the boys' pattern of play. In the video data collected for this study, this episode is the only example located so far where the girls engage in this type of talk, and it is this out-of-the-ordinary talk that first drew me to this episode of play. As I had not seen girls using ritualised threats of power in the same way that I had observed the boys doing, I became curious and began to explore the data more closely.

METHODOLOGY AND PROCEDURES

The study

Data reported in this chapter are part of a larger study exploring how children, as members of a preschool childcare room, produce their everyday interactions, displaying to each other their locally accomplished order, that is, their everyday work of making sense of their interactional encounters. This study utilises the methodological approaches of applied ethnomethodology (Garfinkel, 1967) and conversation analysis (Psathas, 1995; Sacks, 1974, 1984, 1992). This requires paying close and detailed attention to the production of locally accomplished order (Silverman, 1994b). The 'how' of the talk and action reveal 'the practices by which social order is accomplished' (Silverman, 1994b, p. 180). The focus is explicating sequences of talk and interaction by the children in their everyday interactions in the preschool room. Speier (1982/92, p. 184) describes this approach as reducing the context for the study 'to interactional units of *occasioned and situated activity.*' Sequences of interactions during play times are analysed to illustrate how the children build their talk and action together to make sense of their social orders.

The setting

The setting is a preschool room in a childcare centre in an Australian inner city area. The children are aged between 3 and 5 years. On any day, there are two teachers and up to sixteen children in the preschool room.

Method of data collection

Video data focused on children participating in their everyday play activities in the preschool room of a childcare centre. These activities occurred in a period of play known as 'free play,' where a number of learning opportunities, activities and play materials are available from which the children self-select. Children may elect to play with others or play alone. Two teachers organise and manage this play environment by providing resources to encourage such play. In addition, they may participate in the children's self-initiated play activities to extend learning through interactive questions and comments. Another important role is to mediate to settle disputes. As the focus of this study is children's construction of their social orders in play activities, my purpose was to collect and analyse video data of the children interacting in these free play activities.

I walked around the preschool room with a small video camera held at my waist, looking to video interactions among the children. I began with 'unmotivated looking' (Psathas, 1995). Sampling was not used to develop collections of instances; because the theorising is not done in advance, categories cannot be assembled in advance. Use of sampling by predetermined categories of activity privilege adult constructions about children's social order and does not allow for a perspective that lets the talk and action of the children be examined for the categorisations pertinent to their everyday practices.

The analysis is one account of this episode and, as Reid, Kamler, Simpson and MacLean (1996) found, the researcher's positioning within particular discourses influences how she represents classroom life in analysis.[2]

THE EPISODE

What makes this episode stand out is that the girls' actions and talk differ from their typical talk and action of the classroom, at least as I have it on videotape. At first, I was not sure what my analysis would reveal, but I was curious to explore the episode in more detail.[3] The girls' atypical talk-in-interaction would be described by Heritage (1984) and Silverman (1985, 1994a) as a departure from the norm, a deviance, thus making it visible and opening it up for scrutiny. And as Jayyusi (1991, p. 238) states, deviations 'reconstitute and make the "norm", the "ordinary", visible *as just that.*'

The episode involves John, one of the block area boys who, in a previous interaction, acted as David's apprentice in initiating Connell, a younger boy, into the masculine practices of block area. In this episode, John joins Amelia and Portia at the drawing table. The significance of this episode is that it illustrates how Amelia and Portia show that they know the boys' hegemonic discourse of masculinity. They appropriate the discourse and turn it into a game, which they display, with great excitement and laughter, to John, the researcher, the teacher and others in the classroom.

The episode begins when John appears to comment unfavourably on the drawings of Amelia and Portia. The girls use this opportunity to launch into a game using the same ritual pattern of threats that the boys use in their block area interactions. The transcript[4,5] is first presented in full, and later, extracts are analysed more closely. The transcript has been divided into subheadings that are taken up later in the analysis.

Approximately 10.30 a.m.

Portia and Amelia have been drawing at a small rectangular table with A4-sized paper and markers in a container in the middle of the table. Portia is at one end, and Amelia is sitting on her right-hand side. John sits down at the other end of the table facing Portia and starts drawing. A teacher, Mary, is sitting at a nearby table with Connell. I am standing close to the table where the three children are drawing.

Portia and Amelia are both 4 years old and have been together in this preschool room for over a year while John, who is almost 4 years old, has been there for nearly a year. This episode occurs the day after John acts as David's apprentice to teach Connell the local masculine practices of block area.

[The Game Begins]

1	John	( )
2	Amelia	((to Portia)) You know (1.0) / /you know
3	Portia	You don't say Ah-ah-our DRAWINGS a SCRIBBLE.
4	Amelia	You know? ((to Portia)) ( ) (2.0)
5	Portia	((to Amelia)) I don't know how to play this game ((in a playful squeaky voice, looks sideways briefly at researcher))
6	Researcher	/ /Ahh
7	Amelia	because (you do so) ((Amelia glances at John and then leans close to Portia, talking to her while continuing to draw.))
8	Portia	((Portia laughs in a high pitched squeal.))

[*Visiting the discourse of hegemonic masculinity*]

9	Amelia	((Amelia looks up at the researcher, then speaks quietly to Portia)) We're going to ( ) we're going to policeman to get John.
10	Portia	((to Amelia)) We're going to ( ) John in in jail
11	Amelia	((squeals with delight))

12	John	I am not! If you don't be quiet, I'll spread my arms out (0.5) every ( ) on your ey:es, on your mouth ((looks towards Amelia))
13	Amelia	(You/We) won't mind it
14	Portia	M- (Or) (0.5) ((wiping her face with hands)) And (0.5) we'll scrub it all off ((looks at John, and makes wiping motions over her face and chest with her hands))
15	John	(2.0) How?
16	Portia	We can scrub it all off soap and daddy we can scrub it all off, see?
17	John	(3.0) Are you my ( ) maybe I will get the teacher
18	Amelia	You know ((looks at John)) my dad will take you to th- to the hospital ((Amelia and Portia laugh; they both look at each other and then at the researcher))
19		(2.0)
20	Portia	And my mum will takes John to the 'ospital agai::n! ((Amelia and Portia laugh; Amelia looks at John))
21	Amelia	((looks briefly at John and then turns to Portia)) And she will=
22	Portia	=And John will get (0.5) we'll take him to the 'ospital! ((squeals and laughs with delight))
23	Amelia	And and //and
24	Portia	And the doctor won't let him OU:::T ((laughs loudly and gleefully))
25	John	((°will so°) (1.0) You kno::w (0.5), if you won't be quiet, I'll get the teacher and then she'll be really angry
26		(2.0)
27	Portia	((very quietly, as if to self)) (°No, she won't°)
28	Amelia	(No, she won't)
29	John	(Yes, she will)
30	Portia	(No, she won't) ((looking down and drawing))

[*Risky Business – Power Plays: Calling in the teacher*]

31	John	((loudly to the teacher, Mary, who is nearby, pointing towards Portia and Amelia)) They're fighting with me.
32	Teacher	Are they?
33	John	Yeah
34	Teacher	(1.0) Is there a problem? (1.0) Hey?
35		((Portia shakes her head confidently at the teacher as Amelia looks towards Portia; Amelia looks towards John.)) (4.0)
36	Portia	((to Amelia and John)) I told them (0.5) there's not a pro:b(.)lem ((laughing loudly as she leans back in her chair)) ( ) ((Amelia looks towards John.))

37	Amelia	((to Portia)) °And I'm making (I'm making a birthday cake birthday cake °) ((John stands up and puts the lid on the felt pen.))
38	Portia	An-and I'm going to draw the (0.5) the jail! O::o-o::o
39	John	(6.00) ((John is standing using the felt pens.))
40	Portia	See, here's the jail. ((as if talking to herself))
41		(2.0)
42	Amelia	See that jail
43	Portia	See those stripes? ((as if talking to herself))
44	Amelia	I'm going to do one.
45	John	((stands up and takes his drawing to the teacher, Mary, nearby)) Look.
46	Teacher	Show me John. That looks wonderful. Would you like to hang it up? ((John shakes his head while waving his drawing in the air and then gives it to the teacher before walking away.))
47	Portia	((singing to herself)) P.P.P.
48	Amelia	((turning towards the teacher)) Mary, you write my name?
49	Teacher	//Yes, you bring it over here.
50	Portia	((singing)) Amelia And then the police::man says ( ) yeah yeah yeah yeah yeah ((in a singing voice))
51		((Amelia stands up))
52	Portia	Draw on the back Amelia
53	Amelia	((Amelia takes her drawing to the teacher))
54	Teacher	Would you like me to write what it is Amelia?
55		(4.0)
56	John	((John goes to Amelia with the drawing board)) ( )
57	Amelia	((shakes her head)) No:o
58	John	Yeah
59	Amelia	((shakes her head)) No ((John drops the board and picks it up, Amelia watches))

[*Risky Business–Power Plays: Taking the game to the teacher*]

60	Portia	((brings her drawing over to the teacher, stepping over John picking up the drawing board)) Mine's a jai-, mine's a mummy, that's a jail ((turning her drawing over and quickly showing Connell who is sitting at the table; Connell looks carefully.)) right ((turns towards the teacher))
61	Teacher	A jail! ((a teacher from next door walks past with a

		child)) Bye ( ) ((to passing teacher; and then talks to Portia)) ( ) ((hands Amelia's drawing to Portia))
62	Portia	( ) there's a picture for ( ) ((Portia returns to the table and gives Amelia her drawing.)) (Here) Amelia ((Portia walks away from the table.))
63	Amelia	((Amelia turns around in her chair to look at Portia))
64	John	((John and Portia are off camera)) Amelia (3.0) ((then louder)) Amelia are we playing ((Amelia then turns the other way to look behind where she is sitting))
65	Portia	((Portia now has the drawing board)) I want to play with that ((placing it on the table))
66	John	((There is a book on Portia's chair. John grabs it and Portia grabs it back from him.)) No you can't have ( ) my book. ((John leaves the area and walks to the block area. Portia places the book behind her on the seat.))

A SENSE OF PERFORMANCE

A sense of performance is evident throughout this episode, with Portia's talk and action particularly enacted with a sense of display for an audience. In this instance, I appear to be the silent overhearing audience (Heritage, 1985) but my presence becomes a critical aspect of what is to come. The performance begins when Amelia and Portia launch into a game of pretence, imagining and naming all the possible things they could do to John. I overhear their performance, and the teacher and another child sitting at a nearby table are also within earshot. Sawyer (1997, p. xix) describes pretend play as a form of improvisational performance genre. Features of this genre include:

> (a) there is no script, thus they are created in the moment; (b) nonetheless, there are loose outlines of structure that guide the performance . . .; (c) they are collective – no one person decides what will happen. Because the performance is collective, each performer's acts are influenced by the others'. . . . Because group improvisational genres are collective and unscripted, improvisational creativity is a collective social process.

The performances by Amelia and Portia could certainly be described as fitting within this genre. There is no script, yet they use a structure of talk that involves aspects of what I have earlier identified as a discourse of hegemonic masculinity (Danby, 1995). The nature of the game also attests to the collectivity of the social process. John could choose not to participate, yet he does. All three participate collectively, although it seems that John's role is not in performance mode. His talk and action appear to move between that of pretence and 'reality analysis' (Hester and Francis, 1997).

THE GAME BEGINS

Amelia begins a game (the game that turns out to be directed towards John) with 'You know' in turn 2 and tries again in turn 4. Known as a preliminary, this type of utterance serves to preface or 'lead up to' the 'the projected action' (Schegloff, 1980). Here, Amelia uses it to signal her plans for what is to come. The game – which I come to see as a foray across the gender border – is about to begin.

1	John	( )
→ 2	Amelia	((to Portia)) You know (1.0) / /you know
3	Portia	You don't say Ah-ah-our DRAWINGS a SCRIBBLE.
→ 4	Amelia	You know? ((to Portia)) ( ) (2.0)
→ 5	Portia	((to Amelia)) I don't know how to play this game ((in a playful squeaky voice, looks sideways briefly at researcher))

Amelia's use of 'you know' in this episode has a different intent to how young children generally use this type of preliminary (e.g. 'you know what?') with adults. Children have restricted talking rights (Sacks, 1974); that is, they have 'a right to begin, to make a first statement and not much more' (Sacks, 1974, p. 231). Consequently, children use this type of question as a form of beginning with adults to prompt a request to proceed. The adult in saying 'what?' then gives explicit permission for the child to talk. In other contexts where there are no limited speaking rights, the speaker's use of the preliminary utterance 'you know. . .' typically suggests that the speaker supposes that the recipient knows about the referent (e.g. people, things, places) to be mentioned (Schegloff, 1980). The use of 'you know' in this episode would then suggest that Amelia supposes that Portia knows about what is to come, in this case, a game.

Turns 4 and 5 could be heard as an 'adjacency pair' (Schegloff and Sacks, 1974), that is, there is a 'sequence of two utterances . . . produced by two different speakers . . . [and] tied, so that a first part requires a second part (or range of second parts)' (Heritage, 1984, p. 246). The use of a preliminary such as 'you know' affords the recipient an opportunity to grasp the intention of the reference (Schegloff, 1980). Amelia's use of the preliminary 'you know' (turn 4) lets Portia claim that she doesn't know how to play the game (turn 5), but Portia (turn 5) also identifies the reference as 'a game,' and further, as 'this game.' Sacks (1992, p. 476) asks, 'what makes something a game' and this question can also be asked of this episode. What is the interactional force of Portia referring to her and Amelia's intended actions as a 'game'?

Portia's use of a playful squeaky voice suggests that she does know the game but is signalling something else. Sheldon (1996, p. 67) discusses how girls, in pretend play, often use 'a high-pitched falsetto voice . . . [which] blurs the distinction between oneself, the child, and one's character or role . . . tak[ing] some of the responsibility away from the child for what she is saying.' Perhaps Portia's animated voice is for a similar purpose, suggesting that the projected action is in pretend mode, and consequently does not have the same implications as if she were *really* saying it. The game, then, is begun.

Portia's initial rejection of Amelia's suggestion is based on the grounds of 'inability' (after Labov and Fanshel in Heritage, 1984, p. 271). These grounds seem more for my benefit than Amelia's. While speaking from within the knowledge of the game, Portia's disavowal of it (while looking at me) suggests that she is very aware of my presence and that possibly her comment is intended for me as well as for Amelia. This seems possible because I actually respond to Portia (turn 6).

4	Amelia	*You know*? ((to Portia)) ( ) (2.0)
→ 5	Portia	((to Amelia)) I don't know how to play this game ((in a playful squeaky voice, looks sideways briefly at researcher))
→ 6	Researcher	/ / Ahh
→ 7	Amelia	because (you do so) ((Amelia glances at John and then leans close to Portia, talking to her while continuing to draw.))
8	Portia	((Portia laughs in a high pitched squeal.))

Portia's demurral could be heard by Amelia as hesitancy and as 'prefatory to rejection' (Heritage, 1984, p. 274), so Amelia quickly asserts that Portia does know how to play the game (turn 7). Portia acknowledges this by laughing in a high pitched squeal of delight (turn 8). Amelia then launches into the game without further preliminaries (turn 9), suggesting that she does not take Portia's claim seriously. Portia (turn 10) returns this confidence by continuing in the same pattern, signalling that she does in fact know exactly how to play this game. Both turns involve what they will do to John.

7	Amelia	because (you do so) ((Amelia glances at John and then leans close to Portia, talking to her while continuing to draw.))
8	Portia	((Portia laughs in a high pitched squeal.))
→ 9	Amelia	((Amelia looks up at the researcher, then speaks quietly to Portia)) We're going to ( ) we're going to policeman to get John.
→ 10	Portia	((to Amelia)) We're going to ( ) John in in jail
11	Amelia	((squeals with delight))

Amelia's squeal of delight (turn 11) shows her appreciation of being understood and also Portia's involvement in the game. Portia and Amelia share a common world of meaning as they work together to produce their game. It is one of pretence and begins with the girls saying that they will call a policeman to put John in jail. Such a 'linked action' becomes 'the basic building blocks of intersubjectivity' (Heritage, 1984, p. 256).

In early childhood education literature, there are a number of accounts describing how boys traditionally inhabit the block area (Grieshaber, 1986; Mac Naughton, 1994) whereas the girls reside in other areas such as homecorner or the table areas of collage, drawing and painting (Paley, 1984), suggesting that each group 'owns' the respective areas. From Portia's response to John (turn 3), it is possible to infer that John has made a derogatory remark about the girl's drawings, calling them scribbles. John's allegation inflames the girls to action. Portia's highly charged response shows this. This response is hearable as a challenge: Portia's retort, 'You don't say...,' is heard as a response to a dare from John.

1	John	( )
2	Amelia	((to Portia)) You know (1.0) //you know
→ 3	Portia	You don't say Ah-ah-our DRAWINGS a SCRIBBLE.

Portia's come-back is similar to that of the older boys in their episodes, where a challenge by Connell, the younger boy, triggers a quick and emotive response from David:

Transcript 17/1/94/45.30

12	Connell	And I'm bigger
13	David	No we'll just BASH YOU RIGHT off the ( ) ((David swings fists; Connell turns to look at David))
14	John	((pointing towards Connell)) ( ) in jail
15	David	(Well)=
16	Connell	=No
17	David	Yes, (well) you just (we just) if you punch John, well I'll just THROW you ((making throwing movements)) through that television (1.0) that's standing right over there.
18	John	(3.0) And then I'll kick ya ((Connell looks at John))
19	David	((now beside Connell)) And I'll kick you right through the//(window)
20	John	((leans towards Connell)) And then I'll get Batman.

The girls' use of a similar type of ritualised and threatening play to that I had observed the boys using puzzled me. Can this be called an older boys' practice if I show older girls also using the same discourse? Have the girls learned it from the boys? Alternatively, the boys may have learned it from the girls. Is it age (and not gender) related?

VISITING THE DISCOURSE OF HEGEMONIC MASCULINITY

Using Jayyusi's (1984) work on moral categorisation and order, and Sharrock's (1974) work on collectivities and 'ownership' of a corpus of knowledge, I present one way to describe and analyse the interactions of the girls in this episode. Sharrock (1974), in explaining his notion of 'ownership' of a corpus of knowledge, uses the example of Baka medicine. By calling the medicine 'Baka medicine,' the implication is that the Baka people not only have a knowledge of this particular type of medicine, but that they claim ownership of it (or others infer ownership of this knowledge upon them). Others may practise this type of knowledge but they are not said to 'own' it because in order to own it, collectivities would have to adopt and practise this 'corpus of knowledge.' Using these understandings about 'ownership' of knowledge, I now apply them to the episode for analysis here.

For the older boys, their knowledge is understanding and practising the local masculine hegemonic practices. Yet this episode shows that some girls practise some elements. I argue that while they may practise elements, they are not in a position to 'own' it, as they appear not to be consistent practitioners. A few girls practising occasionally does not constitute 'ownership;' a collectivity of girls would have to do this more regularly. Taking this discussion of ownership into the analysis, we have some clues about the above suppositions. The girls demonstrate ways to suggest that they are visiting the discourse of hegemonic masculinity.

John appears to have initiated the interaction by his comment (unheard on the video recording), with Portia and Amelia hearing and responding to this as a challenge. Amelia (turn 4) proposes a planned action (unheard on the video recording) which Portia calls a 'game' (turn 5).

4	Amelia	You know? ((to Portia)) ( ) (2.0)
→ 5	Portia	((to Amelia)) I don't know how to play this game ((in a playful squeaky voice, looks sideways briefly at researcher))
6	Researcher	//Ahh
7	Amelia	because (you do so) ((Amelia glances at John and then leans close to Portia, talking to her while continuing to draw.))
8	Portia	((Portia laughs in a high pitched squeal.))

In this episode, Portia and Amelia enter into a game of their choosing. They use ritualised threats of police and jails.

→ 9 Amelia ((Amelia looks up at the researcher, then speaks quietly to Portia)) We're going to ( ) we're going to policeman to get John.
→ 10 Portia ((to Amelia)) We're going to ( ) John in in jail

These threats involving police and jails are also evident in the older boys' talk and action, as illustrated by the following extract from one of the boys' episodes:

Transcript 17/1/94/45.30

→ 22 John ((to David)) And I'll get the police ((Connell looks at John and then the floor))
23 David And all the ( ) will come out
→ 24 John And I'll and I'll piss on 'im ((points to Connell) and and then the police will (get) it
→ 25 David Yeah, and then you'll ((points to Connell)) be going to jail. Rmmp Rmmp, //Rmmp ((David starts to make car noises, claps hands close to Connell's face, jumping up and down, making play sounds that are high and song-like.))

Despite the similarity of the threats described earlier as the discourse of hegemonic masculinity, the girls' method of delivery is different to that of the boys. The girls do not draw upon the discourse of hegemonic masculinity as work, but as a game. Portia has already signalled that their entry is a game (turn 5). The beginning of the game brings laughter, a distance. The girls are not 'living' the work of hegemonic masculinity but just visiting it. For the boys, however, the discourse is serious; the boys did not refer to their practices as a game; nor did the play involve laughter.

Sacks (1992) uses the term 'imitation' to describe how a child may engage in the activity of a particular category but is still not seen to be a member of that category. For example, one girl that I know follows closely the baseball series and always dresses in a cap and shorts. She has been described as a tomboy, as she 'acts like' or imitates the interests of a boy. This is not suggesting that she is a boy, but that she is copying the actions and display of a boy. She does not belong to the category of 'boy;' instead, she could be described as imitating or visiting the category of 'boy.' With imitation, Sacks suggests, 'no matter how many times one does the activity, no matter how well one does it, it's never a possession; it's always borrowed' (Sacks, 1992 vol. 1, p. 481). Again, in the context of the episode being analysed in this chapter, the girls' talk and actions could be said to be that of imitating or borrowing the boys' talk of hegemonic masculinity, but not really owning it.

John's response, provoked by the girls' talk of police and jails, is highly charged. His quick and loud denial, followed by threats to the girls, appears out of all proportion to the girls' comments about policemen and jails, suggesting that their comments had quite an impact. The girls' foray into the hegemonic masculine discourse appears to have incited John to move into the girls' game, perhaps to defend his position and ownership of the masculine discourse.

10	Portia	((to Amelia)) We're going to ( ) John in in jail
11	Amelia	((squeals with delight))
→ 12	John	I am not! If you don't be quiet, I'll spread my arms out (0.5) every ( ) on your ey:es, on your mouth ((looks towards Amelia))

John has the initial turn (turn 1), but then he does not talk again until turn 12. Amelia and Portia use the interim turns to talk about John, but not to him. As they do this, Amelia glances at John (turn 7) but there appears to be no eye contact. By talking about John in his own presence, they are constituting him as less than a full player in their game. He does not have equal status in the conversation (Payne and Ridge, 1985; Speier, 1982/92). The girls' use of the plural pronoun *we* (turns 9 and 10) also suggests their joint actions and togetherness, while at the same time excluding John (Watson, 1987). The use of *we* and the talking about John (and not to him) is designed for his hearing but also designed to exclude him from their talk. It is a way to exclude John from *their game*, but not *the game*.

9	Amelia	((Amelia looks up at the researcher, then speaks quietly to Portia)) We're going to ( ) we're going to policeman to get John.
10	Portia	((to Amelia)) We're going to ( ) John in in jail

After the girls' talk of police and jails, John's retort is quick and strong and involves a threat (turn 12). The girls' response is seemingly unconcerned (turns 13 and 14).

12	John	I am not! If you don't be quiet, I'll spread my arms out (0.5) every ( ) on your ey:es, on your mouth ((looks towards Amelia))
13	Amelia	(You/We) won't mind it
14	Portia	M- (Or) (0.5) ((wiping her face with hands)) And (0.5) we'll scrub it all off ((looks at John, and makes wiping motions over her face and chest with her hands))
15	John	(2.0) How?
16	Portia	We can scrub it all off soap and daddy we can scrub it all off, see?
17	John	(3.0) Are you my ( ) maybe I will get the teacher

The girls' responses silence John. After a two second silence, John asks

'How?' (turn 15). He steps out of the pretend frame here to ask what appears to be a real question. Using Sack's work on Class I and Class II rules, my analysis proposes that John wants to find out whether the consequences of his threats are 'a natural fact of life' (Sacks, 1989, p. 327) or whether the consequences are something that he can 'get away with.'

Sacks (1989) provides examples to illustrate:

> A prototype of Class I is, 'Don't stick your hand on the stove.' Prototype of Class II is 'Honor thy father and mother' . . . With respect to an adult's conception of reality we would say that these two are different, in that for Class I the consequences, whatever they are, naturally flow from the act done. If you stick your hand in the fire, you get burned. Whereas for Class II, that's not so. For a lot of things that you do that are said to be wrong or harmful, somebody has to do something to you for you to get the negative consequence. You can 'get away with' things of the Class II sort.
>
> (Sacks, 1989, p. 327)

Sacks (1989) continues, acknowledging that adults do not usually differentiate between the types of rules and so children have to work out for themselves as to whether the rule is Class I or Class II. They have to find out 'case by case . . . checking out the causal properties of the world as though they were normative properties in the sense that Class II rules are' (Sacks, 1989).

It seems that what John is doing is trying to work out whether his threats have real-life consequences, or whether the girls' rejection of his threat is valid. This type of 'reality analysis' (Hester and Francis, 1997) has John trying to determine if their threats are part of the game or whether they were issued outside the game. With this type of banter used by the older boys in block area, threats do have real-life consequences, as they form the work of constructing hegemonic masculinity. But with the girls, the banter appears to have different rules. John does not seem sure of what they are and his question seems to signify this. Uncertainty occurs as he tries to work out what is meant by the talk and actions of the girls. John's confusion appears to depict what can happen when girls and boys foray across the border from one gendered social order to another: there can be confusion about which rules operate, and how, at the gender crossing. After a three second pause, he considers two possibilities in turn 17.

16	Portia	We can scrub it all off soap and daddy we can scrub it all off, see?
→ 17	John	(3.0) Are you my ( ) maybe I will get the teacher
18	Amelia	You know ((looks at John)) my dad will take you to th– to the hospital ((Amelia and Portia laugh; they both look at each other and then at the researcher))

The first possibility is his unheard question, which could be one of asking the girls if they are his friend. Children most often use friendship references to gain or refuse entry to play groups or as a form of social control (Corsaro, 1985). John at first appears to be protecting his interactive space, perhaps as a response to the earlier exclusionary talk when the girls talk about him in the third person. He cuts off his question by saying that 'maybe' he will get the teacher. This is the second possibility; his appeal is an attempt to control what the girls were saying. John's use of the modal form *maybe* (Wright, 1989) suggests that John is canvassing a form of social control (the teacher) that is more powerful than his appeal to friendship.

Portia and Amelia ignore John's threat of calling in the teacher and continue to draw upon their own verbal threats of power. Their earlier threats (the policeman, jail) were similar to those of the older boys in block area, but their new threats invoke the categories of dad (turns 16 and 18) and mum (turns 20 and 21) and hospitals and doctors (turns 18, 20, 22, 24). Certainly, themes of domesticity are the categories of play that girls use, and are familiar with, in dramatic play (Paley, 1984; Walkerdine, 1987). Key features of the girls' performance are evident here, particularly those aspects that relate to the structure, flexibility and collective nature of an improvisational performance (Sawyer, 1997). Based upon a structure of hegemonic masculinity, the girls collectively use some of the elements of that discourse, such as threats of police. At the same time, the script is flexible enough to improvise, so that they draw upon familiar categories of play, such as family, for their content.

16	Portia	We can scrub it all off soap and <u>daddy</u> we can <u>scrub</u> it all off, see?
17	John	(3.0) Are you my ( ) maybe I will get the teacher
18	Amelia	You know ((looks at John)) my dad will take you to th- to the hospital ((Amelia and Portia laugh; they both look at each other and then at the researcher))
19		(2.0)
20	Portia	<u>And my mum will takes John to the 'ospital agai::n!</u> ((Amelia and Portia laugh; Amelia looks at John))
→ 21	Amelia	((looks briefly at John and then turns to Portia)) And she will=
22	Portia	=<u>And John will get</u> (0.5) <u>we'll take him to the 'ospital!</u> ((squeals and laughs with delight))
→ 23	Amelia	And and / /and
24	Portia	And the doctor won't let him <u>OU:::T</u> ((laughs loudly and gleefully))

Amelia and Portia continue each other's turns, just as the older boys did in previous episodes. Amelia and Portia work to establish a linked pattern of talk (turns 17–22). This serves to demonstrate their solidarity and intersubjectivity. As Goodwin and Goodwin (1987) found in a study of children's arguing, separate speakers do not interrupt the pattern of talk but serve to preserve it. The girls trust that each will continue the pattern, although this does not always happen. In turns 21 and 23, Amelia begins but Portia finishes each turn (turns 22 and 24). Amelia knows that it is her turn to provide the next threat, but appears to struggle in these turns to provide one. Portia immediately steps in to continue the pattern of threats, although Portia appears to combine the role of doctor with that of jailer. Although Amelia was the one to initiate the game, it is Portia who guides her participation.

The girls are visibly and audibly having fun as they play the game with John. Their threats to John within a pretend frame are produced with delight. Sacks proposes that imitative activities are ones that are done 'mockingly, kiddingly, and the like, in play, . . . more or less explicitly to recognize that in doing them one is making no claim to doing them seriously' (Sacks, 1992, p. 481). Certainly, the girls' playful voices (turn 5), squeals of delight (turn 8) and laughter (turns 22, 24, 36) attest to their joy in this event. This serves to suggest that they see it as a pretend game, that it is not something to take seriously.

At the same time, the work that the girls are doing, that of displaying and performing the discourse of hegemonic masculinity, is serious gender work. They need to get it right in order to display it to maximum effect to John and others nearby. So, while the game is fun, as suggested by the girls' laughter, initiating and maintaining this game could have repurcussions such as the teacher intervening, or other boys joining to side with John, or John successfully up-ending the game so that he would then hold the more powerful position.

John, unlike the girls, is not joining in the laughter. This is indeed a serious matter for him – how to respond to the girls' taunts. At turn 25, he issues another threat. This one is stronger than that of turn 17. Instead of 'maybe' getting the teacher (turn 17), he now says that he will get the teacher if they are not quiet. In addition, he predicts that she will be 'really angry' (turn 25). He does not name the teacher but refers to her by her category. In so doing, he uses a right as a student (to call in the teacher) and invokes the expectation that the teacher would be bound by her category to respond.

24	Portia	And the doctor won't let him <u>OU:::T</u> ((laughs loudly and gleefully))
→ 25	John	((°will so°) (1.0) <u>You kno::w</u> (0.5), if you won't be quiet, I'll get the teacher and then she'll be really angry
26		(2.0)
27	Portia	((very quietly, as if to self)) (°No, she won't°)

RISKY BUSINESS – POWER PLAYS

Classrooms are sites of power and tension where girls and boys test each other and the authority of the teacher to find out which political moves are possible, in particular contexts. This final part of the transcript looks at two power plays occurring. The first is initiated by John, who threatens to call in the teacher to defend his position. The second power play is carried out by Portia, who takes the game to the teacher. Both moves are risky business, as the individual children involved can never be completely sure of what the teacher's actions will be (cf. Waksler, 1991).

Calling in the teacher

Thorne (1993), in her study of elementary school children in playgrounds, found that girls were more likely to call on the authority of the teacher. When boys did, they were ridiculed more by their male peers than girls were when they called in the teacher. In this episode, it is John who asks the teacher to intervene. So while John predicts that she will be 'very angry,' he cannot be sure. The next turns (27–30) have John, Amelia and Portia arguing about this possibility.

25	John	((°will so°) (1.0) You kno::w (0.5), if you won't be quiet, I'll get the teacher and then she'll be really angry
26		(2.0)
27	Portia	((very quietly, as if to self)) (°No, she won't°)
28	Amelia	(No, she won't)
29	John	(Yes, she will)
30	Portia	(No, she won't) ((looking down and drawing))

All of the talk in the episode so far has occurred within the auditory range of the teacher, Mary, who is close enough to hear, although there appears no indication that in fact she has. The pronoun *she* is used to describe what her possible actions may be. They use *she* within her presence as if she were not there. But, finally, in turn 31, John decides to test his hypothesis. He calls in the teacher.

31	John	((loudly to the teacher, Mary, who is nearby, pointing towards Portia and Amelia)) They're fighting with me.
32	Teacher	Are they?
33	John	Yeah
34	Teacher	(1.0) Is there a problem? (1.0) Hey?
35		((Portia shakes her head confidently at the teacher as Amelia looks towards Portia; Amelia looks towards John.)) (4.0)

As this stage, it appears that John calls upon the teacher's intervention as a political move. Maynard (1985, p. 216) writes that children are 'political actors' from an early age. He suggests that children call on teachers to intervene in order to support 'whatever position they have taken during the dispute process'. For John, the teacher's intervention was not what he could have hoped for. She did not become 'very angry' and did not intervene except to ask if there was a problem (turn 34). The teacher's response of asking about a problem is a typical one in early childhood pedagogy (cf. Feeney *et al.*, 1991; Stone, 1990). Portia, however, knows what to do to satisfy the teacher. She shakes her head confidently (turn 35) indicating that there is no problem. The teacher pursues it no further. As an advocate for John, she was not supportive.

→ 34	Teacher	(1.0) Is there a problem? (1.0) Hey?
35		((Portia shakes her head confidently at the teacher as Amelia looks towards Portia; Amelia looks towards John.)) (4.0)
36	Portia	((to Amelia and John)) I told them (0.5) there's not a pro:b(.)lem ((laughing loudly as she leans back in her chair)) ( ) ((Amelia looks towards John.))

'What's the problem?' is a 'marked invitation' to speak (Psathas, 1995), the assumption being that the one who responds to the question either has the problem or has created the problem. Paley (1988) writes that a crying child calls in the teacher and the teachers in this preschool room are no different (Danby and Baker, 1998). The teachers intervene when there is a crying child. As there is no crying child, the teacher does not ask *about* the problem; instead she asks, '*Is* there a problem?' Her question appears one that politically weakens John's accusation. His political stance has not been supported by the teacher as she queries his claim. When the teacher asks, Portia takes the responsibility of responding to the teacher. She confidently shakes her head and then laughingly recounts her version to Amelia and John (turn 36). Portia took the lead earlier in the talk to complete the turns for Amelia, and she takes the initiative here too. By so doing, she shows the others (Amelia, for example) what to do when the teacher intervenes; her account informs the others, who are a silent overhearing audience (Heritage, 1985).

After the teacher's intervention, Amelia changes the talk to that of drawing a birthday cake (turn 37). This appears to be a very safe move. She seems to have moved out of the game performing the discourse of hegemonic masculinity and back into a discourse that could be considered 'proper' talk for preschool children in the classroom. If challenged by the teacher, she is participating in an activity and accompanying talk that would most probably be accepted. John's calling in the teacher may have temporarily silenced Amelia, but not Portia. She continues with the language of the game, again referring to jails (turn 38). After a two second pause, Amelia returns to the game, taking up Portia's lead (turn 42) and she continues the same pattern established by Portia (turn 44).

36	Portia	((to Amelia and John)) I told them (0.5) there's not a pro:b(.)lem ((laughing loudly as she leans back in her chair)) ( ) ((Amelia looks towards John.))
→ 37	Amelia	((to Portia)) °And I'm making (I'm making a birthday cake birthday cake °) ((John stands up and puts the lid on the felt pen.))
→ 38	Portia	An-and I'm going to draw the (0.5) the jail! O::o-o::o
39	John	(6.00) ((John is standing using the felt pens.))
→ 40	Portia	See, here's the jail. ((as if talking to herself))
41		(2.0)
→ 42	Amelia	See that jail
43	Portia	See those stripes? ((as if talking to herself))
44	Amelia	I'm going to do one.

John, in turn 46, takes his drawing to the teacher. Meanwhile, the girls are left alone at the drawing table. Amelia asks the teacher to write her name (turn 48), but Portia continues the policeman theme (turns 50 and 60).

Taking the game to the teacher

Portia now goes one step further and takes the game to the teacher.

45	John	((stands up and takes his drawing to the teacher, Mary, nearby)) Look.
46	Teacher	Show me John. That looks wonderful. Would you like to hang it up? ((John shakes his head while waving his drawing in the air and then gives it to the teacher before walking away.))
47	Portia	((singing to herself)) P.P.P.
48	Amelia	((turning towards the teacher)) Mary, you write my name?
49	Teacher	/ / Yes, you bring it over here.
→ 50	Portia	((singing)) Amelia And then the police::man says ( ) yeah yeah yeah yeah yeah ((in a singing voice))
⋮		
→ 60	Portia	((brings her drawing over to the teacher, stepping over John picking up the drawing board)) Mine's a jai-, mine's a mummy, that's a jail ((turning her drawing over and quickly showing Connell who is sitting at the table; Connell looks carefully)) right ((turns towards the teacher))

61 Teacher A jail! ((a teacher from next door walks past with a child)) Bye ( ) ((to passing teacher; and then talks to Portia)) ( ) ((hands Amelia's drawing to Portia))

In turn 60, when Portia takes her drawing to the teacher, she provides a description of her work. She first appears to call it a jail, but quickly changes her description to mummy, and then back to jail. Connell, who has been sitting next to the teacher, is very interested and looks at Portia's drawing. Portia's actions and talk serve to show the others (Amelia, Connell and John) the power of her game as the teacher accepts her drawing and description of the jail uncritically. Sacks saw games as operating 'under a test of practical efficacy' (Sacks, 1980, p. 324) and Portia has demonstrated the pragmatic worth of the game as a way to foray across gendered borders. In all games, it is getting caught (or not caught) that counts. While Amelia seems aware of this possibility (her drawings becoming a birthday cake), Portia is fearless in her pursuit of the game. Her performance goes beyond the group of participants and includes those on the periphery, the silent audience.

CROSSING THE GENDER BORDER

This chapter presents an analysis showing that Portia's and Amelia's play appears to have been appropriated from the real-life work of the older boys as they construct and display their ritualised masculine practices of the preschool room. Amelia's and Portia's game required them to cross over, or foray across, the gender border to play with the language of masculine discourse. John's participation in the girls' game appears to be one where he is at the crossing of the gender border.

Crossing gender borders is one way in which to describe the forays that boys and girls make across gendered social orders. Described by Thorne (1993) as 'borderwork,' this type of interaction involving boys and girls is described as

> accompanied by stylized forms of action, a sense of performance, mixed and ambiguous meanings (the situations often teeter between play and aggression, and heterosexual meanings lurk within other definitions), and by an array of intense emotions – excitement, playful elation, anger, desire, shame, and fear.
>
> (Thorne, 1993, p. 66)

Thorne (1993, p. 85) describes borderwork as 'ritualized, not as high ceremony, but by virtue of being stylized, repeated and enacted with a sense of performance.' Certainly, the 'sense of performance' was evident in this episode as Portia, particularly, enacted her interactions with an awareness of the audience (the silent others).

Borderwork crossings are usually highly charged with emotions such as excitement and anger (Thorne, 1993), and this episode is no exception. The cross-border work showed how the girls exhibited great excitement as they forayed across the gender border to play with the discourse of hegemonic masculinity. The shared game between Portia and Amelia, because of the risky business involved, serves to strengthen their shared worlds and intersubjectivities. Portia, in going one step further by actually taking the game of hegemonic masculinity to the teacher and not getting 'caught out,' shows the game to be a powerful way not only to cross gender boundaries but to display it to the teacher, researcher and others in the room. John, despite appearing to initiate the exchange, appeared angry as he tried to deal with and make sense of what was happening at the border.

CONCLUSION

The girls' talk in this episode showed them visiting the discourse of hegemonic masculinity. They performed elements of the boys' ritualised and powerful practices of block area in such a way to display to John and others that they knew the discourse, while at the same time appearing to antagonise John. This is the only example where I have found girls engaging in this type of talk. By comparison, I have a number of examples where boys participate in this discourse. Portia calls the suggested action a game. The girls' obvious enjoyment and delight also suggest that it is a game. While the girls appropriate the boys' discourse of threats, their performance is flexible enough to incorporate objects of play from their own pretend themes of home and hospital.

This episode with the girls displays some of the same elements of ritual as the episodes with the boys in block area; but there are some differences. While the threats of terror have similar features to the interactions of the boys, there are four important distinctions. First, it is the girls (and not the boys) initiating the script. Second, the girls recognise and name their talk as a 'game.' The work of hegemonic masculinity is not being done by Portia and Amelia. Rather, they are engaged in a performance of it. By comparison, in analysis of the boys' episodes, there were no references to their talk-in-interaction as a game. Third, my presence is a foil to the girls' performance in a way that my presence was not for the boys. Having an audience appears to be an important part of the girls' game. The fourth distinction is how the teacher responds when called by one of the children to intervene in the episode. The teacher usually intervenes only when there is a crying child. In this episode, when the teacher is called in, her input is minimal and does not support the child, John, who sought her help.

The influences shaping this episode come not from any one individual but are 'located in the momentary relational encounters' (Shotter, 1996, p. 403) and shaped by indefinite possibilities. Participants act spontaneously with one another to create meaning out of the situation. Yet this episode comes out of previous encounters, and future encounters will be implicated from the work of this one. These encounters are 'all so momentary and fleeting, so intricate and elaborate, so spontaneous and immediate, that we find it difficult to attend to them' (Shotter, 1996, p. 404). Only through close and finely grained analysis can some of the possibilities of the encounter be opened up for examination.

For early childhood educators, exploring the play practices of young children using such careful analysis opens up everyday talk-in-interaction for inclusion as a new preschool teacher skill. Play can then be investigated as children organise it, move by move, without a predefined early childhood theory informing or directing the observations and analysis. What became evident in this analysis of the episode of play is the sophisticated and competent ways in which children can use talk and action to build and shape their gendered social orders. This demonstrates to early childhood educators that gender is an essential element of children's everyday social worlds. Such a description of the girls' work of visiting the discourse of hegemonic masculinity invites early childhood educators to consider the everyday gendered work that children do in preschool classrooms. While such understandings may not immediately influence early childhood educators' practices, it may help them to recognise the richly textured and competent work of preschool children, as they engage in the work (and play) of being gendered classroom members.

NOTES

1 The term *preschool* is often used in early childhood literature to describe different types of programmes catering for young children preceding compulsory schooling. This definition differs in Queensland, where *preschool* usually refers to the year of schooling preceding entry into elementary school. However, use of the term *preschool* in this chapter follows the wider definition, so that preschool refers to a programme for 3- to 5-year-old children operating in an early childhood setting.

2 Analysis begins in a local site investigating the everyday talk and action of the participants in play. A fine grained analysis of the transcripts provides opportunities to explore how this reading of the local organisation of talk is organised. From this approach, the complex issue of gender is conceived not in abstract theoretical terms, but is approached from explicating first the daily experience of being a gendered social member of this preschool room. The work of the members of this classroom, that of producing locally accomplished order, reveals expressions of institutional discourses of gender – discourses young children have access to from adults and other children.

3 Particular segments of video data were chosen for closer analysis because they were of initial interest. Sacks (1984, p. 27) explains the choice of particular data in the following way:

Now people often ask me why I choose the particular data I choose. Is it some problem that I have in mind that caused me to pick this corpus or this segment? And I am insistent that I just happened to have it, it became fascinating, and I spent some time at it.

4 The production of the transcript is more than a technical exercise. It involves close and careful listenings to reveal the detailed features of the talk and action (Baker, 1998; Silverman, 1993). The transcription process, and, most notably, the notation used by ethnomethodologists and conversation analysts, has been described as being messy, fragmented and difficult to read (Atkinson, 1981). However, slow and repeated readings allow readers to suspend their commonsense assumptions to consider the data in new ways (Atkinson, 1981) and consequently to consider multiple readings (Baker, 1998). Atkinson (1981, p. 100) likens this approach to that of 'an anthropologist, confronted with a new, alien and exotic culture, force[d] to suspend one's own commonsense, culturally given assumptions.'

5 Transcript notation

Data are transcribed using a system devised by Jefferson and described in Psathas (1995). Punctuation marks describe characteristics of speech production. They do not refer to grammatical units. The following are the features used in these transcripts.

( )	word(s) spoken but not audible
(was)	best guess for word(s) spoken
((singing))	transcriber's description of the scene and characterisations of talk
but	emphasis
BUT	greater emphasis
//no	the point at which an overlap occurs
=	no interval between turns
do::n't	sound is prolonged. Multiple colons indicate a more prolonged sound.
(2.0)	pause timed in seconds
°quiet°	talk that has a noticeably lower volume than the surrounding talk
him-	a dash indicates a cut-off of the prior word
four.	a period indicates a stopping fall in tone
please?	a question mark indicates a rising intonation
away!	an exclamation mark indicates an animated tone
. . .	a horizontal ellipse indicates that parts of the speaker's turn has been omitted
⋮	a vertical ellipse indicates that intervening turns of talk have been omitted
→	arrow used to call attention to particular sections of the transcript

REFERENCES

Atkinson, M. A. (1980). Some practical uses of 'a natural lifetime'. *Human Studies*, 3, 33–46.

Atkinson, P. (1981). Inspecting classroom talk. In C. Adelman (ed.), *Uttering, muttering* (pp. 98–113). London: Grant McIntyre.

Baker, C. (1998, in press). Transcription and representation in literacy research. In J. Flood, S. B. Heath, and D. Lapp (eds), *A handbook for literacy educators: Research on teaching the communicative and visual arts*. New York: Macmillan.

Bredekamp, S. (ed.). (1987). *Developmentally appropriate practice in early childhood programmes serving children from birth through age 8* (Expanded ed.). Washington, DC: National Association for the Education of Young Children.

Connell, R. W. (1995). *Masculinities*. St Leonards, NSW: Allen & Unwin.

Connell, R. W. (1996). Teaching the boys: New research on masculinity, and gender strategies for schools. *Teachers College Record, 98*(2), 206–235.

Cook-Gumperz, J. (1992). Gendered talk and gendered lives: Little girls being women before becoming (big) girls. In K. Hall, M. Bucholtz, and B. Moonwomon (eds), *Locating power. Proceedings of the Second Berkeley Women and Language Conference. Vol 1.* (pp. 68–79). Berkeley, CA: Berkeley Women and Language Group.

Corsaro, W. A. (1985). *Friendship and peer culture in the early years*. Norwood, NJ: Ablex.

Danby, S. (1995). How to be masculine in block area. In *Celebrating the past: Sharing the future. A Postgraduate Research Conference Proceedings* (pp. 1–25). University of Queensland, Brisbane: Graduate School of Education.

Danby, S. (1996). Constituting social membership: Two readings of talk in an early childhood classroom. *Language and Education, 10*(2and3), 151–170.

Danby, S. and Baker, C. D. (1998, in press). 'What's the problem?' – Restoring social order in the preschool classroom. In I. Hutchby and J. Moran-Ellis (eds), *Children and social competence: Arenas of action* (pp. 157–186). London: Falmer Press.

Davies, B. (1989). *Frogs and snails and feminist tales: Preschool children and gender*. Sydney: Allen & Unwin.

Denzin, N. K. (1982/92). The work of little children. In C. Jenks (ed.), *The sociology of childhood: Essential readings* (pp. 189–194). Aldershot: Gregg Revivals.

Feeney, S., Christensen, D., and Moravcik, E. (1991). *Who am I in the lives of children?* Englewood Cliffs, NJ: Prentice Hall.

Garfinkel, H. (1967). *Studies in ethnomethodology*. Englewood Cliffs, NJ: Prentice Hall.

Garvey, C. (1990). *Play*. Cambridge, MA: Harvard University Press.

Goodwin, M. H. (1985). The serious side of jump rope: Conversational practices and social organization in the frame of play. *Journal of American Folklore, 98*(389), 315–330.

Goodwin, M. H. (1990). *He-said-she-said: Talk as social organization among black children*. Bloomington: Indiana University Press.

Goodwin, M. H. and Goodwin, C. (1987). Children's arguing. In S. U. Philips, S. Steele, and C. Tanz (eds), *Language, gender and sex in comparative perspective* (pp. 200–248). Cambridge: Cambridge University Press.

Gracey, H. L. (1972). Learning the student role: Kindergarten as academic boot camp. In D. H. Wrong and H. L. Gracey (eds), *Readings in introductory sociology* (pp. 243–254). New York: Macmillan.

Grieshaber, S. (1986). Girls' day in the block area – is it the right decision? *Links*, (2), 14–16.

Heritage, J. (1984). *Garfinkel and ethnomethodology*. Oxford: Polity Press.

Heritage, J. (1985). Analysing news interviews: Aspects of the production of talk for an overhearing audience. In T. A. van Dijk (ed.), *Handbook of discourse analysis: Discourse and dialogue* (pp. 95–117). London: Academic Press.

Hester, S. and Francis, D. (1997). Reality analysis in a classroom storytelling. *British Journal of Sociology, 48*(1), 95–112.

Jayyusi, L. (1984). *Categorization and the moral order*. Boston: Routledge & Kegan Paul.

Jayyusi, L. (1991). Values and moral judgement: Communicative praxis as a moral order. In G. Button (ed.), *Ethnomethodology and the social sciences* (pp. 227–251). Cambridge: Cambridge University Press.

Jenks, C. (1982/92). Introduction: Constituting the child. In C. Jenks (ed.), *The sociology of childhood: Essential readings* (pp. 9–24). Aldershot: Gregg Revivals.

Kessler, S. A. (1992). The social context of the early childhood curriculum. In S. Kessler and B. B. Swadener (eds), *Reconceptualizing the early childhood curriculum: Beginning the dialogue* (pp. 21–42). New York: Teachers College Press.

Koralek, D. G., Colker, L. J., and Dodge, D. T. (1993). *The what, why, and how of high-quality early childhood education: A guide for on-site supervision.* Washington, DC: National Association for the Education of Young Children.

Mac Naughton, G. (1994). 'It's more than counting heads in block play': Rethinking approaches to gender equity in the early childhood curriculum. Paper presented at the 20th Triennial Conference, Australian Early Childhood Association Perth, WA.

Mac Naughton, G. (1995). A post-structuralist analysis of learning in early childhood settings. In M. Fleer (ed.), *DAPcentrism: Challenging developmentally appropriate practice.* (pp. 35–54). Watson, ACT: Australian Early Childhood Association.

Mann, D. (1996). Serious play. *Teachers College Record, 97*(3), 446–469.

Maynard, D. W. (1985). On the functions of social conflict among children. *American Sociological Review, 50*(April), 207–223.

National Childcare Accreditation Council (1993). *Putting children first: Quality improvement and accreditation system handbook.* Sydney: National Childcare Accreditation Council.

Oakley, A. (1994). Women and children first and last: Parallels and differences between children's and women's studies. In B. Mayall (ed.), *Children's childhoods: Observed and experienced* (pp. 13–32). London: Falmer Press.

Paley, V. G. (1984). *Boys and girls: superheroes in the doll corner.* Chicago: The University of Chicago Press.

Paley, V. G. (1988). *Bad guys don't have birthdays: Fantasy play at four.* Chicago: The University of Chicago Press.

Payne, G. and Ridge, E. (1985). 'Let them talk' – An alternative approach to language development in the infant school. In E. C. Cuff and G. C. F. Payne (eds), *Crisis in the curriculum* (pp. 11–32). London: Croom Helm.

Piscitelli, B. (1992). Reflections on play: Why is it necessary? *Australian Journal of Early Childhood, 17*(4), 24–31.

Psathas, G. (1995). *Conversation analysis: The study of talk-in-interaction.* Thousand Oaks, CA: Sage.

Reid, J.-A., Kamler, B., Simpson, A., and MacLean, R. (1996). 'Do you see what I see?' Reading a different classroom scene. *Qualitative Studies in Education, 9*(1), 87–108.

Sachs, J. (1987). Preschool boys' and girls' language use in pretend play. In S. U. Philips, S. Steele, and C. Tanz (eds), *Language, gender, and sex in comparative perspective* (pp. 178–188). Cambridge: Cambridge University Press.

Sacks, H. (1974). On the analysability of stories by children. In R. Turner (ed.), *Ethnomethodology: Selected readings* (pp. 216–232). Harmondsworth: Penguin Education.

Sacks, H. (1980). Button button who's got the button. *Sociological Inquiry, 50*(3–4), 318–327.

Sacks, H. (1984). Notes on methodology. In J. M. Atkinson and J. Heritage (eds), *Structures of social action: Studies in conversation analysis* (pp. 21–27). Cambridge: Cambridge University Press.

Sacks, H. (1989). Lecture 10 Accountable Actions. *Human Studies, 12.*

Sacks, H. (1992). *Lectures on conversation/Harvey Sacks.* (trans. G. Jefferson) Oxford: Blackwell.
Sawyer, R. K. (1997). *Pretend play as improvisation: Conversation in the preschool classroom*. Hillsdale, NJ: Lawrence Erlbaum.
Scales, B., Almy, M., Nicolopoulou, A., and Ervin-Tripp, S. (1991). Defending play in the lives of children. In B. Scales, M. Almy, A. Nicolopoulou, and S. Ervin-Tripp (eds), *Play and the social context of development in early care and education* (pp. 15–31). New York: Teachers College Press.
Schegloff, E. A. (1980). Preliminaries to preliminaries: 'Can I ask you a question?'. *Sociological Inquiry, 50*(3–4), 104–152.
Schegloff, E. and Sacks, H. (1974). Opening up closings. In R. Turner (ed.), *Ethnomethodology: Selected readings* (pp. 233–264). Harmondsworth: Penguin Education.
Sharrock, W. W. (1974). On owning knowledge. In R. Turner (ed.), *Ethnomethodology: Selected readings*. Harmondsworth: Penguin Education.
Sheldon, A. (1990). Pickle fights: Gendered talk in preschool disputes. *Discourse Processes, 13*, 5–31.
Sheldon, A. (1992). Preschool girls' discourse competence: Managing conflict. In K. Hall, M. Bucholtz, and B. Moonwomon (eds), *Locating power: Proceedings of the Second Berkeley Women and Language Conference.* (pp. 528–539). Berkeley, CA: Berkeley Women and Language Group.
Sheldon, A. (1996). You can be the baby brother, but you aren't born yet: Preschool girls' negotiation for power and access in pretend play. *Research on Language and Social Interaction, 29*(1), 57–80.
Shotter, J. (1996). 'Now I can go on:' Wittgenstein and our embodied embeddedness in the 'hurly-burly' of life. *Human Studies, 19*, 385–407.
Silverman, D. (1985). *Qualitative methodology and sociology*. Aldershot: Gower.
Silverman, D. (1993). *Interpreting qualitative data: Methods for analysing talk, text and interaction*. London: Sage.
Silverman, D. (1994a). Analysing naturally-occurring data on aids counselling: Some methodological and practical issues. In M. Boulton (ed.), *Challenge and innovation: Methodological advances in social research on HIV/AIDS*. London: Falmer Press.
Silverman, D. (1994b). Competing strategies for analysing the contexts of social interaction. *Sociological inquiry, 64*(2), 179–198.
Speier, M. (1976). The child as conversationalist: Some culture contact features of conversational interactions between adults and children. In M. Hammersley and P. Woods (eds), *The process of schooling: A sociological reader* (pp. 98–103). London: Routledge & Kegan Paul.
Speier, M. (1982/92). The everyday world of the child. In C. Jenks (ed.), *The sociology of childhood: Essential readings* (pp. 181–188). Aldershot: Gregg Revivals.
Spodek, B. and Saracho, O. N. (1994). *Right from the start: Teaching children ages three to eight*. Boston: Allyn & Bacon.
Stone, J. G. (1990). *Teaching preschoolers: It looks like this. . .in pictures*. Washington, DC: National Association for the Education of Young Children.
Thorne, B. (1993). *Gender play: Girls and boys in school.* New Brunswick, NJ: Rutgers University Press.
Waksler, F. C. (1991). Dancing when the music is over: A study of deviance in a kindergarten classroom. In F. C. Waksler (ed.), *Studying the social worlds of children: Sociological readings*. London: Falmer Press.
Walkerdine, V. (1987). Sex, power and pedagogy. In M. Arnot and G. Weiner (eds), *Gender and the politics of schooling* (pp. 166–174). London: Hutchinson.

Watson, D. R. (1987). Interdisciplinary considerations in the analysis of pro-terms. In G. Button and J. R. E. Lee (eds), *Talk and social organisation* (pp. 261–289). Clevedon: Multilingual Matters.

Wien, C. A. (1995). *Developmentally appropriate practice in 'real life': Stories of teacher practical knowledge*. New York: Teachers College Press.

Wright, J. (1989). The construction of gender through tenor choices in physical education lessons. *Australian Review of Applied Linguistics*, 12(1), 83–101.

Chapter 11

Gendermaps

Kathy Lowe

INTRODUCTION

Early childhood educators have a complex and changing role in the development of young children. The construction of a workable gender position for each child is of primary concern to educators in the 1990s, with gender discussions over the past two decades assuming that the 'inequalities between adult men and women are, in part at least, the product of inequalities established and perpetuated through the education system' (Jordan, 1995, p. 69). It is difficult to identify the discourses and practices that have led to this inequality in adult life between males and females, and pressure is mounting on educators to address these issues in the early childhood setting, rather than in secondary schools which is where they have traditionally been foregrounded.

In the past, socialisation theory told us that children were discrete individuals who learnt social behaviours, including gender interactions, as a result of outside forces impacting on them. Children were seen not as an integral part of this process, but as individuals absorbing appropriate stances to be used in social settings. Davies (1989) notes that one of the problems with socialisation theories is that 'they obscure our recognition of the complex and contradictory ways in which we are constantly constituting ourselves in the social world in which we live' (p. 6). More recent work has suggested that children constitute and structure a gender position in response to the discourses within which they participate, and this position is dynamic with the child taking an active part in discursive practices. In this context, enculturation is an ongoing process through which children construct a reality that is meaningful to them within the many contexts they are exposed to. Children are enculturated through interaction in their homes with families, interaction in their schools with educators and peers, through the variety of media they are exposed to, and through community interaction. Observation of any early childhood centre will show children practising gender positioning, and these positions will be easily recognised as those from the wider context of society and our particular culture.

Most children interpret gender positions as mutually exclusive. That is, boys should not show traditionally 'feminine' characteristics, and girls should not display 'masculine' traits. To move beyond this dualism is to thoroughly remove all traces of the discursive practices that allow them to be regenerated in the first place. Gilbert (1992) states that:

> If language practices – reading, writing, talking, listening – are seen to be predominantly cognitive, predominantly individualistic, predominantly natural, then it is difficult to accept that it is also through language practices that we learn how to take up positions in our culture as women and men.
>
> (p. 18)

When expressed this way, it is apparent that educators need to inform children about the discourses in which they are participating and make them aware of the importance of being critical of all discursive practices that involve them. Children also need to develop awareness of their position within discourse. Socio-linguistic conventions are linked to concepts of masculinity and femininity and the relative power of each of these positions. Gilbert (1992) makes the point that girls have traditionally been seen as more able at writing than boys. However, control of the powerful discourses of our society, the writings in philosophy, science, history, poetry and drama, have been situated with men.

Davies and Banks (1992) further argue that:

> all children learn to take up their maleness and femaleness as if it were an incorrigible element of their personal selves, and they do so through learning the discursive practices in which all people are positioned as either male or female.
>
> (p. 2)

Children are constantly exposed to a wide variety of discourse, and need opportunities to explore positions they might take within these discourses. Positioning as male or female is dependent upon the experiences the child has had and the response of other participants to the position the child has taken.

'We need theory that will let us think in terms of pluralities and diversities, rather than of unities and universals' (Scott, 1988, p. 33). The child's world needs to be explored without the restraints of patriarchal hierarchies and the issue of alternative ways of knowing articulated, without simply regenerating what already exists. Post-structuralist theory argues that the individual is an integral part of the social world rather than an object within it to be fashioned according to the dominant position of the time. Therefore, the child is constantly acting and reacting to the social world to construct a gender position that is responsive to the dynamism of discourse. This is a useful position from which to explore the issue of gender with young children.

The continuum ranging from femininity to masculinity is one of four major ways of thinking beyond duality. Davies (1990) suggests that this perspective has some problems in terms of the polarisation of male and female, the assumption of biological determinism and acceptance of the fact that it is 'natural' to fall somewhere on the continuum. However, the model does acknowledge that gender is not inherent, but a process of learning and gaining knowledge about oneself, one's environment and what male and female means to the individual. Whilst working with young children as their teacher, I found this model to be most useful, as it helps both adults and children to articulate the position they feel best describes them. Children and adults felt comfortable with the terminology 'feminine' and 'masculine', and were able to assign known traits and positions to those descriptors. There was an issue here regarding acceptance of societal definitions of these positions, but for ease of understanding the terminology seemed appropriate to use in this context. In my research I explored three major contexts within children's lives. They were the home and family context, the educational context and the media context. I will discuss the home and family and educational contexts here.

SCENES FROM THE HOME AND FAMILY

Children create gendermaps based on the many and varied contexts that they experience in their lives. The family and home context is the first and, I would argue, one of the most powerful sites of discourse that informs children about masculinity and femininity. For many children, the educational context either reinforces the position they have constructed for themselves, or creates dissonance between the prevailing dominant gender culture and the child's individual position. Davies (1989) informs us that 'much of the adult world is not consciously taught to children . . . but it is embedded in the language, in the discursive practices and the social and narrative structures through which the child is constituted as a person, (p. 4). Children participate in these social structures and become skilled in decoding the meaning of a variety of complex sub-texts. For example, all children 'know' that girls have long hair and boys have short hair, that girls are 'kinder' than boys and that boys are 'stronger' than girls. In many cases this has not been articulated overtly, but has been inculcated through participation in the medley of interactions that have comprised their enculturation to date.

In many Australian classrooms, the girls are assigned the role of 'caretaker' to the boys. Foster (1996) says that this is part of 'the unspoken sexual contract whereby the patriarchal meaning of femininity entails the provision of service, . . . to men' (p. 48.) If schooling is seen by society as practice for adult role taking, then assigning girls this role in classrooms is preparing them for an adult life spent in service and subservience to males.

To try and identify whether or not this 'caretaker' position was also assigned in the home context, I asked the parents of twelve of the children to keep a diary of chores and work done by their families over a seven day period. Tasks outlined in Table 11.1 are those that were identified by families as having taken place over the period of the week. The data were useful in illuminating who was doing the work, both paid and unpaid, around the house. It seemed clear that the home setting was providing discourse which was informing the choices children were making at school, particularly in the context of practice for adult life, and the relative power of male and female positions. Many girls felt most at home in the home corner setting, where they were familiar with the rituals and positions involved. The boys, on the other hand, were more comfortable exploring the boundaries of socially acceptable behaviour and developing the skills they felt they would need as adults to work outdoors and outside the home. This was not surprising when it was apparent that the chores assigned to boys were generally similar to those of their fathers: for example, tidying the yard, helping wash the car and setting the table and working on the periphery of meal preparation. The chores girls were doing were preparing them for their possible future role as caretaker: for example, feeding and caring for pets, helping with cleaning the home and minding younger siblings.

When parents were asked what they felt were appropriate role models and tasks for their children, they gave remarkably diverse responses. One mother stated 'You would be hard pressed to change (children's' gender role) at that stage (school entry).' She also said that her daughter had

Table 11.1 Family tasks in the home . . . identified by pre-school children

Mother	*Father*	*Girls*	*Boys*
House cleaning	Yard work	Feed pets	Tidy yard
Washing	Office work	Help with cleaning	Dress and clean teeth
Cooking	Washing up	Put away washing	Tidy room
Shopping	Help with baby	Open gates	Set table
Craft activities	Wash and polish car	Tidy toys	Help wash car
Ironing	Visit dump	Mind siblings	
Sewing			
Supervise homework			
Drop off and collect children			

always played well with her two older brothers, and was often the only girl at gatherings. However, she would tire of the rough games and 'seek the quiet comfort of her dolls and dress ups.' It was also interesting to note another comment by a different mother. Pamela said that when I first talked about studying the children generally, and her daughter specifically, she suggested that I had chosen Geraldine because she was not overtly feminine and 'girly.' This mother indicated to me that she felt 'a bit peeved. So I took notice over the year and I could see where you were coming from. But I could also see her wanting girly things like wanting to wear dresses, pretty bows and the like.' I felt this was indicative of the pressure on parents in our society to 'get it right' and ensure that we have gendermaps constructed in line with dominant discourses. However, the question must be asked 'What is *wrong* with being a girl who doesn't want to wear frilly dresses and play with dolls?' Many of the comments from parents indicated a need to position oneself correctly within discursive practice, according to general norms, in order to feel comfortable within society.

It is thus apparent, from observations within the home and family context, that children see a multiplicity of positions being taken, and that one factor in this positioning is gender. Parents appear to see these gender positions as 'normal' and replicate them in their own interactions within discourse. Children also appear to use the home and family context to identify social norms and expectations related to gender in terms of dress and behaviour.

SCENES FROM THE PRE SCHOOL

When children leave the home and family context, they begin the process of becoming a school child and a member of the wider community. As they participate in the educational context, one factor that becomes available for exploration is an individual gender position. For some children, this will be the first time that gender has been an important facet of their lives. Exposure to the dominant school discourses, and interaction within these discourses, will, from this point onwards, help to shape and focus the individual's gender position.

Competing discourses are a fact of life for all children as they struggle to develop and maintain a personal gendermap. Dependent on the contexts they are exposed to, all children will have competing discourses available to them. They position themselves within these discourses in a variety of ways, and this positioning is largely subjective, and is often dependent on the context within which the discourse takes place. The position taken will also depend on the child's life experiences to date and the individual child's ways of understanding the world around them. Weedon (1987) proposes this subjectivity as 'precarious, contradictory and in process, constantly being reconstituted in discourse each time we think or speak' (p. 32). This subjectivity is not static but in a state of constant reconstitution.

Children entering school often clearly show defined gender positions, and can discuss these positions in terms of opportunity and power relations. Experiences in their lives have led them to an understanding of gender interactions and the greater desirability of masculinity over femininity. Children have come to this understanding through seeing males taking dominant positions in sport and literature. Children are exposed to literature that shows them male protagonists winning the day in an endless stream of real and imaginary situations. Sport on television and radio is dominated by male oriented pursuits, and children in playgrounds constantly see male domination of time and space. Lee (1993) tells us that 'subjectivity is an effect of constant struggle between competing discourses. It is multiple, fragmentary, both fragile and aggressive, constantly in a process of renewal' (p. 17). Many of the children I worked with were able to articulate clearly their perceptions of the gendered society in which they live, and the impact it has had on their personal gendermap. Children will often refer to a parent or a significant adult in their lives as a model for their own participation in discursive practice. Observations of early childhood settings illuminate the references children use, particularly in the home corner and during outdoor play. Children position themselves subjectively within these discourses. That is, the position they take depends on several factors such as previous experience in similar contexts, the participants in the discourse and a multiplicity of other changing and dynamic factors.

I found the issue of power to be central to the gender dynamics between young children. The setting for my research was a pre-school centre in a large, country town in Queensland. The children I worked with were 4 and 5 year olds and they attended the centre two and a half days per week. There were twenty-five children in each group and the centre was part of a pre school to Year twelve campus.

According to Foucault's (1978) view:

> Power is not something that is acquired, seized or shared, something that one holds on to or allows to slip away; power is exercised from innumerable points, in the interplay of nonegalitarian and mobile relations.
>
> (p. 94)

Power, in this instance, was defined as the acceptance of the 'commonness' of the fe/male dynamics of everyday life. Paechter (1996) tells us that this view of power sees it as 'inhering in all social activity, pervading human life as an inescapable aspect of existence' (p. 75).

Children show great awareness of the power relationships that exist between males and females. When the issue of power in the classroom was discussed, children could clearly define the characteristics of a person with power. We first discussed what the word *powerful* meant to the children, and they were able to articulate that powerful people were in charge and could make other people do what they wanted them to do. We discussed people they knew who were powerful, and many children related to media figures such as Power Rangers and Transformers as well as people from their families and communities. The discussion moved onto people who held power over them, and the children identified people such as teachers, parents, principals and children who were stronger and bigger. The children were then asked to draw someone powerful. This person was usually male and often larger than the child drawing the picture. Whilst some children drew parents, teachers or other adults, three 5 year old girls – Kassie, Debbie and Carrie – all focused on bullies. They were relatively large, they were male, and the ineffectuality of the powerful one's victim, who was usually female, was clearly evident (Figure 11.1). These girls regarded 'power' as relative to control over the individual's environment and, when questioned, associated power with 'bullies' who hurt other people – usually girls. Power in the educational context was perceived to be in male hands, even though their teacher

Figure 11.1 Children's images of power

was female and the principal of the school was female. The children saw the male Deputy Principal as being 'in charge' of all the women teachers on campus.

This prompted me to observe the children I taught carefully and I observed many incidents where power relations were involved.

> During a free play session, Kelly was walking past Matthew who kicked her as she went by. When she turned around, he turned away and would not make eye contact with her. She asked him if he had kicked her and he replied, 'No.' She then turned and walked on and Matthew kicked her again. Kelly started to walk away more swiftly and Matthew got up from the floor and chased her outside. I spoke to both children about this incident to attempt to determine what it meant to them. I saw it as an assertion of power by Matthew over Kelly and his environment, and perceived it as malicious. Matthew articulated quite a different view of the event. He stated that Kelly had kicked his Lego as she walked by and he gave her a kick to let her know that he was there, and therefore she 'should not be, or she should look where she's going!' When she asked him if he had kicked her, he answered no because she might have 'told' if he had been honest and this would have led to him having to make an apology and 'waste his time.' He said he chased her outside so he could get back to his building 'in peace.' He very strongly stated that he did not want to hurt Kelly, but merely remove her from the area where he was working, as expeditiously as possible. Kelly had trouble even identifying the event when I spoke to her about half an hour later, but with prompting she recalled what had happened. She did not see anything wrong with Matthew's behaviour, and supported his assertion that she was 'in his way, and he needed me to move.' This was of concern to me because it seemed that an incident which I saw as unacceptable was acceptable in the eyes of both of the children involved in the incident.

I observed a second incident also during 'free' time.

> Geraldine was drawing at a table with some other girls. Jeremy came up behind her and placed both his hands over her eyes and said 'Guess who?' Geraldine did not reply so Jeremy pushed his hands harder onto her eyes and repeated his question. Geraldine still ignored him and he pressed even harder. She responded by shouting 'Go away!' and he ran off. I asked Geraldine why she did not respond when Jeremy first placed his hands over her eyes and she replied that she 'thought he would go away if (she) ignored him.' Jeremy said that he 'just wanted to play a trick and got angry when Geraldine wouldn't play.' He said he did not feel sorry about the incident because she should have 'played (his) game.'

In both of these incidents there was an assertion of power and acceptance by the children of the validity of male domination of space and language. Both of the girls positioned themselves as submissive within the discourse, and in Kelly's case excuses were made to justify the boy's behaviour. It was interesting to note that the situations reflected in this microcosm were indicative of some relationships in the wider societal context. The question arose as to where children gained the information that informed their participation in these discourses. Were home contexts informing responses and positioning, or were children responding to peers in a specific way in a particular environment?

Because of my intervention in these incidents, children were made aware of the possibility of other positions, for both parties, within these discourses. In other classrooms, the incidents may not have been noted by the teacher as significant instances of power interplay, or they may have been construed within the dominant cultural context as *normal* behaviour for children. It is critical for children to be made aware of the power relations within such incidents, or they also come to see the marginalisation and subservience of some parties as *normal* or *natural*.

Gender conformity is very apparent in the early childhood setting, and the pressure to conform to typical gender stereotypes constructed by the dominant discourses of society appears to be stronger for boys than for girls. This may be why we see boys focused on strength and control of their physical selves. Boys often harass girls either physically or verbally and this impacts on what girls see as viable gender positions for themselves.

Thorne (1986) has investigated the 'interaction across, yet based upon and even strengthening, gender boundaries' (p. 172). The games that girls and boys play in the early childhood setting are designed to practise and reinforce the rules of engagement for adult behaviour. This is particularly apparent in home corner play. Mac Naughton (1995) advised that 'recognising and analysing power relationships in children's play takes practice, time and understanding . . . ' and that it is 'important to be alert to both direct and indirect ways in which children's play can express gendered power relationships' (p. 5). Mac Naughton further states that girls use power overtly in the home corner in the pre school setting and take on the all-powerful role of 'mum.' Boys tend to be marginalised and are often present only as a pet or absent father. Girls told Mac Naughton that boys 'got it wrong' and were unaware of the rule that 'mum' is always the 'boss.' Conversely, block play has been an area where boys are reluctant to let girls participate (Mac Naughton, 1994; Grieshaber, 1986). This was not entirely the case in my research. In another incident:

> The boys in the centre were initially very reluctant to let the girls into the block play area, particularly Anthony, Ewan and Charlie. However, the girls refused to be intimidated and stood their ground through several attempts to eject them from the area. The boys tried a variety of techniques from verbal abuse and physical threats, to actually barricading the block area off, placing one of them on guard. When none of these techniques distracted the girls from their purpose, they surrendered and allowed the girls some blocks and space to play in. The surrender was ungracious, and they continued to harass the girls who played with the blocks. Geraldine and Nancy were the most persistent girls, and they would go to great lengths to obtain blocks for their constructions. On one occasion, the boys had Charlie moving all the blocks to another part of the pre school and ferrying them to the builders as necessary, so the girls would not have access to them. Geraldine and Nancy negotiated with Jason to allow them a few blocks to begin construction.

By the end of the year, girls and boys were playing together in the block area, but the play was rarely collegial and most often parallel. Geraldine and Nancy were the only two girls who actually got to play *with* the boys and this happened on only three occasions. When they did, it was often the opposite of what occurred in home corner. That is, the boys were the 'boss' and had power, whilst the girls were the ones having difficulty positioning themselves in the resulting discourse. They found it difficult to see themselves as submissive to the boys' dominance, but complied with this version of events in order to continue to participate in the block area. On many occasions in the pre school context, I observed boys banding together to assert collective dominance when they were unable to dominate alone. Even the most submissively positioned girls rarely complied with requests from the boys immediately, but, depending on the degree of coercion, they would eventually submit to the request or order. The less submissive girls often used their superior verbal and negotiating skills to obtain what they wanted from the boys – in this instance it was the blocks. In our discussions, I regularly encouraged the children to rethink and articulate their feelings about how they were being positioned within the discursive practices of the pre school, and to explore and define new positions for themselves.

Foster (1996) has suggested that the 'ideology and boundaries surrounding a woman's place and her appropriate roles and activities has proved to be even more resistant to change than the preserves of men' (p. 46). In the context of the home and family, the children I worked with were participating in a variety of family structures. The type of family structure and the role and activities of the mother seemed to have a significant effect on the behaviour and gendermap of the individual.

Mothers were seen by all of the children as the caretakers in the home context, whether they worked outside the home or not. The degree of the girl's assumption of this caretaker role was varied.

> Jenine was a keen participant in home corner and often assumed the role of 'mum.' In this role she was clearly the director of activities, giving clear directions about who could play and what the game would be. It was interesting to note that, away from home corner, Jenine was not as assertive and tended to work quietly with a couple of female friends. She told me that mums care for children, cook, wash, iron, clean the house and care for their babies, whilst dads mow, wash cars and do yard work. She modelled the behaviour she saw in the home context – if boys joined her home corner play, she allocated outdoor tasks to them and they were made absent from the game in this way. As time passed and I discussed the issue of home corner play and her dominance as mum with Jenine, she became more likely to allow boys to take a wider role in home corner. She trained a couple of boys – Jason and Jerry – to be caring fathers who were sometimes allowed to bath and feed the babies. They were still not completely subsumed into the play, but they did have a broader role than they had initially been allowed to take. However, they had no power over the direction of the game or play and control remained firmly positioned with Jenine.

By taking the position of power within this discourse, Jenine was able to keep her knowledge of gender positions intact. She was able to replicate the position she saw being taken in her home context, and have it validated within the educational context. In many cases, children at play in educational settings, are validating for themselves the positions they see in their home and family contexts.

Walkerdine (1990) tells us that 'particular individuals are produced as subjects differently within a variety of discursive practices' (p.5). In many instances in the early childhood setting, girls are read into discourse as subservient or submissive and treated accordingly. It is interesting to observe situations where girls refuse to be positioned in this way. When girls consistently refuse to be positioned as powerless, the relations of power within the discourse change. Assertion of a power relationship is possible only if the individuals within the discourse accept and read the discourse in the same way. For example, the girls in this centre who refused to be positioned as non-participants in block play were eventually seen by the other participants in the discourse – the boys – as having a different relation of power that enabled them to be accepted into the block play area. In the same way Jenine, by positioning herself in the play as 'boss,' is able to exert power over the boys who wish to participate. In order to participate, they must position themselves as subservient and submissive – a role and relation of power usually assigned to the girls.

These incidents were indicators of the pressure that boys exert over girls to participate in events on their terms. They also illuminated the gender conformity that is apparent in the early childhood setting. Children appear to feel pressure to conform to the gender stereotypes constructed by the dominant discourses of society, and this pressure seems to be stronger for boys than it is for girls. This pressure is often not apparent prior to children entering the educational context. Jordan (1995) suggests that whilst children have particular ideas about gender roles and show a fixed gender position by about 2 or 3 years of age, the social consequences of this position are not yet available to them. As they enter the educational setting and have a wider variety of discourses at their command, they are constantly in the position of being required to interpret contexts to make sense or meaning for themselves. Children may also become aware, for the first time, of the social consequences of their gender position. They want to gain the acceptance and recognition of their peers and may need to reposition themselves, gender wise, in order to do this in the educational context.

TAKING A NEW ROLE

As a pre school teacher, I believed that the children in my care needed to experience and practise a broad range of positions in order to identify and explore possible positions for themselves within discourse. We discussed the possibility of being a member of the opposite sex and what opportunities this would make available to the children. We discussed changing positions within the context of opportunities for play, rather than changing clothes or positions, as children could better relate to differences between 'girl' and 'boy' play than inherent physical or psychological differences between the sexes.

Some children found it very difficult to take the perspective of being a member of the opposite sex. Adrian said that he was 'happy as a boy' and that he 'didn't want to do girl things because they were too boring.' Caleb said that 'even though (he) did some things that girls did,' (such as drawing and painting), he was able to do them 'a bit better because (he was) a boy.' Caleb was the only boy who was able to place himself in a female role and imagine what activities he would be able to undertake in that role. All of the other boys chose not to try.

Conversely, the girls indicated that they would enjoy the opportunity to try a 'boy day.' Geraldine said that she would like to 'play in the sand until (she) was sandy all over' and Nancy wanted to be a 'fighting fairy.' All of the girls also indicated that they would not like to *be* a boy, but they would enjoy the opportunity to position themselves in this way for a while. Geraldine thought it would be fun because if she was a boy she would be 'in charge of the games,' and Theresa wanted to be the 'boss of all the people playing.' Theresa said that she 'could be the boss of all the people playing when she was a girl, but only if there were girls playing with her and no boys at all.' This data suggested that boys found it difficult to position themselves as 'feminine' within discourse. This may have been because they had little experience and had not explored the whole range of power positions within the discursive practices they had participated in. However, the girls were able to take a variety of positions, incorporating various power relations. This may partly explain why girls find it easier to encroach on traditionally male areas, whilst males find it more difficult to fill traditionally female positions within discourse. Girls also saw some value in exploring what they saw as 'male' play, whereas boys were disinterested in participating in 'girl' play.

Kenway (1995) comments that masculinity, particularly, is under siege in schools due to a lack of understanding of the issues that inform masculinity and an *ad hoc* approach by teachers towards addressing the problematic interactions between girls and boys. Connell (1987) has suggested that men largely define themselves and their masculinity through power relationships over women. It would seem that the boys in this context found it difficult not to use power in their relationships with other children, both male and female.

It is sometimes difficult for a predominantly feminised profession, such as teaching, to address the needs and concerns of young boys attempting to define their masculinity and move away from the constraining context of the home and family into the wider educational and societal context. The boys use power relations within discourse with teachers to gain power and control of the situation. Often, when children were on the carpet during sharing time, the boys would attempt to gain control of the situation. One such incident occurred when Mark had brought a doll to school to show and tell.

Mark volunteered to show his doll and discussed its name and relevance to him with the children. Anthony and Ewan roared with laughter and began chanting 'Girls play with dolls, girls play with dolls . . .'

Teacher: No, they don't. Anyone can play with dolls.
Anthony: No! Only girls play with dolls!
Ewan: Yeah, sissy girls play with dolls.
Teacher: Mark, do you enjoy playing with your doll?
Mark: Yes
Continued laughter and harassment from Anthony and Ewan.
Teacher: Who has a teddy bear?
Most children raised their hands.
Teacher: Aren't they dolls?
Anthony: No! Sissy dolls, sissy dolls . . .
Ewan: Boys don't have dolls. (*To teacher*) You're a girl, you can have a doll if you want.

In this discourse, Anthony and Ewan had positioned the teacher as a 'girl' and responded accordingly. They could not put themselves in Mark's position and could not envisage a situation in which they would play with a doll. After discussion of the things that dolls could be used for by men and boys, for example CPR dummies, store window models, etc, the two boys reluctantly accepted that there may be some dolls that were alright for boys, but still maintained that most were not. Even in home corner, where these boys very rarely played, they would not touch the doll 'babies', as they were for girls. Another interesting facet of this exchange was the fact that Mark was not at all perturbed by the harassment he received and continued to bring the doll for several days after this incident. He obviously felt quite confident positioning himself towards the feminine end of the gender continuum.

This highlighted the need for children to be able to express a different position and expect it to be accepted by the other members of the class or community as valid. Only through thoroughly exploring the possibilities can children fully come to understand the best position for them within the discourses in which they participate.

SUMMARY AND CONCLUSIONS

It is imperative that teachers inform children of broader options, and support them in becoming critical participants in their own lives. There are windows of opportunity in which they can be powerful agents of change in developing and extending children's gendermaps.

If we are to move beyond the dominant dualistic perception of gender that exists today, educators in early childhood contexts must help children define the multiplicity of positions available to them within discursive practice. Teachers must raise their own awareness as well as the awareness of parents, so that children can thoroughly explore the myriad issues that impact upon their gender positioning. As with any facet of life, repeatedly practising responses to situations makes them seem *natural* when observed. The challenge for educators is to deconstruct these seemingly *natural* responses with children and enable them to see that there are other positions they can take within discursive practice.

Strategies can be as simple as discussing gender based issues as they arise in the classroom. By allowing children to access other people's responses and positions in given situations, they are able to access a wider variety when a particular situation arises. Children need exposure to the inadequacies of language and need to be able to relate to the fact that language often excludes women or trivialises their position. They benefit from determining their own definitions of sexist language, and through this awareness will be able to generate more appropriate responses in a range of situations. Many children are exposed to perjorative language regarding women such as, 'the little woman', 'chicks', 'babes' and 'old maids'. Children should also be aware of unnecessary modifiers in language related to women. For example, lady doctor, woman lawyer, etc. (Schwarz *et al.*, 1990, pp. 11–12). This awareness raising cannot be a 'one-off' session to 'do' language, but must be ongoing, constant and vigilant in order to permeate the child's responses and become part of the child's gendermap.

The work children do within the early childhood context, whether traditionally feminine or masculine, needs to be valued equally by educators. It should address female life and experience as well as the male paradigm. Opportunities must be taken within discussion with children to explore and illuminate the possibilities of life, rather than narrowing the field of positions a child chooses from to the narrow boundaries of acceptable masculine and feminine responses. The educator should always be aware of their own gender position and values and must take these into consideration, monitoring carefully their student/teacher interaction as well as the student/student interaction taking place.

It would seem from my research that children's gendermapping occurs as a product of the contexts they are exposed to and the positions they explore within these contexts (see Figure 11.2). Children are firstly exposed to the home and family context and position themselves within those discourses. Often, gender is not a significant factor at this time, as

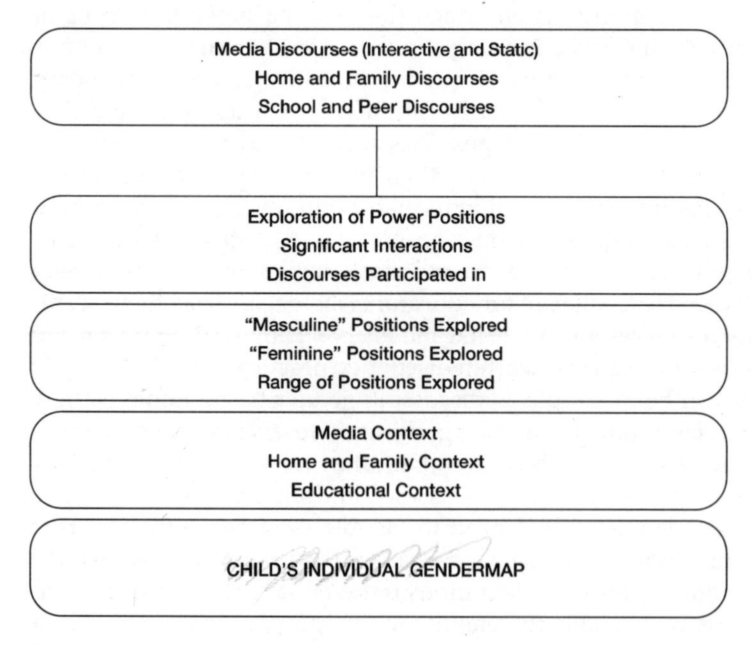

Figure 11.2 Gendermapping

children develop a basic knowledge of the world in which they live. Exposure to media discourses brings a wider range of positions to explore. Children may be involved in static media, such as literature, television, and video, or more interactive media, such as computers and CDROM games and programs. This further develops the number of viable positions available to the child. The media also informs the child about what it is to be fe/male in the wider context of the world. Children find these images powerful, and we have all seen them acting out dominant and aggressive positions from their favourite games and television shows. Finally, the child enters the realm of the school and education. Here they are exposed to an even wider variety of positions in terms of gender, and they now have the added factor of peer acceptance to influence the positions they may choose to take within discourse.

The number of positions the child has had an opportunity to explore will influence the position they take within the discourses they participate in. They will also draw upon knowledge of significant others in their lives and their responses to situations. As with all other aspects of their lives, they will initially model their positioning and responses in line with those they perceive as being most 'right' within their lives. This may be from parents, teachers, the media or other community members. Children will also draw upon the relative power of the positions they have explored and repeat positioning that has afforded them the most success.

As children explore the contexts available to them in more depth, they bring to their position in discourse the experience and practice that they have had within these contexts. All of these factors enable the child to formulate a responsive position, within discursive practice, at a given point in time. This is the child's gendermap – an individual, dynamic and ever changing response to discourse. This dynamism enables children to benefit from further exploration of the texts in which they participate daily, and to become more highly informed about positions they might or might not take.

The data from this research has reinforced the view that power relations are present in the early childhood setting and that children are involved in these power relations as part of the discourses they participate in. The question arises, do children accept gender positions as they are presented to them or are they indulging in exploratory behaviour to define both their own and their society's gender positions? Investigative work needs to be done with young children to illuminate further their perceptions of the gendered world in which they live, and to make them more critical of the discursive practices they are part of. The challenge for educators is to help children draw a gendermap that is both relevant to the child and allows the child to explore the full boundaries of his or her potential.

REFERENCES

Connell, R. W. (1987). *Gender and Power.* Stanford: Stanford University Press.

Davies, B. (1989). *Frogs and Snails and Feminist Tales: Preschool Children and Gender.* Sydney: Allen and Unwin.

Davies, B. (1990). Education for Sexism: A theoretical analysis of the sex/gender bias in education. *Educational Philosophy and Theory, 21, (1).* 1–19.

Davies, B. and Banks, C. (1992). The Gender Trap: A feminist, post-structuralist analysis of primary school children's talk about gender. *Journal of Curriculum Studies, 24, (1).* 1–25.

Foster, V. (1996). Space Invaders: Desire and threat in the schooling of girls. *Discourse: Studies in the Cultural Politics of Education, 17, (1),* 43–63.

Foucault, M. (1978). *The History of Sexuality Volume One.* London: Penguin.

Gilbert, P. (1992). The Story so Far: Gender, literacy and social regulation. *Gender and Education, 4, (3).* 185–199.

Grieshaber, S. (1986). Girl's Day in Block Area – is it the right decision? *Links, 2.* 14–16.

Jordan, E. (1995). Fighting Boys and Fantasy Play: The construction of masculinity in the early years of school. *Gender and Education, 7, (1).* 69–100.

Kenway, J. (1995). Masculinities in Schools – under siege, on the defensive, under reconstruction? *Discourse: Studies in the Cultural Politics of Education, 16, (1).* 59–79.

Lee, A. (1993). *Gender and Geography, Literacy, Redagogy and Curriculum.* Unpublished Ph.D. thesis. Western Australia: Murdoch University.

Mac Naughton, G. (1994). *It's More Than Counting Heads in Block Play: Rethinking Approaches to Gender Equity in the Early Childhood Curriculum.* Paper presented to 20th Triennial Conference, Australian Early Childhood Association, Perth, Session 195, September.

Mac Naughton, G. (1995). The Power of Mum: Gender and power at play. *Australian Early Childhood Association Resource Book Series, 2, (2).*

Paechter, C. (1996). Power, Knowledge and the Confessional in Qualitative Research. *Discourse: Studies in the Cultural Politics of Education,17, (1).* 75–84.

Schwarz, V., Allard, A. and Matthews, B. (1990). *A Fair Go For All: Guidelines for a Gender Inclusive Curriculum.* Victoria, Ministry of Education.

Scott, J. W. (1988). Deconstructing Equality Versus Difference: Or, the uses of post-structuralist theory for feminism. *Feminist Studies, 14, (1),* 33–51.

Thorne, B. (1986). Girls and Boys Together .... But Mostly Apart: Gender arrangements in elementary schools, in Hartup, W. W. and Rubin, Z. (eds). *Relationships and Development,* Hillsdale, New Jersey: Lawrence Erlbaum.

Walkerdine, V. (1990). *Schoolgirl Fictions.* London: Verso.

Weedon, C. (1987). *Feminist Practice and Post-structuralist Theory.* Oxford: Blackwell.

Chapter 12

'The pink's run out!'

The place of artmaking in young children's construction of the gendered self

Margaret White

Children's experiences of the world are reflected in their artmaking. This chapter explores the extent to which children's involvement in artmaking is influenced by gender-differentiated environments. The overall context in which artmaking occurs will be examined by addressing some of the myths of early childhood representation such as, 'only girls use pink', 'only boys draw wars', 'girls draw people and boys draw guns'. Visual discourses, which are evident in children's imagery, will be analysed to understand better the pivotal role that artmaking has in children's negotiation of their position in society. Imagemaking is a central aspect of early child development. Adults can develop this faculty by carefully observing children's use of media such as drawing, painting and clay, being aware of how children are actively shaping their view of themselves, and recognising their own role in the co-construction of children's learning in this area.

'I want pink', 'I bags pink', 'Chris won't give us the pink', 'I really need the pink'. 'Oh, no! The pink's run out'!

What is it about pink? Any adult who has watched young children drawing will be familiar with these refrains. And any adult who has provided young children with drawing materials will be familiar with the way in which a new packet of twelve felt pens quickly becomes eleven, as the pink is used intensively by the coterie of pink users!

A short exchange such as this can alert adults to some initial questions about gender and artmaking:

Does the 'coterie of pink users' consist exclusively of girls? Under what circumstances do boys use pink? Is the choice of colour significant? Do boys have a 'special' colour? How is children's symbolic imagery influenced by their use of colour?

And how do we work with all children to ensure that their art-making supports and expands their conception of themselves as gendered individuals?

ARTMAKING AND THE DEVELOPMENT OF SYMBOLIC THOUGHT AND EXPRESSION

The value of artmaking in the development of children's symbolic thought and expression has frequently been challenged by a perception of the human mind as consisting of an intuitive, affective and creative realm that is the province of the arts, in contrast to a rational, cognitive realm that is seen as the province of the sciences. During the 30 years from the 1960s–1980s, considerable research was undertaken to clarify and challenge this perception (Perkins and Leondar, 1977; Gardner, 1982; Geahigan, 1992). In this period, now commonly referred to as the 'Cognitive Revolution' (Davis and Gardner, 1992), a substantial body of interdisciplinary research demonstrated the construction of meaning as an active process in which emotion and cognition are directly interconnected (p. 119). Whereas the arts had formerly been regarded as affective and noncognitive, in the light of the new cognitive research, the arts came to be seen as embracing cognitive, intuitive, creative and emotional realms.

Parallel stereotypes in gender socialisation

This shift in perception of the arts has a parallel in views about gender-stereotyping. The perception of male behaviour as rational and female behaviour as emotional and, by implication irrational, has been challenged, as has the belief in women as being constituted as the 'negative' of men, which has come to be recognised as providing insufficient analysis of female abilities (Topliss, 1996). As more is understood about the socialisation of young children, the role of adults in the process of gender differentiation in early childhood has become clearer (Golombok and Fivush, 1994). Just as the arts are now seen as embracing many different realms, so the development of gender identity is now recognised as embracing complex biological, social and cultural characteristics. To stereotype emotional behaviour as feminine, artistic and marginalised in contrast to rational behaviour as masculine, logical and mainstream, is no longer an acceptable or informed position on which to base an educational programme.

During the pre-school years, as children are forming their gender identity, their use of symbolic expression can make this developing understanding explicit. This chapter will focus on the unique ways in which the visual arts offer children opportunities to make meaning of their lives and the ways in which adults and the wider socio-cultural context influence this process.

The spontaneous drawings shown in Figures 12.1 and 12.2 illustrate some gender contrasts and similarities in children's conceptions of the world. Anna, who chose to draw frequently, was at this time exploring

Figure 12.1 Girl: drawing in crayon by Anna, age 5

Figure 12.2 Martians: drawing in pencil by George, age 7

her depiction of girls by trying out many subtle variations of facial features, hair and clothes. She often commented on differences in both her drawings and in the faces she observed. George also drew spontaneously and frequently. He experimented with the depiction of media characters and the use of dialogue 'bubbles'. George talked at length about the story that his drawing illustrated, showing his preoccupation with the 'lives' of his characters.

When we consider the ways in which each of these children has incorporated aspects of their socio-cultural environment, such as:

- style in depictions of gender,
- attention to detail of clothing, human features and machines,
- awareness of media depictions,
- experience of human emotion,

it is interesting to note some of the differences and similarities that are evident in the children's approach and use of drawing as an expressive medium.

A CONTEMPORARY APPROACH TO THE VISUAL ARTS IN EARLY CHILDHOOD SETTINGS: PROGRAMMING AS A CYCLICAL PROCESS

Close observation of children is fundamental to planning in early childhood settings. Bringing knowledge of children's development to the observational process enables teachers gradually to understand how children are shaping their view of themselves and plan to engage with children in developing their learning about the world.

Social attitudes reflected in early childhood programmes: the background to some 'truths' in early childhood art education

Any consideration of artmaking in early childhood also needs to acknowledge the broader context of early childhood. For example, it has been observed that adults frequently perpetuate stereotypical images of girls and boys in early childhood settings (Golombok and Fivush, 1994). Artmaking, as with other experiences, does not occur in a vacuum. Attitudes to teaching and learning, perspectives on the value of the arts as a form of expression, and views of the child will all inform approaches to art education.

Using case studies of early childhood educators who examined their practices in relation to traditional sex-stereotyping, Mac Naughton (1996) observed the ways in which 'truths' about early childhood practice are perpetuated. When boys dominate block play and girls dominate home corner, an assumption is frequently made that this is 'natural' behaviour.

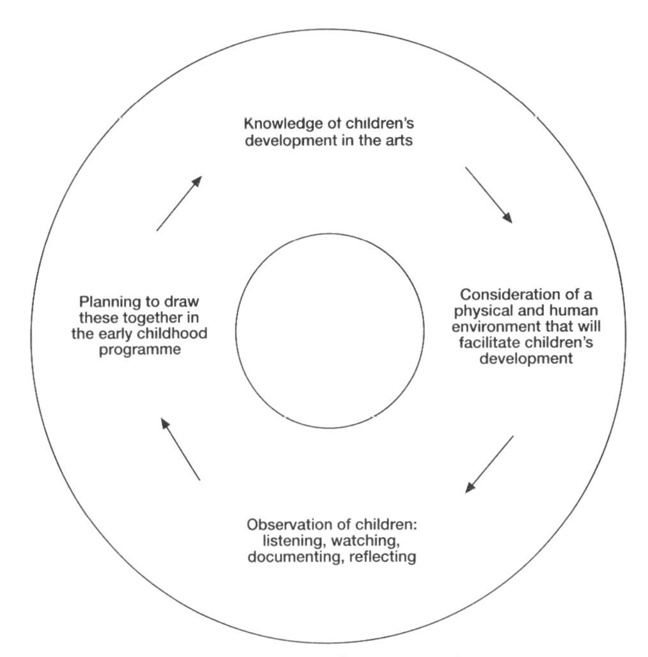

Figure 12.3 The cyclical process of programming

> Careful observation of children's play can enable teachers to discover how the physical and social environment may be supporting the stereotypical use of equipment, thereby reinforcing stereotyped gender behaviour. For example, the placement of art materials inside or outside the room may influence the extent to which boys and girls participate.

In art education, as in other areas, these accepted 'truths' about early childhood practice have been powerful in perpetuating values that have not necessarily reflected a contemporary appreciation of wider contextual issues such as social and cultural diversity. For example, many observations of sex differences in children's drawings are documented, yet little consideration has been given to the precursors of these gender differentiated images.

> When girls or boys consistently depict specific images such as detailed human figures or machines, to the exclusion of experimentation with other images, it is useful to listen to the response they receive from parents and others, and to consider how their experiences may have influenced both their choice of subject matter and their ability to depict these images. Again, careful observation may show how the physical and social environment can effect gender stereotyped imagemaking.

The challenge for early childhood educators is to take a dynamic and proactive approach in relating wider social and cultural issues to their practice with children and to understand the context in which their practice occurs.

By taking the child's perspective through conversation about something of genuine interest to the child, an adult can grasp an opportunity to extend the inquiry. For example, a child's frequent use of a specific colour such as pink could provoke a discussion about:

- the particular qualities of that colour;
- where the child has seen it in nature, familiar objects, paintings, and in other graphic images; as well as
- experimentation with a prism, and with mixing colours to discover many different pinks.

Rather than accepting a stereotype such as 'girls always use pink, boys prefer brown', children can be engaged with the experience of using colour in a way that:

- expands their understanding of the qualities of colour such as tone, hue, intensity; and
- extends their vocabulary of colour, both in their use of colour and in looking at works of art and observing colour in their environment.

'NATURAL' DEVELOPMENT AND THE CONTEXT OF ARTMAKING

Figures 12.4 and 12.5 show one child's responses to two different teaching approaches. The expressive quality of Hugo's image of a panda (Figure 12.4) provides a clear contrast to his response to a teacher's direction to draw a panda using an adult-prepared stencil (Figure 12.5).

The degree of emphasis on the process by which children make art, as opposed to the end-product, has generated one of the central debates in early childhood arts education in the twentieth century. Integral to this debate have been the polarised views of the role of teachers which have clearly created a tension for educators in the arts in early childhood.

The view of education that sees the goal as preserving the 'free nature' of the child is contrasted with one that sees learning as involving constraint imposed by adults on children (Gardner, 1976). This tension has, in some situations, restrained practitioners from interfering with the 'natural' development of children. The consequences of this tension are still evident in contemporary practice (Makin, White and Owen, 1996).

Figure 12.4 Panda: drawing in crayon by Hugo, age 4

Figure 12.5 Panda: drawing on stencil in crayon by Hugo, age 4

Views of a 'natural' gender imbalance in art and education

The belief in minimising the 'interference' of teachers in early childhood education grew from the eighteenth-century writings of Rousseau (1911), who believed in the original perfect nature of children and advocated that they be allowed to develop 'naturally'. However, Rousseau's concept of 'natural' included 'natural' differences between the sexes (for example, boys were seen as independent and girls as dependent), which led to his advocating significant differences in the education of boys and girls.

Similarly, Froebel's view of 'natural' learning reinforced a masculine perspective of sex differences. Freedman (1994) has observed the late nineteenth- and early twentieth-century connections between the notion of 'natural' development and a range of apparently objective norms that were in fact 'laden with social meaning' (p. 159). These included notions of sex-differences in children's drawings that viewed boys as superior to girls, who were considered, for example, to be 'inferior in originality' (Hall, 1911, p. 498).

Here the links between the world of fine art and education start to intersect. The 'natural' superiority of boys' drawings that G. Stanley Hall (1911) reported, reflected the view of gender identity that prevailed within the art world at that time.

The view of women in art history as inferior, and at best, developing

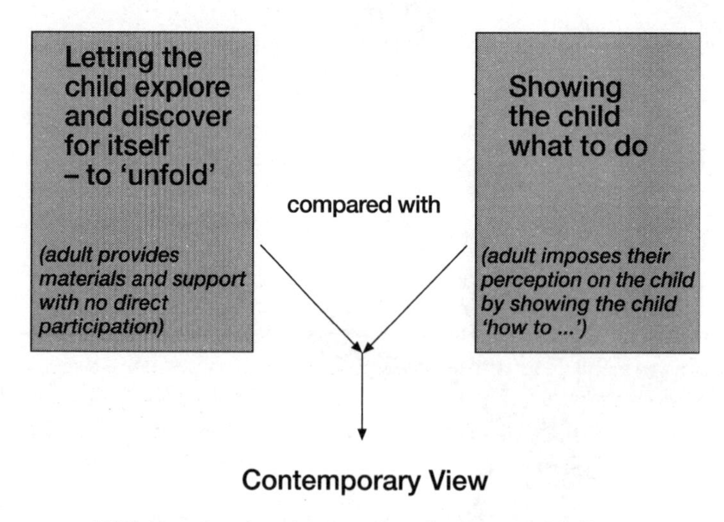

Figure 12.6 Contrasting views of the role of adults in Arts education

artistic accomplishments to enhance the role of wife and mother, served to limit the conceptual framework on artmaking by constructing a male model of artistic practice that discounted, or ignored, social and cultural characteristics. In the late twentieth century, the impetus for inclusion of women in the writing of art history has not necessarily altered this model, as Hoorn (1994) has observed. Her analysis of art texts revealed the subtle ways in which women's artmaking is devalued through relatively limited discussion and reference to women's personal characteristics (such as 'attractive personality') rather than their contribution to artistic practice. While these assumptions about adult artwork are being challenged, the influence of socio-cultural attitudes in relation to gender in early childhood art has received relatively little attention.

Social context in the experience of learning

The antecedents of the tension surrounding the role of the teacher are evident in the metaphors used by theorists such as Rousseau, Pestalozzi and Froebel. Froebel, whose term 'kindergarten' epitomises the use of metaphor to liken the child to a plant and the teacher to a gardener, explained his intention: 'Little children . . . ought not to be *schooled* and taught, they need merely to be *developed*. It is the pressing need of our age, and only the idea of a garden can serve to show us symbolically . . . the proper treatment of children' (Froebel, 1891, p. 291).

There is a sense of understatement in the use of 'merely' in this context and it is possible to imagine how such a statement could be interpreted as advocating a restrained role for the teacher. In fact, the teacher's role was of particular concern to Froebel:

> Not the communication of knowledge already in their possession is the task, but the calling forth of new knowledge. Let them observe, lead their pupils to observe, and to render themselves and their pupils conscious of their observations.
>
> (Froebel, 1905, p. 200)

As individualistic models of cognitive development have been reassessed (Rogoff, 1990), the influence of social, cultural and historical factors on children's development has been recognised. Vygotsky (Davydov, 1995) has shown how the various signs and symbol systems such as language and visual images that are specific to a child's culture are integral to the way in which that child comes to make meaning and to understand his or her world.

The complex interplay between the child, the current situation and the broader cultural context mediates the child's experience of thinking and learning. For example, in the 'pink' vignette in the opening section, the context of the current situation for the children included their previous and present experiences of drawing, of colour, and of relating to each other, as well as the availability of art materials and the child-sized table that they were sharing. The broader context of culture included the language used, the children's exposure to particular visual images, social norms regarding gender stereotypes, and the educational approach that facilitated their participation in artmaking.

Children's interactions with each other affect their understandings of themselves. The reciprocal exchanges involved in social interactions result in children being influenced and influencing their socio-cultural environment (Van Der Veer and Valsiner, 1991, 1994; Newman and Holzman, 1993). Again, as an example, in the 'pink' vignette the children were sitting around a small table on which they could see each other's images, comment on them, possibly respond to them through their own images, and choose to use the same or different colours as their peers.

The interactive role of the adult or more expert peer described in Vygotsky's theory of the Zone of Proximal Development (Vygotsky, 1962) involves the joint construction of meaning through discussion and collaborative exploration with the child. Rather than imposing perceptions upon them, adults respond to children's interest and curiosity and, in the process, encourage them to extend their learning just beyond their present mastery level.

In the light of this contemporary understanding, Froebel's view of the teacher's role could be seen as a relatively enlightened perspective. Froebel sees the influence of teachers as both subtle and dynamic. Engaging in the process of observing, the teacher is an active participant in making meaning, not *for* the child, rather *with* the child. That is, both the teacher and the child appear to be viewed as learners.

The nature of effective interactions between teachers and children is increasingly being seen as a complex interplay of factors that need further investigation. An example of research that seeks to understand this dynamic more clearly is discussed in a later section.

THE DEVELOPMENT OF INTEREST IN ASPECTS OF GENDER IN THE VISUAL ARTS IN EARLY CHILDHOOD

During the twentieth century, many studies of children's drawings and paintings signalled differences in form, colour and imagery according to gender. To a late twentieth-century observer, the research in this area reflects an increasing understanding of the circumstances and nature of the development of creative processes in early childhood. Specifically, research has moved from investigating the *psychological characteristics* of children's artmaking, to observing the *subject matter* chosen by children, and, more recently, to analysing the *influence of the curriculum* in children's artistic development. The following section explores the way in which gender has been seen to influence children's artmaking and shows how early childhood educators have been influenced by wider social attitudes.

Psychological characteristics

The growing influence of psychology on practice in education in the 1930s–1940s was responsible for several categories of research studies that were to influence aspects of the arts in early childhood. Goodenough's 1926 study of the measurement of intelligence through analysis of children's drawings was the precursor to a range of research focusing on different psychological characteristics (Goodenough, 1926; Eng, 1931; Griffiths, 1935).

A parallel interest in sex-differences in young children was evident in studies such as Hattwick (1937). Hattwick's continuing interest in sex-differences is reflected in the influential study *Painting and Personality*, published ten years later with Alschuler (Alschuler and Hattwick, 1947). One hundred and fifty 2- to 5-year-old children, 'black and white', were studied over the period of a year, and the data were extensively analysed in an attempt to show how children's experiences are often reflected in their paintings and drawings. The influence of sex-differences is explicitly drawn out from analysis in three areas of artistic development: line and form; colour; and brush strokes. In reporting on the quantitative analysis of the difference between crayon and easel painting 'products', Alschuler and Hattwick made some significant observations:

> Our study of products revealed that circles, delicate colors, and light strokes are likely to be associated with submissive and/or feminine qualities, while strong colours and heavy, vertical strokes tend to be associated with assertive and/or masculine tendencies.
>
> (Alschuler and Hattwick, 1947, p. 132)

In the context of the late 1940s, the 'and/or' qualification appears to signal an awareness of the complexity of factors, other than gender, that may influence imagemaking. This is borne out in the subsequent observation:

> It is of some interest that all these examples of conflicting circular–vertical designs (or, as interpreted, 'conflicting masculine–feminine drives') occur in girls. One wonders whether this may be due to two cultural factors, namely (1) Do the rather rigid standards concerning the behaviour of little girls make for rebellion and conflict? (2) Does the value placed on being a male in our society also make for the conflict noted?
>
> (Alschuler and Hattwick, 1947, p. 132)

The influence of environmental stimuli on children of both genders is acknowledged and the background of each child is considered within a psychological framework for analysis. While associations are made between types of behaviours and gender (assertive-male, submissive-female), explicit mention is made of the observation of both boys and girls who did not conform to these stereotypes. For example, while vertical strokes are seen to have parallels with 'masculine tendencies', girls with 'strong assertive drives (who appeared to have) no conflicts over their assertive feelings' are observed to use vertical strokes, as seen in the case of:

> *Shirley* was a talkative, self-assured, outgoing child with a wealth of ideas which were carried out in dramatic play, in which she took the lead. Shirley showed relatively little interest in painting. She used warm colors, and her products were consistently characterised by vertical and horizontal strokes often combined into squares.
>
> (Alschuler and Hattwick, 1947, p. 59)

Choice of colour was the second aspect of artistic development that was perceived by Alschuler and Hattwick (1947) to be significantly sex-related. They reported that girls' use of colour was more 'intense and persistent' (p. 15) than that of boys, and this was specifically linked with a perception on the part of contemporary researchers that girls manifested more emotion than boys; it was seen as logical, therefore, that girls should 'tend towards free expression of emotions' in their paintings and drawings (p. 103).

From a contemporary perspective, it is possible to see how Alschuler and Hattwick foreshadowed a more inquiring approach to the study of sex-differences by raising questions about the broader developmental context of the child.

Subject matter

In the second half of the twentieth century, interest in identifying gender differences in the subject matter of children's drawing became evident in studies such as Feinburg (1977) and McNiff (1982). Two special issues of the American journal *Studies in Art Education* addressed the current interest relating to gender issues. In 1977, guest editors for the issue titled 'Sex Differences as they Relate to Art and Art Education' noted the paucity of research into 'male–female differences as they apply to art and art education' and particularly:

> qualitative and quantitive research on: the occurrence and effects of sex discrimination in the art classroom; the differential effects of teaching methodologies and role modelling on boys and girls, and many other important areas of related interest.
>
> (Packard and Zimmerman, 1977, pp. 5–6)

Thirteen years later, Pariser and Zimmerman (1990) note in their guest editorial that a paucity of research still exists in gender issues in art education. While the focus of *Studies in Art Education* covers the whole spectrum of art and art education, these observations are particularly relevant to the area of early childhood art education. In the 1990 issue, no research specific to the early childhood area was included.

Observations of the socio-cultural expectations that influence artmaking suggest that there are qualitative differences in the development of imagery in girls and boys. The expectations that were alluded to by Alschuler and Hattwick (1947) were investigated by Feinburg (1977) in a study of the depictions of fighting and helping by 7- to 8-year-old children. While differences in the choice of subject matter between boys and girls is not an unusual observation, Feinburg's (1977) analysis explored differences in the way in which children related to interpersonal situations. She suggests that boys depersonalise destructive themes in order to explore them, whereas girls identify on a personal level with conflict, and therefore such themes are associated with a stronger sense of personal risk.

By recognising different motivations in children's depictions, teachers are able to take an inclusive approach to art education based on the personally relevant conceptualisations of children's experiences of the world.

Figure 12.7 Untitled drawing in crayon by Becky, age 6

> Becky frequently drew her friends, always girls, in groups arranged according to her prevailing friendships. Consider how you might work with Becky and other children in her group to develop her interest in the nature of friendship and how boys might be included in such an investigation.

In a study of 1,800 drawings done by 26 children aged 6, 7 and 8, McNiff concluded:

> The children's art did not present stereotypic images of sex roles nor could the contrasts be specifically attributed to genetic, social or psychological differences between the sexes . . . girls and boys have very different expressive interests which are not necessarily fully incorporated into their educational environment and which affect all areas of school adjustment.
>
> (McNiff, 1982, p. 271)

This question of how differing expressive interests may be incorporated into the educational environment has been approached through a systemic view of learning by attention to the ways in which the curriculum influences children's choice of images.

Influence of the curriculum

For young children, an approach to the curriculum that facilitates the investigation of aspects of their own lives, including aspects of gender, is likely to start with the teacher observing those interests and questions that are motivating children's play. Observations such as the preoccupation with pink mentioned earlier, the roles children take in socio-dramatic play, or the interest a child takes in constructing a complex building, may all form the basis for planning in early childhood settings. Such an approach contrasts with a more traditional view of curriculum that advocates teacher control of the subject matter.

In concluding a review and analysis of current literature pertaining to gender differences in children's drawings, Speck (1995) raises the issue of 'free' choice in drawing and suggests that such an approach perpetuates stereotypes:

> Therefore ought not drawing (and painting) topics be set that function to create successful masculinity and femininity, rather than permitting children to perpetuate unsuccessful versions thereof in their free choice art.

Speck's solution is:

> more observational, scientific, technical and mechanical drawing for

girls and more still life and decorative drawing and more detailed human figure drawing for boys; and to fantasy drawing for girls and boys that is not gender blind.

(Speck, 1995, pp. 49–50)

Speck is not specific about the age group she is addressing. For early childhood educators, however, such a statement again raises the issue of teacher intervention in children's artmaking and the means by which teachers promote children's construction of meaning through the visual arts. While Speck's research indicates the need for teachers to consider carefully children's experience of the world to ensure that this is expanded through their artmaking, the way in which this occurs in early childhood settings is more complex than merely 'setting topics'.

RECOGNISING TEACHERS' INFLUENCE IN CHILDREN'S CONSTRUCTIONS OF SELF

Teachers' responses to children's behaviours or products has been observed by Csikszentmihalyi (1990) to be a key dependent variable in much research about children's creativity. Several researchers (for example, Halpin and Halpin, and Glover and Gleary, cited in Amabile, 1979) suggest that creativity can be influenced by children's knowledge of what is valued by the teacher. Yet, specific evaluation of children's art is generally discouraged. This raises the question of how teachers can respond constructively to children.

Parsons' (1992) work on the role of interpretation in art education has contributed to the discussion about the means by which teachers can engage children in dialogue about their artmaking. This is clearly illustrated in the contemporary example of practice in the pre-schools of Reggio Emilia, where teachers consciously use discussion to restate, develop and extend children's experiences (Edwards, 1993, p. 153).

A case study of teacher response to children's artmaking

Teachers can be a potent influence in shaping children's points of view (White, 1996). In artmaking experiences, teachers convey attitudes and values to children in subtle ways. Seeking to understand more clearly how teachers conveyed to children, through explicit verbal responses, what they valued in children's artmaking, Makin, White and Owen (1996) observed teachers and children in four Anglo-Australian and Asian-Australian early childhood settings. Five teachers in four settings were observed as they interacted with children engaged in painting/collage experiences. Verbal interactions from video-recordings of the teacher–child interactions were transcribed using message-semantics networks developed by Makin (1994) that allowed for the detailed description and analysis of the evaluative messages in the talk between children and teachers.

The issues explored in the study included:

- What do adults say to young children about their imagemaking?
- How do adult responses affect children's engagement with their imagemaking?
- Do adults in different cultures give similar evaluative messages?

Considerable contrast was observed between the five teachers (three Anglo-Australian, one Japanese and one Chinese-Australian) in terms of their level of engagement with children from a range of cultural backgrounds. While all the teachers indicated that communication was a goal of their arts programme, the ways in which this occurred in practice varied widely. The use of non-verbal communication, such as gesture, proximity, eye contact and timing, both by children and adults, all indicated subtle, yet powerful, forms of communication.

In some settings, however, many of the interactions between teachers and children during the artmaking were concerned with the mechanics of activity maintenance. In these settings, less emphasis seemed to be placed on interactions that focused on the actual process of painting/collage and the image being created. It was also found that in many instances teachers did not wait to hear children's responses to their questions. Rather, they appeared to be responding to their own preconceived ideas about the topic under discussion, which precluded them from genuine interchange with the children. Teachers who actively engaged the children in dialogue about their image-making encouraged longer participation in the activity. This engagement involved imaginative responses in many instances.

The following examples illustrate these contrasts. In both examples, children have indicated that they are ready to leave the activity:

Example 1

(*Note:* Both children in this example are female.)

Teacher: is your painting finished Nanayo?
Nanayo: (*nods*)
Teacher: if it's finished, why don't you tell Masayo what your painting is all about?
Masayo, why don't you ask Nanayo what her painting is all about? Why don't you ask her what she has drawn?
Masayo: what have you drawn?
Nanayo: (*whispers something in Masayo's ear.*)
Teacher: oh, you feel a bit shy Nanayo. What did she tell you Masayo?
Masayo: I couldn't hear it

Nanayo: (*whispers again*)
Masayo: (*to T.*) they're stars.
Teacher: aren't these stars pretty? You are in this picture too aren't you Nanayo?
Nanayo: (*points to one place in the picture*)
Teacher: so that's where Nanayo is? Who are you watching those stars with Nanayo?
(*to Masayo*) Do you know Shia? Shia is a little baby.
(*to Nanayo*) who else with?
Nanayo: Mia and Mum and Dad.
Teacher: (*to Masayo*) can you see the stars from your place? Oh, you don't think you can?, oh if that's the case ask your Mum and Dad tonight OK?
(*to Nanayo*) that's what you can see from your place isn't it Nanayo?

The teacher makes a deliberate attempt to extend the children's involvement at the easel by first encouraging them to look closely at each other's paintings and then engaging with them in dialogue. The co-construction of meaning appears to be this teacher's goal.

Example 2

Mary: Bill's finished.
Teacher: Bill's finished has he? Oh you have finished Bill? Right, would you like to take your painting and hang it up outside? It's a lovely painting. Bill, would you like to hang it on the fence?
Bill: I can't.
Teacher: You can't, oh, would you like me to help you?
Alright Phoebe, I'll help you love, I'll just get some pegs as well, we'll put it down here like that to dry.

In this example, the teacher's goal appears to be maintenance of the activity. Her response to children's comments is to repeat them without amplification. Children are not encouraged to extend their time at the easel.

Is the contrast in the approach of these two teachers influenced by gender or culture? While these two female teachers were from different cultural backgrounds, the contrast in teaching styles that is evident was also apparent when the teacher in the first example was interacting with boys. Her beliefs about teaching and learning were consistent in terms of her practice with both girls and boys. In post-study interviews, both teachers mentioned that they had taught in at least one country other than the country in which they undertook their original teacher education. The first teacher felt that her beliefs and practice had been influenced by this experience. The second teacher said that she had not changed her practice as a result of the experience. It appears that the first teacher's openness to new cultural experiences and willingness to change her practice may be symptomatic of a greater flexibility of approach to teaching and learning.

Implications for teachers concerned to develop the child's construction of gender

In analysing the effect of teachers' verbal messages on children's artmaking, it became apparent that, in many instances, teachers had difficulty in responding to the children's artmaking. They seemed uneasy about using specialised language to discuss aspects of the children's paintings such as colour, form and texture, which restricted their ability to respond to and talk with children in ways that challenged and extended the artmaking experience. This suggests that teachers would benefit from more experience in using art materials to enable them to go beyond developmental theories and gain a more concrete understanding of the potential and challenge of artmaking and art media in early childhood settings.

Skills such as listening, observation and knowledge of strategies that children use are essential if teachers are to assist children in articulating, refining and extending their artmaking experiences. Understanding of the wider context of how children are thinking about gender, how they are evaluating gendered images and how individual children are actively constructing themselves as male or female would enable teachers to engage with children as co-constructors of meaning, thereby extending children's capacity to use the visual arts as an imaginative and expressive form of communication.

Thus, a contemporary view of the role of adults in art education (Figure 12.6) that acknowledges both the value of children's exploration and investigation and their need to develop the skills of artmaking to enable them to satisfy their increasing need for complexity in the expression of their ideas, will also need to acknowledge that the 'natural' development of children is culturally shaped.

TRANSMISSION OF SOCIO-CULTURAL VALUES IN EARLY CHILDHOOD SETTINGS

The influence of the Romantic writers such as Rousseau on visual arts education practice in the 1920s–1930s is clearly evident through the work of Franz Cizek, who developed the concept of 'Child Art'. Cizek subscribed to Rousseau's view of the 'natural' law of children, as is evident in his reply to a question about the need for teacher-direction:

> Children have their own laws which they must needs obey. What right have grown-ups to interfere? People should draw as they feel.
>
> (cited in Viola, 1942, p. 32)

While the view of the child as 'natural' and 'free' pervades many adult perceptions of childhood, this view is naive in terms of recognising the means by which culture informs a child's experience of the world. The notion of 'free' expression would appear to deny the influence of a whole range of factors such as:

- parental interest, encouragement and facilitation;
- the character of the child's wider visual environment;
- the value that the child's community places on visual expression; and
- the practice that the teacher creates in the early childhood setting.

Such factors are likely to influence the ways in which children make sense of their world and represent their ideas through images.

Similar observations have been made in the field of literacy, where the way in which children relate their experience of the real world to the world of books has also been assumed to be 'natural' (Brice Heath, 1982). Different communities follow socially established practices regarding the sharing of literacy through reading or telling stories, reading signs, following information or instruction sheets, interpreting television advertisements and, more contemporarily, using information technology. Depending on the orientation of these early literacy experiences, children arrive at school with varying degrees of enculturation into the assumed world of school-based literacy.

The parallel in the visual arts are the early experiences a child has in sharing aspects of the visual environment. Just as exposure to the world of written language does not automatically result in a direct path to literacy, so looking does not necessarily result in 'seeing' details of the visual environment. The socially established practices of families and communities with regard to attending to and sharing visual details with children, will clearly inform the ways in which children use these images in their own symbolmaking.

Children's development in the visual arts

While all facets of children's development are likely to affect their artmaking in some way, aspects of development that are particularly relevant to symbolic expression include:

Birth to 2 years

- transition from bodily expression towards the use of symbols;

  for example from crying to pointing when wanting to direct attention to an object.

- exploring through the senses;

  feeling an object, putting it in the mouth, shaking it.

2–5 years

- spontaneously representing feelings about themselves and their world;

  making marks on paper to represent their family and friends, squeezing, pulling and rolling clay to represent their pet or toy, using boxes to create a representation of their home.

- developing an individual repertoire of recurring symbols or schema;
- often systematic in their experimentation;

  for example will use trial-and-error, repetition, rotation, observation and reflection to refine their artistry in an effort to produce more specific communication.

5–8 years

- relative confidence in their own forms of expression;
- interested in solving graphic problems such as showing a profile;
- need for more precise and effective communication with their peers;
- need to use symbols in an increasingly more functional way.

Awareness of the value of visual expression in the overall development of the child will enable teachers to facilitate children's acquisition of personally valid and satisfying forms of communication.

Consideration of a physical and human environment that will facilitate children's development of a positive gendered self-concept through the visual arts

By taking an investigative approach to children's interests and considering both the human and physical environment when planning, early childhood teachers can play an active role in children's construction of the gendered self. The following aspects of context are presented so that you have the opportunity to reflect on issues that may influence the way in which children in early childhood settings can explore their ideas, create images and make sense of their world.

Physical environment

Consider the influence of the physical arrangement of the setting:

Teachers sometimes observe that boys prefer outdoor play and girls prefer indoor play.

  what opportunities are there for children to engage in art experiences both inside and outside?

If boys dominate the block area and girls control the collage materials, some children may be prevented from exploring equipment and materials that may be valuable for the expression of their ideas.

how can equal access to a full range of expressive materials be ensured?

When a child has had a satisfying experience with drawing, painting or clay, they are likely to want to repeat this on subsequent days.

how can provision be made for a range of basic materials to be available every day?

When children are comfortably seated in small groups, they often look at each other's drawings or clay constructions and discuss them together.

what provision is made for small group seating arrangements?

The potential for extending children's visual environment reaches well beyond the immediate physical environment.

what opportunities are available for broadening children's experiences through visiting galleries, museums, and going on walks into the natural environment?

Human environment

Considering their role in the joint construction of meaning between children and adults requires teachers to observe and analyse the nature of their interactions with children.

When children make gender related comments on issues such as clothing, preferences for particular colours, toys or games, this is often an indication of an interest in socio-cultural expectations about gender.

are opportunities made for following up such comments, either at the time or in a later experience?

Looking at plants, familiar objects, paintings and other visual images does not necessarily ensure that details such as colour, form, line and subject matter have been closely observed.

how can children be engaged in looking closely at their visual environment?

When children hear comments that stereotype abilities or behaviour as gender specific, they often conform to those stereotypes without trying experiences for themselves.

are boys and girls being encouraged to be involved in a range of expressive visual experiences and to use varied media?

The creative potential of materials and equipment varies in terms of the possibilities for imaginative or realistic expression and play.

how are children encouraged to use equipment in a variety of ways to ensure that both the imaginative and realistic potential are explored?

When responding to children's artworks, adults often make casual comments that may include assumptions about the meaning that the child is expressing and stereotypical perspectives of gender and symbolic representations.

what methods can teachers use to listen to the way in which they respond to children and to understand more fully how their responses influence children's imagery?

Social relationships affect children's artmaking. The subtleties of peer relationships, such as the way in which children watch and evaluate each other's artmaking, how ideas are exchanged, how imagemaking may be regulated through peer control, all influence children's participation in the visual arts.

how can staff in early childhood settings support each other to become more aware of children's social interactions?

Observing and understanding how children are shaping their view of themselves and the world

Seeking a better understanding of the differences in children's symbolic understanding of reality necessitates a sensitivity to the ways in which children are making meaning of their lives. The development of intuitive understanding in 3- to 4-year-olds leads to their 'theorising' about the world in order to make sense of their experiences.

A graphic example of a 4-year-old girl's fascination with pink is found in Figure 12.8: Emily's Bathtime Survey.
Emily frequently involved herself in graphic representations of her world, making pop-up pictures depicting her journey from home to school, three-dimensional images of animals, people and houses, and in this case a survey, ostensibly of the choice of Bathtime, a children's shampoo. Emily connected her experience of the simple method of using surveys that she had been introduced to at school with her preoccupation with pink to 'prove' to herself and others that pink was clearly favoured within her milieu. The fact that she was the only person responding to the survey was not yet relevant to her theorising!

How can teachers harness this intuitive theorising? Furthermore, how

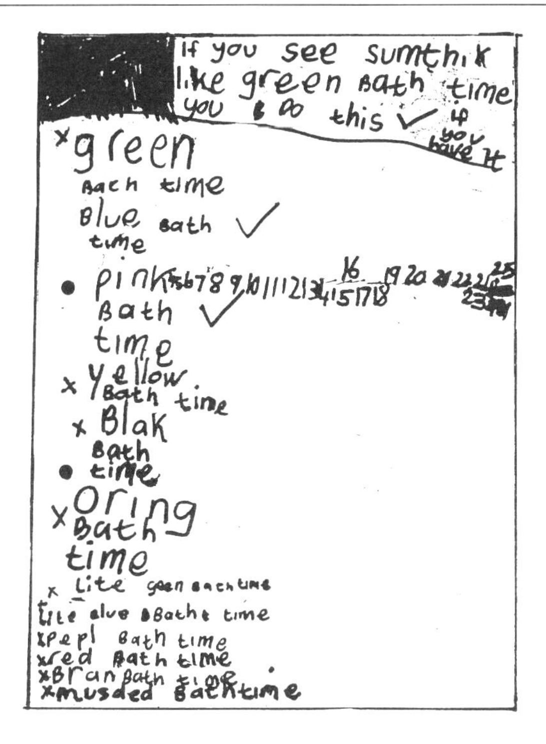

Figure 12.8 Emily's Bathtime Survey in felt pen by Emily, age 4

can children's symbolic representation of their experiences be nurtured in ways that enable them to deal with the stereotyping of behaviour and other conflicting evidence they receive when interacting within their communities? In concluding an analysis of some examples of these conflicts, White (1996) asserted:

> By being aware of the significance of the connections which children are making, how they are theorising about the world and the role imagination plays in their learning, teachers can collaborate with children to open up the possibilities for more responsive interaction, thereby building on and enhancing children's intuitive learning.
>
> (White, 1996, p. 110)

In considering learning environments that are conducive to children's 'research' through artmaking, the issues raised earlier regarding the contextual circumstances of children's learning will be revisited, with specific reference to the capacity of the teacher in creating such an environment.

DRAWING TOGETHER: THE POTENTIAL OF PINK!

Returning to the questions raised in the opening vignette about pink, while colour was the focus of that particular exchange, similar questions can be asked about line, form and other aspects of artmaking in relation to children's developing awareness of gender. The arts are fundamental to early childhood practice, and regular participation in drawing, painting, clay and other expressive media can provide children with opportunities to reflect on and extend their imaginative experiences. In parallel, teachers have the opportunity to develop interactions that support and extend young children's symbolic and imaginative development as one facet of a range of strategies to facilitate children's development of a positive, gendered self-concept through the visual arts.

Teachers as active participants in children's artmaking

Teachers' abilities to engage effectively in the co-construction with children of an expressive environment are influenced by their own understanding of the process of artmaking. Just as children bring prior experiences to their symbolic expression, so too do teachers bring to their interactions with children the prior experiences, both positive and negative, that they have had in the visual arts. In families, they have experienced varying degrees of interest and enthusiasm about visual expression and communication. Among friends, they have possibly shared or rejected particular styles of visual imagery. And in their educational settings, they have experienced positive or possibly questionable reactions to their use and development of symbolic expression.

Children and adults both benefit from a dynamic and supportive environment in which exploration, experimentation, expression and reflection are valued. For adults, such an environment is likely to encourage awareness of the interaction of many elements in their own attitudes to gender, to artmaking and to teaching and learning in early childhood. This recognition can be the starting point for teachers interested in developing an inclusive approach to furthering children's understanding of gender through the visual arts. Rather than accepting the stereotypes that have been associated with pink, they can become active explorers of the issues raised in the pink vignette and, in the process, help to re-define the role of adults in children's artmaking.

Similarities and differences evident between genders also exist within gender groups. When, in 1947, Alschuler and Hattwick asked (regarding examples of conflicting circular–vertical designs):

> One wonders whether this may be due to two cultural factors, namely (1) Do the rather rigid standards concerning the behaviour of little girls

make for rebellion and conflict? (2) Does the value placed on being a male in our society also make for the conflict noted?

(Alschuler and Hattwick, 1947, p. 132)

they indicated their alertness to the overall context in which a child is developing. To a contemporary reader, that these questions were raised is not entirely surprising, given the present awareness of the influence of gender stereotyping on young children (Golombok and Fivush, 1994). In the contemporary context, the challenges for early childhood educators are to continue to raise questions, to realise the potential of working with children through their socially constructed exchanges, such as the 'pink story', and to ensure that children's artmaking does support and expand their conception of themselves as gendered individuals.

REFERENCES

Alschuler, R. and Hattwick, La Berta W. (1947). *Painting and personality,* Chicago: The University of Chicago Press.

Amabile, T. (1979). Effects of external evaluation on artistic creativity. *Journal of Personality and Social Psychology, 37*(2), 221–223.

Brice Heath, S. (1982). What no bedtime story means: narrative skills at home and school. *Language in Society, 11*, 49–76.

Csikszentmihalyi, M. (1990). The domain of creativity. In M. Runco and R. Albert (eds) *Theories of creativity*. Newbury Park: Sage Publications, pp. 190–211.

Davis, J. and Gardner, H. (1992). The cognitive revolution: consequences for the understanding and education of the child as artist. In B. Reimer and R.A. Smith (eds) *The arts, education and aesthetic knowing*. Chicago: National Society for the Study of Education, pp. 92–123.

Davydov, V. (1995). The influence of L.S. Vygotsky on education, theory and practice. *Educational Researcher,* April, 12–21.

Edwards, C. (1993). The role of the teacher. In C. Edwards, L. Gandini and G. Forman (eds) *The hundred languages of children*. New Jersey: Ablex, pp. 151–170.

Eng, H. (1931). *The psychology of children's drawings: From the first stroke to the color drawing,* London: Kegan Paul, Trench Trubner & Co.

Feinburg, S. (1977). Conceptual content and spatial characteristics in boy's and girl's drawings of fighting and helping, *Studies in Art Education, 18*(2).

Freedman, K. (1994). Interpreting gender and visual culture in art classrooms, *Studies in Art Education, 35*(3), 57–170.

Froebel, F. (1891). *Letters on the kindergarten,* trans. Michaelis, E. and Moore, H.K. Swan: Sonnenschein.

Froebel, F. (1905). *Education of man*, trans. Hailmann, W.N., New York: Appleton.

Gardner, H. (1976). Unfolding or teaching. In E. Eisner (ed.) *The arts, human development, and education.* California: McCutchan Publishing Corporation, pp. 99–110.

Gardner, H. (1982). *Art, mind and brain.* New York: Basic Books.

Geahigan, G. (1992). The arts and education: a historical perspective. In B. Reimer and R.A. Smith (eds) *The arts, education and aesthetic knowing.* Chicago: National Society for the Study of Education, pp. 1–19.

Golombok, S. and Fivush, R. (1994). *Gender development.* Cambridge: Cambridge University Press.

Goodenough, F. (1926). *Measurement of personality by drawing*. New York: World Book Co.
Goodman, N. (1968). *Languages of art*. Indianapolis: Bobbs-Merrill Co.
Griffiths, R. (1935). *A study of imagination in early childhood*. London: Kegan Paul, Trench Trubner & Co.
Hall, G.S. (1911). *Educational problems* (Vol.2). New York: Appleton.
Hattwick, La Berta W. (1937). Sex differences in behaviour of pre-school children. *Child Development*, December.
Hoorn, J. (ed.) (1994). *Strange women*. Melbourne: Melbourne University Press.
Makin, L. (1994). Teacher style and small group problem solving in multilingual classrooms: roles and realisations. Unpublished PhD thesis, Macquarie University.
Makin, L., White, M. and Owen, M. (1996). Creation or constraint: teacher evaluation of children's painting in Anglo-Australian and Asian-Australian child care centres. *Studies in Art Education*, Summer.
Mac Naughton, G. (1996). *Curriculum for curriculum change in post-modern times: Some ethical considerations*. Keynote address: Weaving Webs Conference, Melbourne, July.
McNiff, K. (1982). Sex differences in children's art. *Journal of Education, 164*(3).
Newman, F. and Holzman, L. (1993). *Lev Vygotsky: Revolutionary scientist*. London: Routledge.
Packard, S. and Zimmerman, E. (1977). Guest editorial: sex differences as they relate to art and art education. *Studies in Art Education, 18*(2), 5–6.
Pariser, D. and Zimmerman, E. (1990). Editorial: gender issues in art education, *Studies in Art Education, 32*(1).
Parsons, M. (1992). Cognition as interpretation in art education. In B. Reimer and R.A. Smith (eds) *The arts, education and aesthetic knowing*. Chicago: National Society for the Study of Education, pp. 70–91.
Perkins, D. and Leondar, B. (eds) (1977). *The arts and cognition*. Baltimore: The Johns Hopkins University Press.
Rogoff, B. (1990). *Apprenticeship in thinking*. New York: Oxford University Press.
Rousseau, J.J. (1911). *Emile*. London: J.M. Dent
Speck, C. (1995). Gender differences in children's drawings *Australian Art Education, 18*(2).
Topliss, H. (1996). *Modernism and feminism, Australian women artists 1900–1940*. Sydney: Craftsman House.
Van der Veer, R. and Valsiner, J. (1991). *Understanding Vygotsky: A quest for synthesis*. Oxford: Blackwell.
Van der Veer, R. and Valsiner, J. (1994). *The Vygotsky reader*. Oxford: Blackwell.
Viola, W. (1942). *Child art*. London: University of London.
Vygotsky, L.S. (1962). *Thought and language*, New York: Wiley.
White, M. (1996). Imagination in learning: learning to imagine. In W. Schiller (ed.) *Issues in expressive arts*. Amsterdam: Gordon & Breach, pp. 99–111.

Chapter 13

Making sense of gender issues in mathematics and technology

Nicola Yelland

INTRODUCTION

This chapter focuses on young children using computers in a mathematical environment and describes some of the ways in which they interact in technology based activities embedded within a mathematics curriculum.[1] It suggests that traditional views concerning expertise with computers have elevated characteristics that are more compatible with masculine performance and interactions, and in doing so have often considered the performance of females as being deficient in some way. It will present research that focuses on the strategies and interactions of children as they worked on computer based tasks, in one of three gender pairs (girls, boys or boy/girl), and highlight differences in performance as the pairs solved novel problems. It challenges the notion that girls are inferior to boys in activities that use efficiency as a measure of outcome.

The research is presented in the context of the literature pertaining to gender issues of performance in mathematics and computing in order to situate the findings in terms of what is currently known about the use of computers in educational contexts and how they may enhance learning for all students. It has too long been accepted as a truism that boys have both more confidence and ability in mathematics and technology than girls. This chapter will consider research that highlights the equivocal nature of findings in relation to gender issues of performance in mathematics and technology and suggest that results must always be considered with knowledge of the task and the context of its presentation.

ASPECTS OF GENDER IN MATHEMATICS

Research concerning gender differences in mathematics has tended to focus on upper primary and secondary aged children and the results of studies that have been conducted over the last two decades have been equivocal. While some have reported differences in performance based on gender, they have frequently been attributed not only to the mathematical content area, but also to the format of questions and the test context. There is a dearth of information about performance related to gender in the early childhood years that can be used to assist both researchers and educators to understand the variations that have been observed in later years of schooling.

Schuard (1986) stated that it is 'generally thought that there is little difference between the mathematical attainment of girls and boys at the primary stage' (p. 22). She also maintained that when the performance of primary aged children in mathematics is considered, the situation is complicated by a number of variables, such as the types of questions that are asked, the content area and the task format.

Walden and Walkerdine (1985) have noted that 'the main difference between girls and boys was the greater preponderance of boys among the high scorers' (p. 123). They created a 40 item test that revealed 'that there were no sex differences in the numbers of questions answered correctly, answered wrongly, or left unanswered' (p. 31). There were significant differences in favour of the boys on one of three questions related to symmetry and in favour of the girls for two questions: the first of these was related to correcting times on an analogue clock and the second to computing differences. Walden and Walkerdine found that the *between school* differences were more pronounced than the *between sex* differences, and proposed that the description of differences in performance based on gender found in the APU surveys were an artefact of their brief, that is, to 'look at (and for) differences between the sexes' (p. 35), which resulted in them being obliged to find them. They stated that 'This is not the first time it has been suggested that actually setting out to find differences often leads the researcher to ignore data of more importance which may suggest similarities' (Walden and Walkerdine, 1985, p. 36).

More recently in the United Kingdom, the National Evaluation of Key Stage 1 in 1991 and 1992 has provided important information about the attainment levels and performance of 7-year-olds in mathematics as well as English and science. Schagen (1994) analysed seven background variables (sex, ethnicity, special education needs, age, any nursery education, number of years in an infant school and whether or not English was the first language of children), and reported that girls performed better than boys in the two English attainment targets and that age, the number of terms in infant schooling as well as a nursery education all had a positive effect across the results. Sharp, Hutchinson and Whetton (1994) agreed that both age and the starting date of school were positively related to performance, but they also reported a significant gender effect in their analysis of the results whereby girls performed significantly better than boys in both English and mathematics.

Leder (1990) suggested that there is an overlap in the performance of males and females. She contended that consistent between group differences are dwarfed by within group differences, and that these often depend on the type of task that was used in the study as well as the age level of the children. Leder also stated that a meta analysis of the literature using 100 studies confirms her findings and suggested that gender differences have declined in recent times.

The area of spatial ability has been an area of mathematics in which the male superiority over females has long been regarded as a truism. However, the conjecture that males' superior ability in the area has been a major factor affecting achievement in mathematics has not been supported by the literature (Tarte, 1990). A close examination of the literature reveals that the nature of such differences may be more complex than originally thought. As early as 1966, Maccoby stated that, even in the early years, boys were consistently better than girls on spatial tasks and later that spatial ability was the main source of differences between the sexes. However, by 1974 they had changed their view to conclude that male superiority was related to only one aspect of spatial ability – spatial visualisation – with no differences apparent until adolescence. Linn and Petersen (1985) conducted a meta-analysis of the literature in spatial ability. They concluded that large sex differences were found only on measures of mental rotation, while smaller differences were located on measures of spatial perception.

Tarte and Fennema (1995) identified consistent gender differences in the roles of spatial and verbal skills in predicting mathematics ability, and suggested that 'many have believed that male superiority in spatial visualisation skills has contributed to the gender differences found in mathematics achievement' (p. 212). However, they recommended caution for those who make such an assumption, since their study did not provide any evidence to support such a contention. Moreover, their work has revealed that cognitive variables were more reliably related to achievement in mathematics than any affective factors.

Linn and Petersen (1985) also noted that when sex differences were found, they could be detected across the life span. The review detected differences from about the age of 8 years of age for individual studies, but this rose to 18 years for studies of group learning. Linn and Petersen (1985) noted that:

> sex differences in spatial ability appear on tasks for which efficient solution requires rapid manipulation of symbolic information and on tasks that require recognition of the vertical or horizontal. Spatial visualisation tasks, where efficient solution depends on effective use of analytic procedures to select strategies for manipulating symbolic information, do not appear to yield sex differences.
>
> (p. 1492)

They suggested that females' use of analytic strategies was characterised by a cautious approach to problem-solving and that this was disadvantageous in terms of performance parameters that highlighted efficiency.

The literature has also focused on affective features when describing differences between the performance of boys and girls in mathematics. Fennema (1980) suggested that the confidence–anxiety dimension is one of the most important affective variables that can help to explain sex differences in mathematics. Fennema concluded that the literature strongly supported the notion that differences in confidence–anxiety level accounted for differences in performance. She maintained that often sex differences in performance could be related to the greater anxiety and less confidence that girls exhibited in *mathematical* activity. Hilton and Berglund (1974) suggested that gender differences in mathematics achievement may have been due in part to interest that could be viewed as gender typed. This was, and remains, important, because if girls regard themselves as inferior to boys in the area, or if they perceive maths to be a male dominated area, it may restrict their participation and ultimately affect the choices that they are able to make later in life.

GIRLS USING COMPUTERS

With the increased use of computers in schools, there has been an interest in describing performance where students use applications in various subject areas. Research that has focused on gender differences in performance with computers has not been as extensive as that in the subject area of mathematics. However, both in primary and secondary schools the use of computers has been closely aligned to mathematics and science. To this extent, the use of computers, like mathematics and science, has been viewed as a male oriented activity, except in the case of word processing which is seen not only as a 'soft' option, but one that is more attractive to females. Even though there are no substantive reasons for this phenomenon, it seems to be the predominant model in both school and the wider social context. There is little research to suggest that girls cannot do as well as boys in terms of any applications of learning with technology.

Studies have also noted differences based on gender related to performance on computing tasks and attitudes towards computing. Hoyles (1988) outlined some in a comprehensive review. With respect to attitude differences, Hoyles cited the work of Gardner *et al.* (1985) who surveyed 1,500 16- and 17-year-old students and found that, even though the majority of them regarded computer skills as essential for future prospects, a higher proportion of boys than girls held this belief. In a survey of young children, Hughes and MacLeod (1986) reported that, when asked if boys would like computers more than girls, more children associated computers with boys. In a study on the effects of computer use on gender differences in attitudes, Siann, MacLeod, Glissov, and Durndell (1990) found substantial differences in attitudes towards computing prior to participation in computer activities. The boys were more confident in their own ability, showed more interest in the area of computing, and were more likely to associate computing with a need for a high level of ability than were the girls, even though Siann *et al.* reported that 'General attitudes to computer use were similarly positive for both sexes' (p. 183). After the computer experience (with Logo, for 12 weeks), the gender differences in attitudes to computing diminished, although the girls' 'anxiety levels relative to the boys' were reported to increase. An interesting finding of this study with 9-year-old children was that in the mixed pairs the boys tended to dominate the sessions but that this did not result in significant attitudinal differences between girls who worked with boys, and girls who worked with other girls. The authors did note, however, that 'girls in single-sex dyads seemed to gain most cognitively' (p. 191) and as a consequence they stated that 'it is probably more effective for girls for them to be paired with each other than with boys' (p. 191).

In an earlier study by Siann and MacLeod (1986), ten children from a severely disadvantaged area of Edinburgh were observed working in boy/girl pairs on Logo tasks. The authors concluded that the research indicated important gender differences. They found that:

> girls on the whole were less interested and motivated than the boys; secondly, the girls were more disposed to turn to and seek help from the boys than the reverse; and finally, although the girls did seek help from the boys, they resented it when the help was given practically (i.e., by pressing the appropriate keys) rather than verbally.
>
> (p. 137)

It should be noted that the results were reported in a situation in which all the girls were paired with boys, so it was not possible to compare the findings with those of single-sex dyads. It could be that the boys' tendency to dominate the proceedings that was reported in four out of the five pairs, and in the later research (Siann *et al.*, 1990), contributed in a major way to the results. Yet there is evidence that male students are more confident about using computers as a learning tool than females (e.g. Ring, 1991).

In terms of performance, in the study by Siann and MacLeod (1986), the boys completed the task faster than the girls, but this was not statistically significant. Other researchers (Chadwick, 1986; Gunterman and Tovar, 1987; Hattie and Fitzgerald, 1987) have not found significant differences in performance based on gender, while the work of Hughes, Brackenridge, Bibby, and Greenhaugh (1988) has reported significant differences in the performances of girls and boys, on a particular Logo task, to the detriment of girl pairs.

A cautious, or more careful, approach by girls to tasks was also revealed in a study by Hay and Lockwood (1989), who analysed the performance of 6- and 10-year-old children in a computer simulation game concerned with hunting. Their findings emphasised the need for a distinction to be made between optimal and careful decision-making. They asserted that a careful approach was not usually the optimal strategy. In the Hay and Lockwood study, the careful approach that characterised the girls' performance did not affect their success and thus there were no apparent differences based on gender. The research of Hay and Lockwood has highlighted the need to consider the influence of contextual features in any consideration of performance, since it showed that differences in performance based on gender are likely to be enhanced or minimised by manipulation of task characteristics. It is easy to imagine how the context can be manipulated to favour one sex or the other. For example, increased time constraints might favour males, while increased error 'penalties' might benefit females.

Logo was designed as an environment that would engage children in authentic mathematical experiences. In most of the studies of young children exploring with Logo, their performance, whether working individually, in pairs or small groups, has been described and related to either specific methodological issues pertaining to curriculum and teaching (e.g. Hawkins, Homolsky, and Heide, 1984; Noss, 1984) or to cognitive theories of learning (e.g. Clements and Nastasi, 1985, 1988; Webb, 1982, 1984). Only a limited number of these studies have considered performance with reference to the gender composition of pairs, small group or indeed individuals (e.g Gunterman and Tovar, 1987; Hoyles and Sutherland, 1989; Hughes *et al.*, 1988).

The work of Turkle (1984) suggested two types of programming styles: hard and soft mastery. In Turkle's analysis, hard mastery was viewed as the 'mastery of the planner' (p. 104). It was reflected in the imposition of will over the machine by controlling it with the plan. The plan was manifested in the production of a programme that would result in the generation of the product. In contrast, soft mastery was viewed as being more interactive. The user decides, evaluates, and then enters the cycle again. The process of interaction takes precedence over planning or the creation of the final product. Soft mastery is the 'mastery of the artists: try this, wait for a response, try something else, let the overall shape emerge from an interaction with the medium. It is more like a conversation than a monologue' (p. 105).

Hoyles and Sutherland (1989) noted differences in the programming styles of boys and girls and also differences related to the nature of the collaboration and attitudes while working. However, at the end of a three year project, they found no gender differences related to the student's ability to use the ideas of structured programming when working on a well defined task, the ideas of a variable and either a top-down or bottom-up approach to planning. They also indicated that a girl was 'more likely to share her problem with her partner, her representation of the problem, and her ideas for problem solving' (p. 171). They provided useful advice about the dangers of coming to quick and superficial conclusions about supposed gender differences on the basis of short term performance, and warned against the use of slogans such as 'Girls do not plan and boys do not collaborate in their computer work or boys are better than girls in programming' (p. 177). They enforced the idea that statements need to reflect the context in which the activities have occurred and to consider development over a series of tasks and time.

Gunterman and Tovar (1987) did not observe any differences in the productivity of individuals, dyads and triads working on Logo tasks. In comparing the interaction of two and three person groups, they found similar types of behaviour with different gender pairings. However, they also found significant differences in the type of interaction between males, females and mixed groups, whereby males displayed more solidarity than females or mixed groups, the female group members were much more likely to express agreement with their peers than the males, the male groups asked for more information than the female groups, and finally, the males expressed much more antagonism than females or mixed gender groups.

Underwood, Underwood, and Turner (1993) and Underwood, Jindal, and Underwood (1994) have conducted studies in both computer based language tasks and with Roamer, which is akin to the programmable robot turtle. They reported a general improvement in performance in both contexts when pairs were instructed to co-operate and that this requirement had the most beneficial effect for boy pairs in their study, while girl pairs tended to co-operate whether asked to or not.

Previous studies (Yelland, 1993; 1994a; 1994b; 1995) revealed that when children worked, in gender pairs, on computer based tasks, girl pairs made more moves and took more time than either boy or boy/girls pairs to complete a maze type task. However, girls were more accurate in tasks that required them to copy items.

It was found that performance in Logo tasks was moderated by factors such as the task structure, the style of interaction in dyads and personality characteristics that affected the way in which the problem was solved. The results of these studies also indicated that performance was differentiated according to different levels of operation to task solution, which were the result of a number of features, such as comprehension of the task requirements, the selection of appropriate strategies for solution and the application of selected executive processes. The use of such processes ensured a more effective level of task solution that reflected a greater level of sophistication in the application of problem-solving skills. The studies highlighted qualitatively different levels of performance, ranging from naive to knowledgeable, that were distinguished according to the types of processes that were deployed in the problem-solving context, and the influence and application of prior knowledge relevant to task solution. The data also indicated that performances were differentiated on the basis of gender only when performance was considered in terms of specific criteria and related to certain types of tasks. However, with experience in the domain and with changes in tasks design and presentation, such differences disappeared. Additionally, they highlighted the fact that collaborations varied according to the gender composition of the pair in initial experiences in a new domain with specific types of tasks. Girl pairs frequently sought more information from each other and used verbal strategies to work through their problem-solving. This was contrasted with the style of interaction of boy and boy/girl pairs, who tended to make more independent moves and whose talk often centred on disagreements rather than clarification of ideas and strategies. However, another study (Yelland, 1995) of young children revealed no differences in performance based on gender in terms of accuracy or efficiency, when accuracy tasks were presented prior to efficiency based tasks.

It is thus apparent that research findings have illustrated the fact that there may be differences in performance based on gender, and that these need to be carefully considered in terms of the task and context of the study under review.

The research reported here did not set out to analyse gender related performance issues but rather sought to understand the ways in which young children collaborated to solve novel problems that were posed in a technology based context. The activities were based on a version of Logo called *Geo-Logo*[2] embedded within a mathematics curriculum designed to enable the children to investigate actively mathematical ideas. Within the *Geo-Logo* environment, the children can embark on novel problem-solving tasks designed to stimulate their thinking and provide opportunities for them to apply their understandings in a new context.

The studies focused on the strategies and interactions of pairs of children, and thus the Vygotskian perspective of learning based in the social context of the situation was important. Vygotsky (1978) maintained that 'All the higher functions originate as actual relations between human individuals' (p. 57). Additionally, his work highlighted the crucial role that speech takes in mediating learning. In the context of this research, the children's spontaneous comments, as recorded on videotape and transcribed, provided details of their problem-solving strategies and how these may be differentiated according to the gender composition of the pair.

The tasks that will be discussed are 'Get the Toys' – a maze activity in which the turtle had to be directed to pick up a 'toy' – and an open ended project in which the children were required to draw a picture of their choice.

'GET THE TOYS'

'Get the Toys' had three levels. Level 1 was used as a demonstration for the whole group, level 2 for familiarisation for each pair before they all attempted to solve level 3 independently. When the turtle was directed to the toy, the toy was transported to a storage area at the bottom of the screen and the children were instructed to return the turtle to the elevator in the centre of the screen.

The activity will permit only 90 degree turns, and consequently the turtle moves only in orthogonal orientation around the screen. This meant that the choice of turn, rather than being a matter of calculating degrees, was reduced to left (lt 90) or right (rt 90), while still reinforcing that a right-angle turn *is* 90 degrees. Additionally, the children were supported in their choice of distance via the placement of dots in a grid so that each dot was 10 turtle steps apart. In a demonstration session, the children were advised that they had to take the turtle to the toy and get back to the elevator without running out of energy. They were told that every command they gave the turtle would use up energy, so they would have to be very careful about how many moves they made. A meter on the top of the screen indicated to the pairs how much energy was being consumed with each move. Energy consumption was based on the number of moves irrespective of the size of each move. The purpose of this feature was to promote efficiency in use of moves and estimation of distance. For example, a child who moved the turtle fd 2, fd 5, fd 6, fd 2, would consume energy at a higher rate than one who entered fd 15.

Choosing the most efficient route to the toy was not always obvious, particularly at level 3, where the shortest route to the toy was not the most efficient in terms of energy consumption, as it involved a lot of turns. In the case of Floor 3 there were, in fact, three possible routes to direct the turtle along in order to reach the toy rabbit. These are shown in Figure 13.1.

The first route was 'over the top', and although, as previously stated, this appears to be the shortest in terms of distance, it uses more energy because a considerable amount of turns need to be made in order to reach the toy. The second route is the most efficient in terms of the total number of moves that need to be made. Route 3, a variation of route 2, has more turns but is slightly less efficient. The task allowed the children to use this route without running out of energy if the moves that were made to complete it did not exceed 31. Additionally, the children could also use a combination of the routes.

As each pair of children worked on the tasks in the study, all the commands that they made and the resultant moves were recorded on a videotape. Simultaneously, a camera recorded the interactions of the children as they engaged in the problem-solving activity. The two video inputs

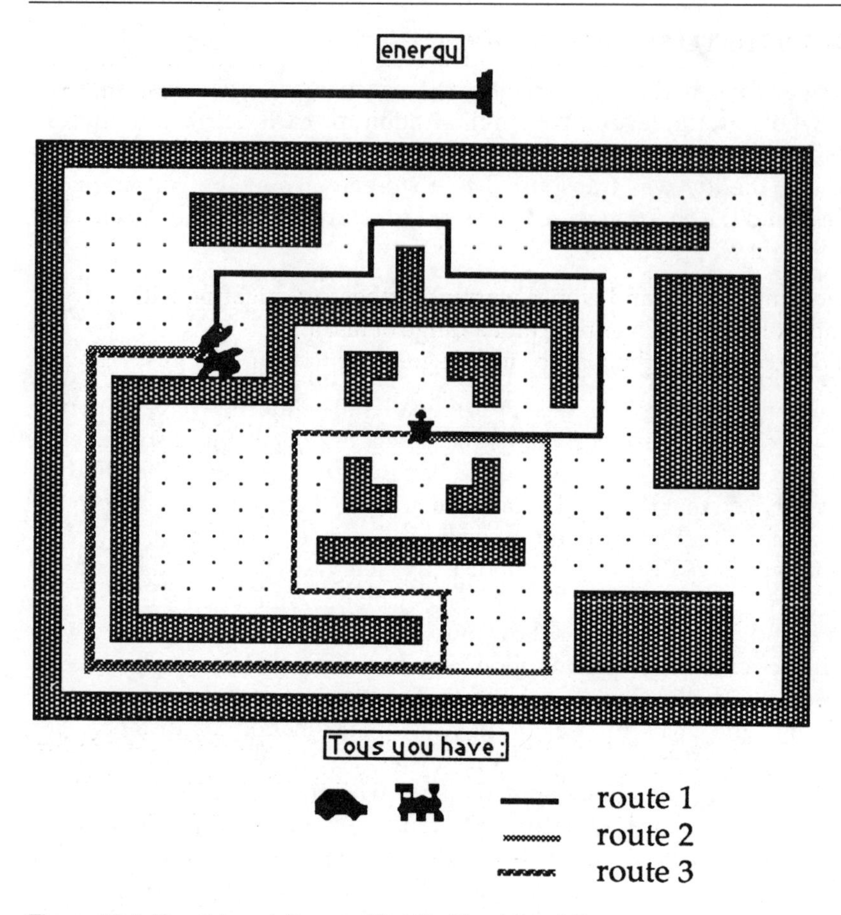

Figure 13.1 Possible solutions to 'Get the Toys' (level 3)

were then mixed using a digital video mixer so that both the computer screen containing the strategies and the camera input showing the interactions of the pair could be analysed cohesively. The children were asked to talk aloud to each other as they worked on the task so that their verbal utterances could be recorded clearly on videotape.

Table 13.1 shows the number of pairs of each gender type that did or did not complete the task. As previously stated, the turtle ran out of energy after 31 moves. The table reveals that, in terms of the performance of the gender pairs, the girls were more successful at completing the task requirements than either of the other two gender groupings. A Fisher Exact Probability Test revealed that the only significant difference was between the girls and the boy pairs ($p<.10$). Stephens (1992) has suggested that acceptance of this level of probability in a small sample is reasonable since it affords the opportunity to improve the power of the test. This is an

Table 13.1 Performance of gender pairs in 'Get the Toys'

groups	*finished*	*did not finish*
girls (n = 10)	8	2
boys (n = 10)	4	6
boy/girl (n = 10)	5	5

interesting finding and would warrant further investigation with a larger sample of children over time and a range of tasks.

When analysing the reasons for the greater success of the girls than the boys, it is interesting to note some general trends in performance as well as to examine specific instances in the transcriptions derived from the video recording that indicated the strategies that were deployed in the problem-solving process.

In the first instance, it was apparent that the *choice of route* was critical to success in the task. All the boy pairs took route 1, whereas two boy/girl pairs and one girl pair took a combination of routes 3 and 1, and one boy/girl pair and two girl pairs took route 3, which was the optimum route in terms of efficiency of moves. The remaining girl pairs chose route 2. An important observation here was that both the girl pairs and the boy/girl pairs spent more time articulating which route should be followed. Every girl pair discussed some general features about the hardware, such as the location of the keys that they needed, and then talked about the direction of turns (this is my left and my right) and how they would complete the task, before they typed in any moves. Figure 13.2 shows the completed task of one girl pair.

At the beginning of this task, this pair keyed in rt 90 only after they had decided on the route by calculating the number of moves:

g1: Where are the keys that we need? . . .
g2: There is the r and the t . . . and this long one is space . . .
g1: So we can go across and then down and then across again, up and right and to the bunny . . . 8 moves here and then 5.

Several boy/girl pairs adopted the same strategy as the girl pairs and talked about the 'best way to go', which necessitated them counting the number of distance moves and turns in order to decide. One pair decided to go the 'bottom way' (route 2) after such an interaction, and in the first move the girl typed in rt 90 to start the quest for the rabbit.

The other boy/girl pairs varied in their approach to the start of the task. In some pairs, one member immediately took control and made the first moves and then let their partner have a turn. In others, one of the children said 'let's go this way' and directed the turtle to follow route 1 by making all the moves, only letting the partner gain control of the keys when they

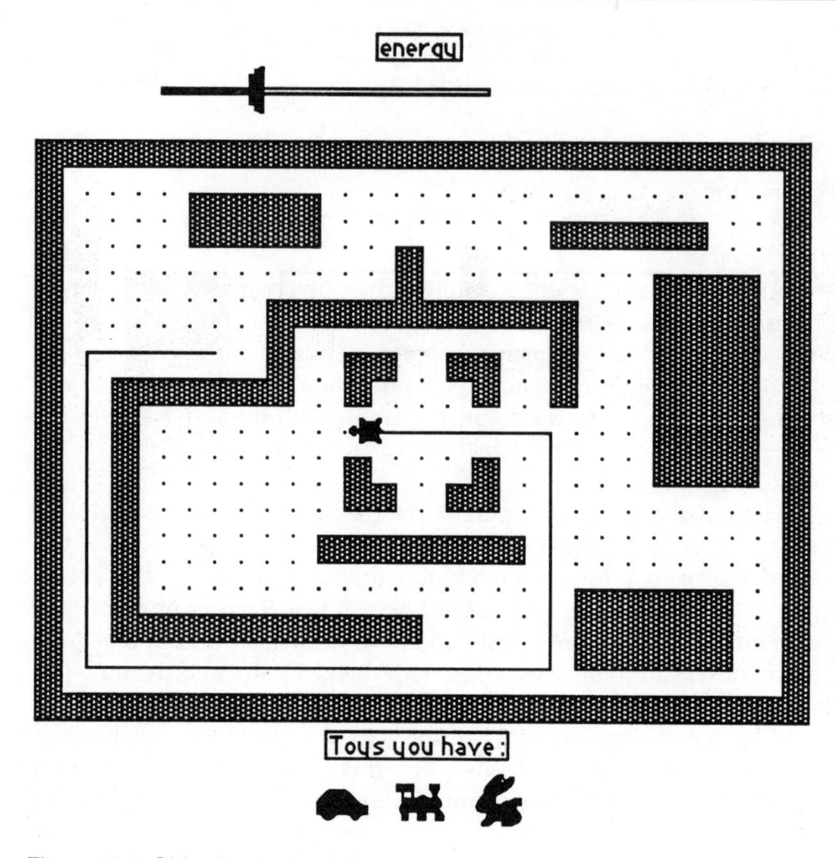

Figure 13.2 Girl pair – task solution

realised they were in trouble, that is, the energy was getting low as indicated by the message that appeared on the computer screen. This style of interaction was not determined by the gender of the child in the pair. In fact, the most interesting observation about the mixed gender pairs was that they did not seem to follow any predictable pattern of behaviour based on gender. In contrast, the girl pairs discussed moves more frequently and it seemed as if they were not concerned about who actually pressed the keys to effect the move. The boy pairs, on the whole, regulated the moves in turns. The turn-taking occurred on a regular basis and varied from one, two or five turns, before the change.

The boy pairs also made physical moves for control of space in order to be the one to execute the first move, more than the other gender pairs. There was more body contact and raised voices for appeals such as 'wait, wait, wait'. Furthermore, there was no evidence of planning regarding the most efficient route to preserve energy. One completed task of a boy pair is shown in Figure 13.3.

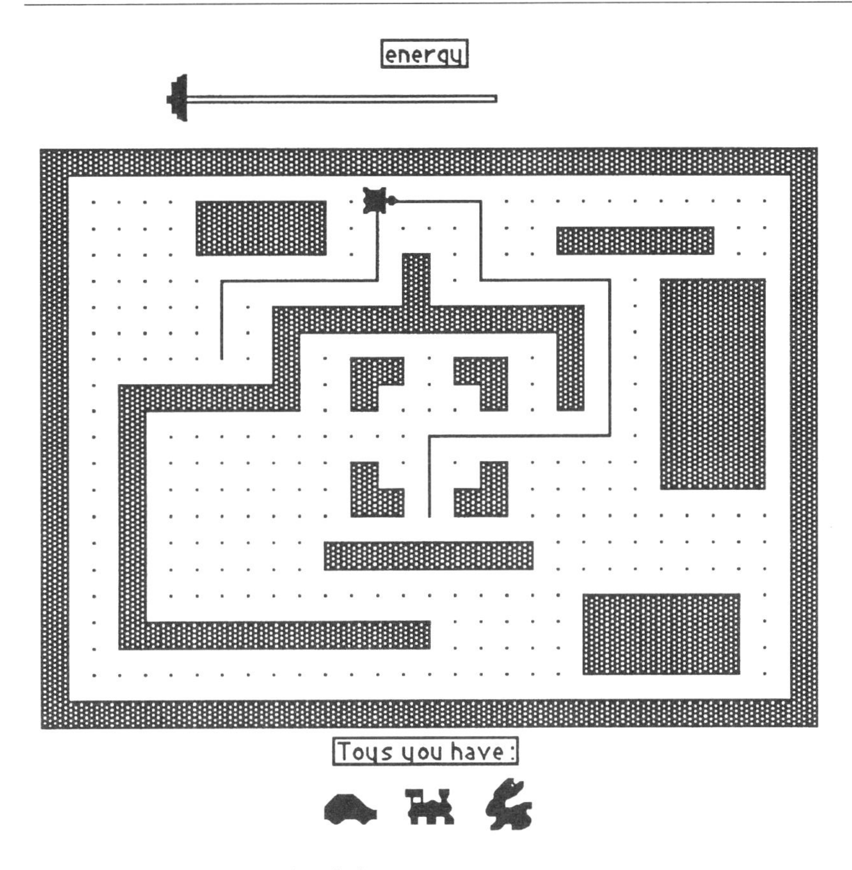

Figure 13.3 Boy pair – task solution

The amount of physical contact in manoeuvring for space was observable only in boy pairs. In the pair from the example above, the two boys edged in constantly when they wanted to take over and often pushed each other out of the way with relative degrees of success. At the very beginning of their interaction, B2 wanted to start pressing keys immediately, but was held back by his partner. However, he gained access and typed in bk 30, and, as he was doing this, his partner called: 'Wait! wait! wait! count the moves ... (as the turtle moves) see!! I told you'.

B2 keeps going and types in fd 20 and fd 10 while B1 says: 'right 70' and pushed him away so he cannot reach the keys. B2 replies: 'no, no no fd 70' and then what follows is an episode characterised by each boy shouting out numbers, and trying to grab each other's hands from the keys.

It should be noted here that, even when route 1 was chosen, as long as the most efficient moves were made in order to reach the toy, there was just enough energy to complete the task and return to the elevator in 31 moves. A combination of route 1 with 2 or 3 was also possible, as long as all moves were combined and reduced to the minimum. However, many pairs of children who went on this route ran out of energy because they did not combine moves. The most efficient route in terms of energy (route 2) allowed the children some leeway in terms of optimum moves. They could complete the task with 11 moves 'spare', which meant that not every move had to be combined.

The girl pairs who chose this option were very effective not only in choosing the correct distance for moves, but also in *combining moves* to make the turtle travel the appropriate distance. They completed the task in 23 and 27 moves. Both of these pairs spent time at the start of the task discussing which route they should select, and worked it out by counting the dots on the grid as they imagined the turtle travelling along the route. They used their fingers to locate the path that would be followed and then counted one for the distance move and another number for the turn. They also doubled the number when they arrived at the turtle to get the distance for the total trip. The transcript from one episode indicated:

g2: 'OK how much should I put in then for this bit?'
g1: '(counting the dots) 'well this is 4 dots . . . 40, so we need to go fd 40. I will tell you what to press . . . That is it!' *G2 types fd 40.*

and later in another episode:

g1: Right, now we have to go forward, how much do you think . . . let's count, you do it *G2 counts the dots with her fingers.*
g2: It's 1,2,3,4,5,6,7,8,9 – 90 . . . type in forward 90 *G1 does this.*
g2: Now go rt 90 again
g1: OK *Types rt 90.*
g2: Now this is a big bit! . . . it's 100 because it's more turtle to there! *(pointing)*
g1: That's not far enough there are more dots.
g2: Well 100 is the biggest, let's try that!

The boy/girl pairs usually decided to take turns pressing the keys to make the moves, and generally the child who was at the keyboard decided on the code that was to be entered. At one point, a girl gave her boy partner access to the keys and he said: 'I think that 50 will do me'. The girl just watched with no expression on her face until the boy indicated that he was going to do 50 again. She said: 'No it is 60' and, as she did so, she assumed typing on the keys as he relinquished his position with no comment. Subsequent moves indicated that they had silently agreed to adopt a strategy of taking alternate turns for the course of the activity, even though it was apparent from the video that she often hesitated and often turned to him as if she wanted to ask or receive advice regarding the move in question. When the boy assumed his turn after she had made distance moves that were not enough, he did not change her move but simply counted the dots and entered his amount to make what he perceived to be the correct move. Their completed activity is shown in Figure 13.4.

However, there were also instances in the boy/girl pairs when one member was not sure what to do and sought out the opinion of his or her partner. As one girl typed in rt 90, her partner seemed confused with the direction of the turtle. He sat next to her in his seat moving his body in an attempt to determine the position. She completed the move and said: 'Great . . . look how much energy we have left' and moved away to let him have 'his go'. He asked out loud: 'Which way?' And as she said 'left', he typed it in with 70. However, she pointed out that you cannot use 70 for turns, only 90. So he rubbed out the 70 and put 90 and then proceeded to count the dots for the next move, which he made independently by typing fd 60. They proceeded to the rabbit by taking alternate turns and when

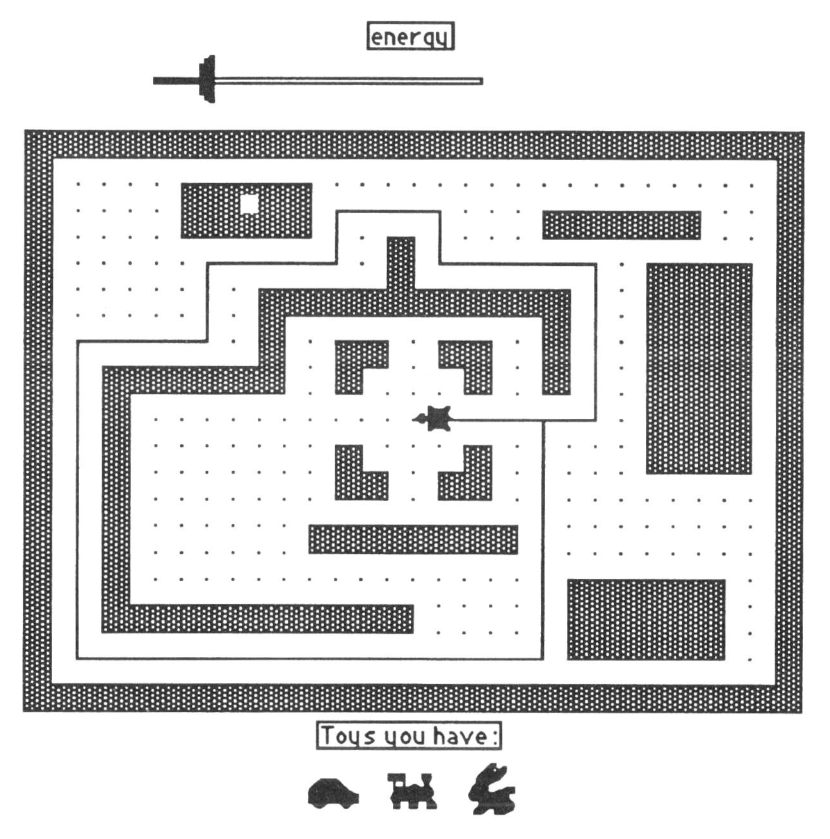

Figure 13.4 Boy/girl pair – task solution

they got there the girl said: 'We need to save some energy.' She examined the code. 'Look here we went fd 40 and then 30 and we should have done 70'. The boy replied: 'Great idea.' However, she moved the cursor back and could not remember how to delete. The researcher came in and deleted the two moves and then asked: 'What do you want to do now?' So she typed in her new move. The boy then suggested they go back 'this way', outlining the reverse of route 1 with his index finger, and as he did so, the girl agrees. On the way back, they combined moves to save energy on the basis of the girl's suggestion and subsequent actions and the boy generally took on the role of counting the dots whether he was using the keys or not. He offered praise such as: 'Good one . . . we got more energy' as she made some of these moves.

As previously indicated, all the boy pairs took route 1 and one of the pair usually made the first move straight into the task without indicating that they had considered which options were available to them. This was apparent not only by the first move but also by the minute amount of time that preceded the depression of the keys. If a partner disagreed with a move, it was apparent that the most obvious strategy adopted was to try and gain physical control of the keyboard. It seemed as if verbal reasoning was not a strategy that the boys considered, although shouting out a possible move in a loud voice was. In one pair, the following scenario was recorded:

b2: 80, 80
b1: No 70
B2 types rt 90 and they are still arguing but B2 still has the keyboard. He counts the dots and types forward 80.
b1: That's too far. I told you!
B2 types bk 10 and then rubs it out to type bk 60 and when that does not work for him he rubs it out again and does fd 70 which seems to be OK for them both. B1 gains control of the keyboard by pushing his partner aside.
b1: 80
b2: 70
B1 types rt 90 and immediately goes on to type fd 70 – which was his partner's suggestion although not acknowledged in any way. He types rt 90 and then pauses to count '20,30,40,50' He stops and counts again '10,20,30 . . . . ' There is more elbowing and b2 takes over as B1 says:
b1: We're going good!
There is much of the same interaction with shouting out of numbers which are either ignored by the typist or used without question. When they arrive at the toy B1 says:
b1: We've won it . . . now we are in trouble *(as he points to the energy level).*

Another explanation for the success of the girl pairs in this task might have been related to the fact that, in addition to carefully considering each move and asking their partner's opinion, the girl pairs in this study also spent time evaluating each move *as it was made* and were very effective in determining the extent of how useful the move was in terms of reaching the goal. By doing this they often negated the need to go back past their previous move to correct an error. Changes made beyond the last move were more complex because 'undoing' the move had to be thought through mentally, with all subsequent changes followed up, which is conceptually difficult due to the abstract nature of the process.

Additionally, the girl pairs often used prediction of future moves as a basis for decisions about the one that they were about to make. In one interaction, as a pair was trying to position the turtle, the following occurred:

g2: That is good! Now we have to make it go like this. (*positions body*)
g1: Well that is right (pointing) and it's 90 (meaning forward). *G2 types in the move.*
g2: Now it's your turn to type.
g1: It's not far enough but I'll do it and then we can go more.
They watch as the turtle moves and when it stops they say:
g1: It's not far enough! We can do another 100 . . . no maybe less . . . how about 80 do you think?
g2: Yes let's try 80. *She types it in and it is just right.*
g1: Yes that is it!
g2: Now right 90 again. *She makes the move while G1 nods in silent agreement.* Shall we do 100 again up here?
g1: OK. I can type it in.
g2: Yes it is your turn . . . type fd space 100. *G1 does this and they watch.*
g1: It's not far enough . . . we need more . . . how many do you think . . .? It is two dots, um we should do 20. *She types it in and G2 looks on.*
g2: Yes!!! We are nearly there! . . . Now we go right 90. *G1 types it in.*
g2: And now go forward 1,2,3,4,5 – 50 and we will be there. *G1 does this.*
g1: We've got it.
g1: We have to go back now. *G1 is looking at the commands on the screen, she points to the previous move and says.* We need to go back 50 like here and then it will be a left turn. *G2 looks surprised but makes no comment and types in bk 50. When it works she types in lt 90.*
g1: We have to go down so put right 90. *She deletes lt 90 and types rt 90.*
g2: OK we want to go forwards.

This episode characterises much of the type of interaction between pairs of girls in the study. They revealed evidence of planning and their interaction was very much reciprocal in nature, with most of the moves being agreed upon. Even if there was a disagreement, there was no conflict in terms of arguing.

In contrast, the boys did not demonstrate behaviour that indicated that they were evaluating each move as it was made, nor did they show evidence of thinking ahead and planning. The boy pairs seemed reluctant to make changes once they had typed in the move. They also made more moves that would have benefited from being combined, which was the main reason that more of them ran out of energy than the girl pairs. This meant that when they got into problems with energy levels, it was much harder to go back a number of moves to rectify the problem, so they just seemed to get themselves deeper into trouble. They demonstrated evidence of their frustration with each other more often than either the girl or boy/girl pairs. At one stage near the end of the game, two boys were engaged in calling each other names like 'idiot!' and 'dork!', as they realised that they would not make it back. They had no suggestions about how they could regain energy, and eventually, as things got more heated, one of them suddenly got up and left his partner to make the final move that would ensure there was no energy left, and thus the game was over.

The issue of delivering insults to each other also raises another issue related to behaviour. Instances of praise were highest in the girl pairs and apparent in the boy/girl pairs. They would often say things like 'Cool . . . that is what we want' or 'Good one! nice going', 'I told you it would work!' Such comments were rare among the boys working together. Even when a move was made that was useful, the (boy) partner would often take his turn without comment.

PROJECTS

In another activity, the children were required to plan and complete a drawing project in their pairs. The ways in which they set out to complete the task requirements were, once again, very different. However, the 'final products' all reflect a sound understanding and excellent use of the features inherent to the *Geo-Logo* environment.

As shown in Figure 13.5, one girl pair meticulously planned their project and included colour and detail to enhance the final product. They planned each element of the picture and then brought them all together to create the whole, which was the final 'face'. This form of modular programming was methodical and suited the style of the pair. They knew exactly what they wanted as they planned their drawing off the computer, and once on the computer the only aspect that they decided not to include was the hair because it was 'too complicated'. They were going to use 'spiky' hair but decided that they preferred the 'bald' look of their final drawing.

In contrast, the boy pairs did not seem to want to spend a considerable amount of time in the planning phase (off the computer). They produced drawings, as required in the task instructions, but were much more eager to get on the computer and start to enter the commands. The turtle (Figure 13.6) that was produced is an example of this observation. The boys were clearly bored and agitated at the paper and pencil phase, whereas the girls saw this as a necessary part of the process. Interestingly, the performance of the boy/girl pairs more closely approximated that of the boy pairs, as in the previous maze task. Figure 13.7 shows not only the sword that was created by one boy/girl pair but the total planning that occurred in the off computer phase, that is before they went on the computer to enter the commands to form the picture.

When we look at the final products, it is neither possible, nor appropriate, to make statements that identify the best or worse, more sophisticated or less, unless we specifically want orderly planning or drawings that reflect a stated number of component parts, because the amount of effort and enthusiasm that went into the task was fairly consistent across the gender pairs. Furthermore, what would be the point of setting such goals? All the projects by the children reflected an interpretation of the task requirements that is equally valid, but more than that they are testament to the ability of young children to use mathematical concepts in new and vital ways. The task structure facilitated this. It was open ended and gave the children plenty of scope in deciding what the final product should consist of and the means of achieving this.

CONCLUSIONS

The work of Hoyles and Sutherland (1989) has suggested that we should not come to quick and superficial conclusions about supposed gender differences on the basis of short term performance, since they can often be misleading. Previous research has tended to devalue the performance of girls working together (e.g Hughes *et al.*, 1998) and has even suggested that girls need boys in order to perform certain tasks effectively. Data have been presented here to illustrate that this phenomenon may be an artefact of context and task. It has shown that, in novel problem contexts based in a computer environment, girl pairs can have more success than either boy or boy/girl pairs when completing the task requirements for a maze type task. It was apparent in this research that girls were more efficient in their moves than either of the other gender pairs. They did not take greater lengths of time in order to achieve this. Analysis of the pairs' actions, activity and strategies revealed that the performance of the girls was significantly different and more successful to that of the boys because of their demonstrated ability to show evidence of:

- *planning*, not only before they commenced the task, but as they proceeded through it
- *reflecting* on the *effectiveness* of their plans and goals as they were executed

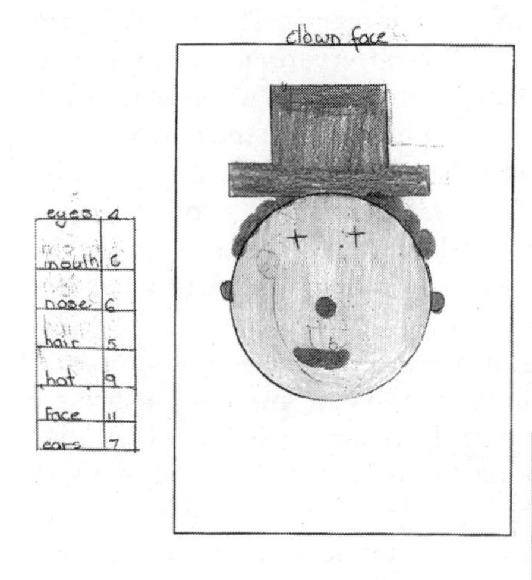

Geo-face

Name		Plan	Procedure
tri	colour	△	
head		○	repeat 360 [Fd1 rt1]
eyes	4	+	Fd 60, BK30, rt 90, Fd 20, bk 60.
nose	6	○	repeat 45 [f1 rt8]
mouth	6	◡	repeat 45 [bk1 rt4]
hair	5	◠	repeat 90 [Fd1 rt 2
hat	9		rt 90, fd50, rt90, Fd 25, lt90, Fd 30 Lt 90, Fd 25 Lt90 Fd 30, rt 90, Fd 20, rt90, Fd 25, rt 90, Fd 50
Face	11	○	
ears	7	◠	45 [rt 1 rt 4]

Figure 13.5 Girl pair – clown face

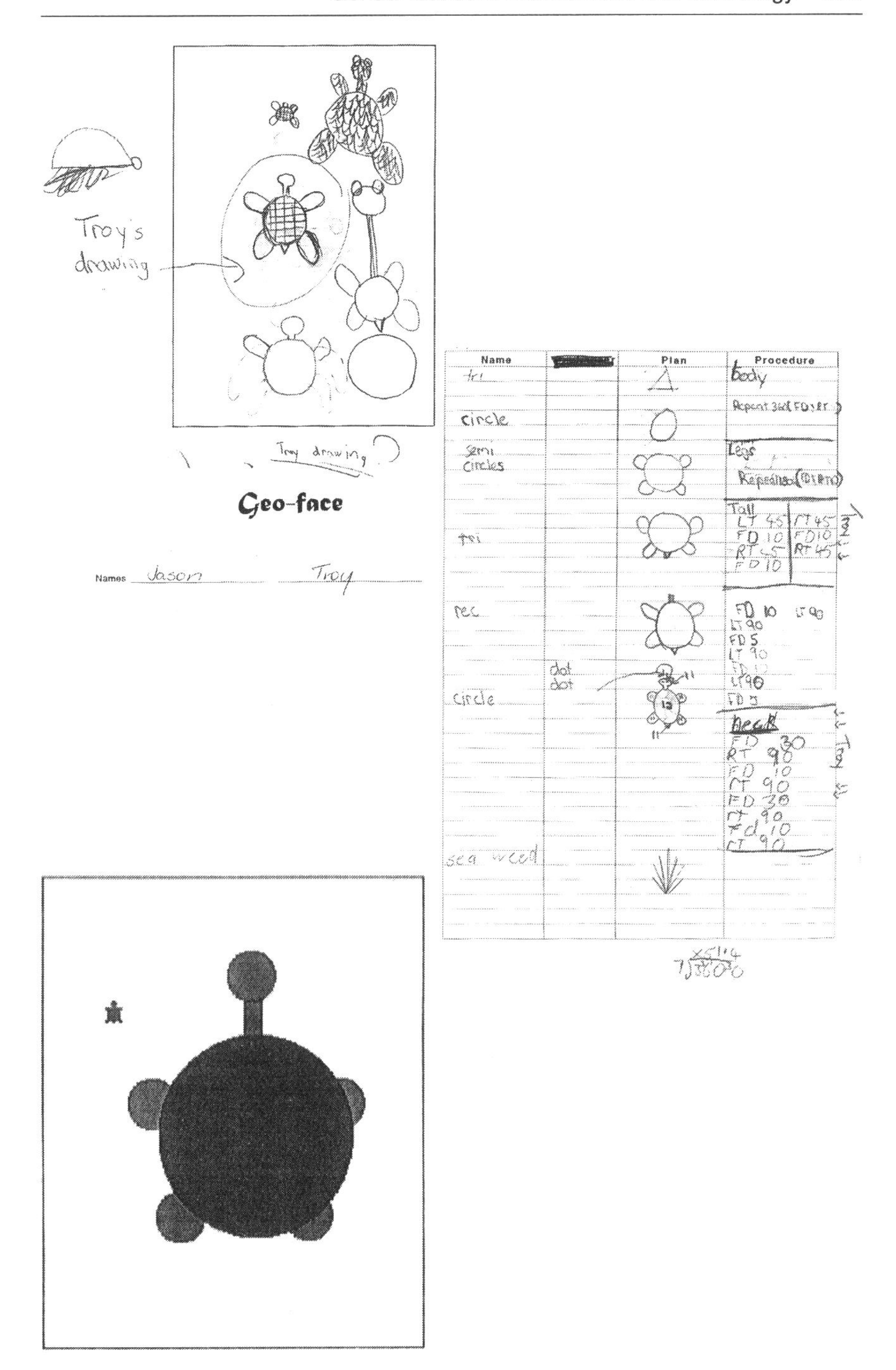

Figure 13.6 Boy pair – turtle

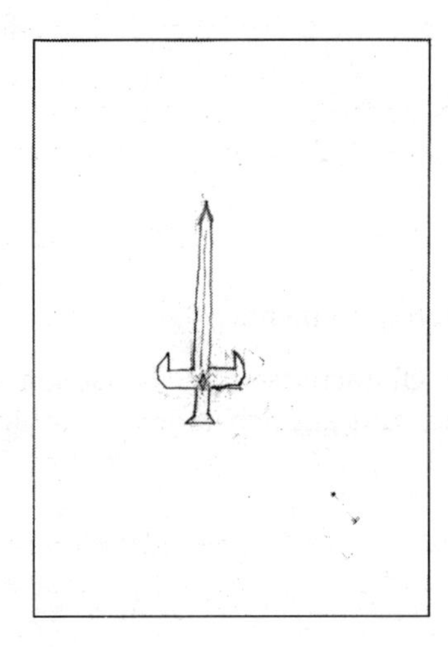

Geo-face

ies [illegible] [illegible]

Name		Plan	Procedure
tri			
Sword (Yellow Grey)			[illegible]
Diamond (Red)			[illegible]
line (Black)			[illegible]

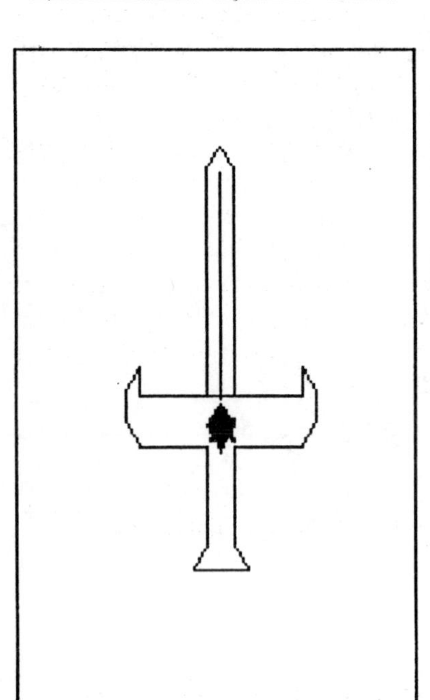

Figure 13.7 Boy/girl pair – the sword

- *predicting* the consequences of their actions before they implemented them
- *monitoring* their progress at each stage of the problem solution
- *engaging in dialogue* to ensure that each decision that was made had been thought through
- working *cooperatively* in order to effect a task solution that represented a consensus
- *interpreting and understanding* the task requirements

Most of these behaviours have been characterised by Davidson and Sternberg (1985) as being metastrategic, and as such represent a higher level of thinking and reasoning than the application of basic strategies such as trial and error.

In a completely different type of task, it was also evident that girls working together approached tasks in a different way to either boy or boy/girl pairs, in terms of planning and completing the task requirements. It has been argued here that, because of the nature of the task (an open ended project), such comparisons become redundant, as *all* children met the task requirements while demonstrating commitment and enthusiasm for the task.

Technology is permeating all aspects of our lives and will have a significant impact on the lives of our children as they enter the workforce of the twenty-first century. It is hoped that the expertise with technology will not be considered in terms of 'hard mastery' (Turkle, 1988), which may advantage males and put them in a position where they are considered masters of these powerful cultural tools. All children, irrespective of gender, class and ethnicity, need to be provided with learning opportunities that incorporate the use of various artefacts of technology as tools for learning. Educators should ensure that in classroom contexts all children have opportunities to work with a variety of applications with different partners as well as individually, and that every child in their care recognises the potential of technological applications to empower them in their acquisition of new knowledge and skills.

NOTES

1 Investigations in Number, Data and Space. Dale Seymour Publications.
2 Copyright D.H. Clements, 1994.

REFERENCES

Chadwick, C. (1986). *Differential group composition in problem solving using Logo.* Unpublished masters thesis, Concordia University, Montreal.

Chambers, S.M. and Clark, V.A. (1987). Is inequity cumulative? The relationship between disadvantaged group membership and students' computing experience, knowledge, attitudes and intentions. *Journal of Educational Computing Research, 3*, 493–516.

Clements, D.H. and Nastasi, B.K. (1985). Effects of computer environments on social-emotional development: Logo and computer-assisted instruction. *Logo in the Schools, 2*(2/3), 11–31.

Clements, D.H. and Nastasi, B.L. (1988). Social cognitive interactions in educational computer environments. *American Educational Research Journal, 25*(1), 87–106.

Davidson, J.E. and Sternberg, J.E. (1985). Competence and performance in intellectual development. In E. Niemark, R. Delisi and J.L. Newman (eds), *Moderators of Competence* (pp. 43–76). Hillsdale, NJ: Lawrence Erlbaum.

Fennema, E. (1980). Sex related differences in mathematics achievement. In L.H. Fox, L. Brody, and D. Tobin (eds), *Women and the mathematical mystique* (pp. 76–93). Baltimore, Maryland: Johns Hopkins University Press.

Fitzgerald, D., Hattie, J. and Hughes, P. (1986). *Computer applications in Australian classrooms*. Canberra: Australian Government Publishing Service.

Gardner, J.R., McEwen, A. and Curry, C.A. (1985) A sample survey of attitudes to computer studies. *Computers in Education, 102*(2), 293–298.

Gunterman, E. and Tovar, M. (1987). Collaborative problem solving with Logo: Effects of group size and group composition. *Journal of Educational Computing Research, 3*(3), 313–334.

Hattie, J. and Fitzgerald, D. (1987). Sex differences in attitudes, achievement and use of computers. *Australian Journal of Education, 31*(1), 3–26.

Hawkins, J., Homolsky, M., and Heide, P. (1984). *Paired problem solving in a computer context*. New York: Bank Street College of Education.

Hay, D.F. and Lockwood, R. (1989). Girls' and boys' success and strategies on a computer generated writing task. *British Journal of Developmental Psychology, 7*, 17–27.

Hilton, T.L. and Berglund, G.W. (1974). Sex differences in mathematics education: A longitudinal study. *Journal of Educational Research, 67*(50), 231–236.

Hoyles, C. (1988). Review of the literature. In C. Hoyles (ed.), *Girls and computers: General issues and case studies of Logo in the mathematics classroom* (pp. 5–12). London: Institute of Education, University of London.

Hoyles, C. and Sutherland, R. (1989). *Logo mathematics in the classoom*. London: Routledge and Kegan Paul.

Hughes, M. and MacLeod, M. (1986). Using Logo with very young children. In R.W. Lawler, M. d. Boulay, M. Hughes, and H. MacLeod (eds), *Cognition and computers* (pp. 179–219). Chichester: Ellis Harwood.

Hughes, M., Brackenridge, A., Bibby, A., and Greenhaugh, P. (1988). Girls, boys and turtles: Gender effects with young children learning with Logo. In C. Hoyles (ed.), *Girls and computers: General issues and case studies of Logo in the mathematics classroom* (pp. 31–39). London: Institute of Education, University of London.

Leder, G. (1990). Gender differences in mathematics. In E. Fenema and G. Leder (eds), *Mathematics and gender* (pp. 10–26). New York: Teachers College Press.

Linn, M.C. and Petersen, A.C. (1985). Emergence and characterization of sex differences in spatial ability: A meta analysis. *Child Development, 56*, 1479–1498.

Noss, R. (1984). *Creating a mathematical environment through programming: A study of young children learning Logo*. London: University of London Institute of Education.

Ring, G. (1991). Student reactions to courseware: Gender differences. *British Journal of Educational Technology, 22*(3), 210–215.

Schagen, I.P. (1994). Multi level analysis of Key Stage 1 National Curriculum assessment data in 1991 and 1992. *Oxford Review of Education, 20*(2), 163–171.

Schonberger, A.K. (1980). Sex related issues in mathematics education. In M.M. Lindquist (ed.), *Selected issues in maths education* (pp. 185–198). Berkeley: McCutchan.

Schuard, H. (1986). The relative attainment of girls and boys in mathematics in the primary years. In L. Burton (ed.), *Girls into maths can go* (pp. 22–37). Eastbourne, East Sussex: Holt, Rinehart & Winston.

Sharp, C., Hutchinson, D., and Whetton, C. (1994) How does season of birth and length of schooling affect children's attainment at Key Stage 1? *Educational Research, 36*(2), 107–121.

Siann, G. and MacLeod, M. (1986). Computers and children of primary school age: Issues and questions. *British Journal of Educational Technology, 2*(17), 133–144.

Siann, G., MacLeod, H., Glissov, P., and Durndell, A. (1990). The effects of computer use on gender differences in attitudes to computers. *Computers in Education, 14*(2), 183–191.

Tarte, L.A. (1990). Spatial skills, gender and mathematics. In E. Fennema and G. Leder (eds), *Mathematics and gender* (pp. 27–59). New York: Teachers College Press.

Tarte, L.A. and Fennema, E. (1995) Mathematics achievement and gender: A longitudinal study of selected cognitive and affective variables. *Educational Studies in Mathematics, 26* (3), 199–217.

Turkle, S. (1984). *The second self: Computers and the human spirit.* New York: Simon & Schuster.

Underwood, G., Underwood, G., and Turner, M. (1993) Children's thinking during collaborative computer-based problem solving. *Educational Psychology, 13*, 345–357.

Underwood, G., Jindal, N., and Underwood, J. (1994) Gender differences and effects of co-operation in a computer based language task. *Educational Research, 36*(1), 63–74.

Vygotsky, L.S. (1978). *Mind in society: The development of higher psychological processes.* Cambridge, MA: Harvard University Press.

Walden, R. and Walkerdine, V. (1985). *Girls and mathematics: From primary to secondary schooling.* London: University of London, Institute of Education.

Webb, N. (1982). Student interaction and learning in small groups. *Review of Educational Research, 52*(3), 421–445.

Webb, N. (1984). Microcomputer learning in small groups: Cognitive requirements and group processes. *Journal of Educational Psychology, 76*(6), 1078–1089.

Yelland, N.J. (1993). Learning with Logo: An analysis of strategies and interactions. *Journal of Educational Computing Research, 9(*4), 465–486.

Yelland, N.J. (1994a). A case study of six children learning with Logo. *Gender and Education, 6*(1), 19–33.

Yelland, N.J. (1994b). The strategies and interactions of young children in Logo tasks. *Journal of Computer Assisted Learning, 10*(1), 33–49.

Yelland, N.J. (1995). Logo experiences with young children: Describing performance, problem-solving and the social context of learning. *Early Child Development & Care, 109*, 61–74.

Yelland, N.J. and Masters, J.E. (1995). New ways with Logo: Powerful problem-solving for young children. *Quick, 54*, 4–7.

Index